JOURNAL FOR THE STUDY OF THE OLD TESTAMENT
SUPPLEMENT SERIES
6

Editors
David J A Clines
Philip R Davies
David M Gunn

Department of Biblical Studies
The University of Sheffield
Sheffield S10 2TN
England

The Story of

KING DAVID

Genre and Interpretation
D.M.GUNN

Journal for the Study of the Old Testament
Supplement Series 6

Sheffield
1978

ISSN 0309-0787

Paperback: ISBN 0 905774 05 1

Hardback: ISBN 0 905774 11 6

Published by

JSOT

Department of Biblical Studies
The University of Sheffield
Sheffield S10 2TN
England

Printed in Great Britain

1978

Fengraphic, Cambridge

To
my mother and father,
Jean and Farquhar Gunn

Contents

Preface

This book seeks to foster a fresh understanding of the narrative about David in 2 Samuel and 1 Kings, commonly known as the "Succession Narrative", by arguing for a fuller appreciation of its nature as a *story*. If some readers find some segments of the argument familiar that is because the book in part builds upon studies which have appeared in print elsewhere. In particular, Chapter Three draws upon two articles in *VT* 24 and 26 (see Bibliography: Gunn, 1974a and 1976a) and Chapter Five upon an essay in *Semeia* 3 (Gunn, 1975). Incorporation of this material, which is in revised form, is made possible by kind permission of Brills of Leiden and the Society of Biblical Literature. The preparation of some parts of the book was aided by grants from the University of Sheffield Research Fund and the Research Fund Committee have my thanks for this help.

My preoccupation with the story of King David goes back to my time as a student of theology at Knox College, the University of Otago, New Zealand, where Professor Lloyd Geering kindled my interest in this finest of Old Testament stories. I owe him my thanks, as I do Professor Max Wilcox whose energy and encouragement launched me on the first stages of this project at the University of Newcastle upon Tyne, ten years ago. Above all, my thanks to my colleagues here at Sheffield University for providing an on-going community of interest; and to David Clines especially I acknowledge a great debt for countless invaluable debates on matters of central importance to my subject as well as for a host of helpful and detailed suggestions as the work reached its final stages of preparation. In other ways, however, my greatest debt is to my wife, Margaret— for sharing her life for so long, too long, with a book-in-the-making.

Department of Biblical Studies,   David Gunn
The University of Sheffield,
Sheffield, England.

Reference and Abbreviations

Reference to secondary literature is by citation of the author's name and the year of publication. The Bibliography at the end of the book (pp. 142-53) is listed in alphabetical order by author's name and provides details of all works thus cited. Standard abbreviations of journals, series, etc., are used (see especially those listed in Eissfeldt, 1965: 854-61).

Notes are marked in the text with a number set off by slashes, thus: /1/. The notes themselves are printed at the end of the book (pp. 122-41).

Reference to the Old Testament follows the numbering of the Hebrew text unless otherwise stated.

CHAPTER ONE
INTRODUCTION

Chapter One
Introduction

It is rare to meet unanimity among Biblical critics. But there is one aspect of
the so-called "Succession Narrative" *(Thronfolgegeschichte)* or "Court History"
(generally taken to include 2 Sam 9-20 + 1 Kgs 1-2) that has been the subject of
almost universal agreement among scholars: it is a fine example of narrative art, a
skilfully told story. Curiously, however, in extended discussions of the character of
the narrative this observation has tended to play a relatively small role. That is not to
say that such discussions devote little space to the analysis of the narrative as a well-
constructed story. But somehow when it has come to the making of decisions
regarding genre (and so purpose) this "story" quality has either been ignored, mis-
applied (for example, as an argument for the classification of the narrative as history
writing) or, for various reasons, strictly subordinated to other postulated dimensions
(for example, historical, political or theological).

In recent years notable characterizations of the narrative have been made in
terms of history writing (von Rad), political propaganda (Rost, Whybray, Delekat,
Würthwein, and most recently Langlamet),and didactic or wisdom literature (Whybray,
Hermisson), or some combination of these. In the present book I wish to assess some
of these arguments and justify an alternative approach to the narrative as first and
foremost a story or tale in the sense of a work of art and entertainment.

After some further introductory observations in the present chapter, Chapter
Two offers a critique and rejection of prevailing views of the literary genre of the
narrative, in particular descriptions of the narrative as history writing, political
propaganda and didactic (wisdom) literature. In the course of this examination I
raise the question of the date of the narrative since the widely accepted view that the
document belongs to the Solomonic period can be shown to have played a significant
part in the designation of its genre (and so in its interpretation). Yet, as I shall argue,
this dating lacks any substantial foundation.

In Chapter Three I present an alternative view of the genre, by arguing that the
often observed character of the narrative as a *story,* and a fine and entertaining one
at that, ought not to be subordinated to other postulated dimensions of the document
but constitutes in fact its primary character. While a term such as "novel" is not
entirely inappropriate as a classification, an exploration of stereotyped patterns and
motifs in the story suggests that the story has a more traditional character than this
particular descriptive label would suggest. The story belonged to a tradition of
Israelite story-telling which was most probably originally an oral one. Whether,

however, the narrative in its present form is *directly* a product of oral tradition, or whether it embodies originally oral techniques and story material which have in time become part of a written ("literary") tradition, must remain an open question. Accordingly I fall back on the, admittedly broad, term "story" as the most satisfactory basic genre-label for the narrative, with the qualification that it is most probably a *traditional* story.

I discuss the question of genre on the basis of the generally accepted boundaries of the "original" narrative, viz. 2 Sam 9-20 + 1 Kgs 1-2 (cf. Whybray, 1968:8; Soggin, 1976:192). As I argue in Chapter Four, however, I believe that these boundaries should be significantly modified. Nevertheless I have not wanted my argument concerning genre to be thought to stand or fall with the acceptance of the argument about boundaries: I believe that the argument applies to the narrative as conventionally defined no less than to the narrative as I would wish to define it. Hence I follow what might appear otherwise a somewhat illogical order – discussion of the work's genre first, and of its boundaries second.

Chapter Four contains a demonstration that the narrative includes the bulk of 2 Sam 2-4 (2:8 or 2:12 to 4:12 or, most probably, 5:3), together with most of 9-20 and 1 Kgs 1-2. The argument challenges some key points in Rost's influential analysis (1926) as well as taking account of more recent proposals. One of these points is his insistence on the importance of "succession" as the major thematic interest of the narrative.

My critique of the "succession" theme leads to Chapter Five which offers an interpretation of the story the boundaries of which have been defined in the previous chapter. The story is a story of David's fortunes through accession, rebellion and succession. Put very baldly, it might be said that the central themes are the interrelation of the political and personal spheres in David's life, and the "giving" and "grasping" which takes place in the various events relating to these spheres and which is the key to his fortunes.

In the paragraphs above I have summarized my argument very briefly so as to give readers some clear indication of where they are going if they venture further. In the remainder of the present chapter I should like to make a few further points concerning the objectives and methods of this study.

First, I wish to stress that the book is about a reconstructed text, a postulated original, and not about the final form of the Old Testament text. Ten years ago I would not have felt it necessary to make this point. Today much has changed. More than a hundred years of the historical-critical approach to the Old Testament has sanctified the search for the original sources and setting of the literature as the key to its true meaning. Yet in the last decade amongst scholars in the liberal tradition of biblical criticism there are signs of unrest and dissatisfaction with the results of this kind of historicism – an unrest and dissatisfaction that has been felt all along and for not always dissimilar reasons by scholars from a more conservative tradition. It manifests itself, for example, in the move towards structuralist or literary interpretations of the text in its final form; also in a growing interest in the history of interpretation and the exegesis of the "pre-critical" period. It is not my purpose here to explore the reasons for this faltering in confidence. Suffice to say that I share the disquiet. A too rigid historicism may lie like a dead hand on our texts. It may too easily focus the bulk of attention on minutiae, not in the realistic expectation of arriving at results which will significantly help the reader to explore and appropriate any existential meaning in the texts, but in the interests of creating a complex and usually highly speculative hypothesis about the historical development of a text or of ancient Israelite "thought" in general. It may too easily obscure the universality of a text by effectively anchoring its meaning to that hypothetical process of development or to some supposed historical context, leaving it vulnerable to the next shift in the programme of reconstruction.

But if I share this dissatisfaction with the current state of historical-critical research I am unwilling to circumvent the method, ignore it or reject it out of hand. It is not easy to be rid of historicism's original setting, original meaning, or author's intention without incurring, probably justly, the charge of subjectivism. Perhaps the best one can do is to try to keep this approach in perspective by learning better to recognize its limitations. Whether or not I have managed to do this in the present book is for others to decide. As I have said, it is about a postulated original text and not its final form — though I would hope that the amount of "reconstruction" involved would be regarded as minimal. Moreover I have devoted a good part of it to an argument about its original context and the possible purpose of the original author despite that person's total anonymity.

In some respects it could be said that these lines of investigation have led me up a blind alley. The extent of the evidence for traditional composition (as I argue it to be) in the narrative is still too restricted to allow the factor of tradition as opposed to innovation to play in practice much part in the interpretation of particular segments of the text. Thus in Chapter Five the reader will find little reference back to the prior discussion. On the other hand it is precisely the recognition that there is a significant traditional aspect to the narrative, no matter how limited the directly comparable material elsewhere in the Old Testament, that has encouraged me to press for a reading of the story as a story or tale and not as an example of some other literary genre. Without exception the traditional elements all points to a world of story-telling as their normal setting. They also make it increasingly difficult to postulate a contemporary or near-contemporary (to the events described) provenance for the work. This, I believe, does have a significant bearing on the interpretation of the text. For these reasons I have persevered with this argument and tried to meet some of the objections raised against it.

The matter of the original boundaries of the document is perhaps even more crucial to its interpretation. Rost's thesis has gone far too long unchallenged. As I shall argue below, he starts effectively with a theme and from this proceeds to define the boundaries, putting the cart before the horse. Whether my own procedure is more circumspect is for the reader to judge. The point is, however, that my inclusion of 2 Samuel 2:12 - 5:3 does have a direct bearing on the meaning of the narrative by making it even more difficult than it is, if the conventional boundaries are assumed, to insist on the adequacy of any interpretation of the story which depends on the primacy of the succession theme.

I have tried to resist too fine an analysis of the original boundaries since in general the finer the discriminations in this kind of analysis the more speculative it becomes. It is interesting to see that Rost's theory has also now met a different kind of challenge, namely the postulation of a high level of redactional interference with the text, which in fact depends upon the finest of source and redaction analyses (Würthwein, Veijola and Langlamet). Yet as far as the interpretation of the narrative is concerned these theses appear to me to be essentially only reformulations of Rost's basic thesis that the narrative is primarily a document of political propaganda. On both counts, therefore, I would wish to dispute such approaches to the text.

In many respects, then, it is the final section of interpretation, Chapter Five, which is the focal point of this book, though I am conscious that it lays no claim to being in any sense definitive nor even extensively original. It is a tentative exploration only and relies at many points on the work of others. I would single out von Rad, Whybray. and Brueggemann as writers who have stimulated my reading of this story, though clearly there have been many others who have contributed to my appreciation of its meaning, and, of course, I hold none of these scholars responsible for my own manipulation of their insights. Furthermore, my approach to the interpretation of the story does raise some important questions of method: these questions I shall discuss briefly at the beginning of the chapter.

I have spoken of what this book is about. I have also felt it important to stress what it is not about. It is not about the text of Samuel and Kings in its final arrangement. How the narrative relates to its present context and how this relation might affect its meaning are questions of importance, but not questions which I have chosen to deal with here. Here I am content to indicate that I believe that it is David's willing subordination to the prophet and his readiness to put himself in Yahweh's hands that has appealed above all to the Deuteronomistic redactor.

Another important area of investigation, given my emphasis upon the story as story, might concern the shape of the plot, as P. R. Ackroyd has suggested to me /1/. For example, it could be argued that the plot has affinities with a section of the biographical pattern of the hero, discerned by Raglan (1936) and others (cf. Taylor, 1964).

Such an investigation would raise the question of the historicity of the document. I shall indeed discuss in principle the question of whether the narrative is well described as history writing. I do not, however, propose to make an assessment of its historicity, which is a complex matter deserving full treatment in its own right. I simply stress that my attack on the view that we have here a near-contemporary, and methodologically rigorous, piece of history writing, does not amount to a denial that we might nevertheless have also historical information of value, though it does make it more difficult to be sure of precisely what that information might be.

Finally, an exploration of this narrative might follow its fortunes elsewhere in the Old Testament, account for its absence from Chronicles, and its relation to the Psalms (especially Ps 51), examine its transformation in Josephus, trace its influence (if any) on the New Testament, its treatment in the Fathers, and indeed follow its interpretation not only in theology but also in literature and the fine arts through succeeding periods. For this is a story that has captured man's imagination in many spheres of culture over thousands of years. But that is a task for another occasion. In the present book I am content to share a glimpse of the story at its outset.

CHAPTER TWO
GENRE: PREVAILING VIEWS

Chapter Two
Genre: Prevailing Views

GENRE

The term genre appears in the title of this book. By it I mean simply a label which gives information about the form and content of a piece of literature and thus very crudely sets limits around the expectations a reader should bring to the piece /1/. The critic's task should be to help the reader explore and appropriate for himself the meaning of a text and classification by genre is merely one means by which he can point to appropriate and inappropriate ways of approaching a text. One does not normally expect historical information ("what actually happened") in a parable; one does expect this, at least after a fashion, in a chronicle or history. Likewise in a piece of history writing one is likely to treat literally accounts of women, adulteresses or prostitutes, who lure men to their death, whereas in a "didactic poem" one is attuned already to the possibility that such accounts might best be interpreted symbolically or metaphorically (as perhaps in Proverbs 1-9). It is not necessary that the generic terminology should be that of the original author or society in which the work was produced. Rather it is most likely to be useful to the contemporary reader if the terminology is drawn from conventions recognizable in modern literature even if this procedure involves some measure of approximation. On the other hand modern generic terms must not be so loosely used as positively to mislead the reader in his expectations. As I shall presently argue, this has been the case where the King David narrative ("Succession Narrative") has been described as "history writing".

Genre may convey information about content (the subject matter) or form (how the author has handled his subject matter). It may also, by implication, convey information about what the critic conceives as the author's intention or purpose as it comes to expression in terms of the work itself. The latter claim is important. Intention or purpose could be so broadly conceived as "to meet a psychological need on the author's part, or even to make money or gain prestige" (Clines, 1976a:484). Thus the use of a term like "history writing" is likely to suggest a primary intention of recording and analysing events for the information of those who had no first-hand knowledge of them and, in particular, for posterity; or "wisdom literature" might be taken to indicate a didactic intention.

HISTORY WRITING

Probably the dominant generic classification of the narrative in the critical period has been some variation upon the term "history" or "history writing". We find this in Wellhausen's description (1878:227) : "That we have in 2 Sam 9-20, 1 Kings 1-2 a very good historical source requires no demonstration"; we find it today in standard text books (e.g. Bright, 1972:179). Tucker (1971:36) writes:

> Certainly the best example of the genre ["history"] in the Old Testament is the throne succession history of David (2 Sam 9-20, 1 Kings 1-2). This document is Israelite history writing at its very best. As a result of this writer's historical scholarship, the last part of the reign of David is one of the best documented periods in the history of Israel. The author, who must have written his work during the reign of Solomon, had access to first hand information about David, but he was not content to simply give a list of events. He worked his data into a consistent whole, painting a picture which not only describes but also interprets the events in terms of causes and effects . . . . From what must have been a wealth of information about the period at his disposal he has selected the data which he considered relevant and organized it thematically.

Perhaps the only difference between the earlier critics and those of more recent times is that today scholars are usually a little more cautious in their addition of a postscript, viz. that one cannot use the label "history" *strictly* in its modern sense (so, in fact, Tucker, in the work just cited, p. 37) /2/. For von Rad whose essay, "The Beginnings of Historical Writing in Ancient Israel" (1944/1966), strongly reinforced this classification in recent times, the narrative was not only the best but also the earliest piece of its kind in Israel's literary history. Indeed it represented a decisive break with past literary traditions. Where there had only been "legend" *(Sage)* now there was "history writing" *(Geschichtsschreibung).* For many scholars it has the historical reliability of a first-hand, eye-witness, account, as Tucker's summary makes clear.

This view has not gone without its critics. We might note especially the emphasis of Luther (1906:194-9) who saw this material (taking chapters 10-12, 13-20, and 1 Kings 1-2 as independent units) primarily in terms of the genre *Novelle* and accordingly cast some doubt on its value as an historical source. Eissfeldt (1965:140-1) drew attention to the large number of private scenes where it was difficult to imagine first-hand accounts emerging and he suggested that the most that could be said about such material was that it might have come through court gossip (and cf. Jacob, 1955:29-30). But much the most thorough-going attack on this classification has come from Whybray (1968).

I agree substantially with Whybray's criticisms (pp. 11-19). If the term "history writing" is to have anything like its modern meaning then the "Succession Narrative" does not readily qualify for inclusion in the genre. Whybray develops Eissfeldt's point about the predominance of private conversations and scenes reported in what can hardly be reliable detail. He also draws attention to the extremely meagre treatment of public and political aspects of David's reign – aspects which are everywhere subordinated to a primary interest in character and the personal motives of a few main actors in the drama.

An excellent case in point is the account of Absalom's rebellion. Following the elaborate and dramatic account of Absalom's reconciliation with his father, we are given merely the barest outline of the events leading up to the rebellion. There is a comment about his grandiose life-style, a glimpse of him winning favour with the people, but nowhere an unambiguous analysis of the causes of discontent. Was there real cause for grievance, or did Absalom deceive people about David's administration? And was this the only issue? Even the account of who supported the rebellion is vague, if not confused (as witness the differing reconstructions offered by modern historians /3/). On the other hand, after a mere twelve verses dealing with the fomenting of the rebellion we find a chapter and a half occupied with David's personal encounters on his retreat from Jerusalem. If there is clearly an area in which the author has little interest (or knowledge?) it is that of the political undercurrents of the reign. One might compare and contrast the approach of two other "historians" in the ancient world, Herodotus and Thucydides.

I would also add some other features of the work which suggest that "history" is an inappropriate classification. There is a lack of interest in sources, a most rudimentary chronology, and an almost total lack of any sense of the historian's presence over against the material being presented, let alone the *sine qua non* of history writing, the discriminating analysis or explanation, explicit as well as implicit, in the narrative. The difference in these respects between this narrative and, say, the final chapters of 2 Kings (or the Deuteronomistic History as a whole) or, again, the works of Thucydides or even Herodotus is striking. Whybray concluded (p. 19) that "The Succession Narrative, although its theme is an historical one and it makes use of historical facts, is not a work of history either in intention or fact. The author's interests lay elsewhere". In the light of the predominant view this was a conclusion of major importance. That is has not had the kind of impact one might have expected is perhaps in some part linked with his qualification, that the narrative's "theme is an historical one and it makes use of historical facts". Indeed Whybray goes on to argue for a classification of the material as political propaganda, written soon after the events described by some one with access to the "facts". Thus in practice he might appear to be advocating something rather less than a wholesale rejection of the category of "history writing" and something more like a modification or sub-genre — that the work is deliberately *tendentious* history writing.

Though Whybray's classification of the narrative as political propaganda may be viewed as having some link with that as history writing, this is not a necessary connection. His argument against the use of the term history writing may be considered on its own merits, and in my view it has considerable force (so also Crenshaw 1969:138). My own conclusion is a more drastic version of Whybray's: it is simply that the narrative is *not* best described as history writing. Perhaps I should add here, lest I be misunderstood, that this does not amount to a blanket denial of the historicity of the events described in the story. That is a separate matter to which I shall return breifly later (Chapter Three). Here I am simply making an assertion about the author's handling of his subject matter, and about his purpose.

POLITICAL PROPAGANDA

This consideration of Whybray's argument leads naturally to a consideration of the classification "political propaganda". In essence this description has arisen in response to former analyses of the narrative's theme in terms of the succession to the throne. "Every incident in the story without exception is a necessary link in a chain of narrative which shows how, by the steady elimination of the alternative possibilities, it came about that it was Solomon who succeeded his father on the throne of Israel" (Whybray, 1968:20-1). While such analysis had long been familiar (cf. Wellhausen, 1878:224-6), it received significant treatment by Rost (1926/1965). The real concern of the narrative, he argued, is with dynastic politics, the theme is Solomonic succession, and the document was written to the greater glory of Solomon. This view was further explored by Vriezen (1948) and again, more recently, by Whybray (1968). Whybray concluded that the narrative was written during the early years of Solomon's reign, soon after the events described in 1 Kings 2 and while the regime was still threatened by disaffected parties; it is primarily a political document intended to support the regime by demonstrating its legitimacy and justifying its policies (pp. 54-5).

A key element in the shift in defining the genre from "history writing" to "political propaganda" was the general acceptance of a Solomonic date for the narrative. This appears clearly, for example, in Whybray's analysis (p.47):

> He [the author] would not have chosen so recent a period of history as the setting for his story if he had some other [sc. than artistic or entertainment], more practical purpose.

Obviously the Solomonic date magnifies the significance of the political subject matter. If the story touches directly on the accession of the reigning monarch (and the intrigue that led to his) how could it be other than embroiled in contemporary politics, especially if written, as generally assumed, in or around the court? Accordingly it is tempting to look in the narrative for a manifesto. Rost, Whybray and others locate this basically in the outcome. Solomon is the winner. The story is told, therefore, in justification of his succession /4/.

Now it so happens that about the same time as Whybray's book appeared, Delekat published an article (1967) which challenged this longstanding claim that the narrative is written from a view-point favourable to David and the Davidic house. Again he assumes without question that the work appeared during Solomon's lifetime (p. 27) and again he is much concerned to relate text and (reconstructed) historical setting, the latter having no little bearing on his exegesis of the former. Starting with an analysis of the Bathsheba episode, which undoubtedly conveys a less than glowing picture of David, he argues with skill that anti-Davidic and anti-Solomonic polemic pervades the whole narrative. The generic classification as political propaganda provides the logic for the swing of the pendulum. If the document is not *pro* the royal house it must be *anti;* if the tone is not white, it is likely to be black.

Focus upon negative dimensions of David and Solomon in the narrative was not new. For Kittel (1898:177-82), for example, an analysis of 1 Kings 1-2 had exposed something of this possible negative dimension and suggested that the author may have belonged to Adonijah's party. More recently Hölscher (1952), though admittedly working with a different literary unit which extended further into 1 Kings, saw 1 Kings 1-2 as essentially hostile to Solomon, as marking the beginning of decline, an intimation of the disaster (the division of the kingdom) to come. But these arguments had largely been dismissed or forgotten. Delekat's article disturbed a growing consensus and proved influential. One can see its impact, for example, on Brueggemann's stimulating interpretations of the narrative and especially of the character of David, in the change from an exploration of the David who is fully man, fully free and responsible, the bringer of life (1969:487,498; 1972a:8) to the David who is the "death bringer, who in his self-seeking calls down upon his people and his family death" (1972b:108 — the essay in which reference to Delekat first appears).

It is clear that no exegesis can afford to ignore Delekat's emphasis /5/. His general perspective is pertinent and many of his particular observations illuminating. Yet I remain unconvinced that he has accurately described the tone of the narrative. Have a host of critics been totally wrong in detecting in the story an underlying sympathy for David, despite his undoubted short-comings? /6/. I doubt it (and will develop the point further in Chapter Five. As Auzou so nicely puts it (1968:43) : "[David] excites liking" ("Il provoque l'affection"), and even with his weakness "He was never mediocre". This too would appear to be Brueggemann's conclusion (1974) after his earlier explorations of both positive and negative aspects in turn. *Author view*

But, whatever the precise attitude of the narrator towards the dynasty, what becomes absolutely clear from this timely clash of judgments (Whybray and Delekat) is that if there is a particular political *Tendenz* in the narrative *it is by no means obvious what it is*. Indeed this had been Eissfeldt's conclusion (1948:25-6) when comparing von Rad's assessment of the *Tendenz* of the narrative (the legitimation of Solomon), with that of Hölscher, just mentioned. And while this conclusion is no "knock-down" evidence against the propaganda classification /7/ it certainly calls it radically into question. Thus Hermisson (1971:148 n.16) simply comments that it is a thesis which in view of the "distanced" attitude of the author can hardly be maintained. Indeed this notion of "distance" takes us back to a characteristic of the writing which has been much observed, particularly in connection with discussions of it as history writing, viz. its "objectivity". Writing a few years before the publication of Delekat's paper McKane commented (1963:275) : "A noteworthy feature of the History of Succession is the impression of objectivity which it gives. It is not tendentious, nor does it strive to enlist the sympathy of the reader for one side or the other . . . ." Writing in the light of Delekat's paper some years later Schulte contended that this renewed exploration of the negative perspective should not be over-emphasized but be seen as contributing balance to the depiction of the author's political stance as essentially "neutral" (1972:175). *Whybray + Positive*

Nevertheless, if Delekat's article threw the political propaganda thesis into confusion, it was only temporarily. In the past few years a new approach has emerged which has restated the argument by recourse to the methods of source and redaction criticism. Würthwein (1974), Veijola (1975) and Langlamet (1976ab) while differing somewhat in their individual theses, all share a similar method and reach the same conclusion. For them there is no real tension between the positive and negative aspects of David, Solomon and the other leading figures (especially Joab), since these aspects belong in fact to different literary stages in the compilation of the present text. Essentially the stages are two — though to say this is to simplify somewhat and both Langlamet's and Veijola's positions are more complex, involving various levels of redaction. There was originally an anti-Solomonic (and to some extent anti-Davidic) primitive text which has been supplemented by material favourable to the dynasty in order to transform it into its present, pro-Solomonic, edition. The primitive stage is not exclusively profane or secular though that is its tendency, whereas the revision of this piece of tendentious political historiography, as Würthwein terms it, is the work of what Langlamet has described as a theological-sapiential editor. Langlamet agrees with much of Veijola's literary analysis but contests his correlations with Dietrich's scheme (1972) of Deuteronomistic redaction – Dtr G (an historian), Dtr P (a later prophetic editor) and Dtr N (a final, nomistic, editor). For Langlamet, the important (first) theological-sapiential redaction of the original narrative is quite definitely anterior to Dtr G /8/.

All this discussion makes for an interesting development in the study of the King David story but it remains to be seen whether the approach will find further support. It involves an intricate and detailed analysis of the text and much close argument. To examine the various cases in detail would require in turn a major study which I do not propose here. A recent reviewer of Veijola's book (Brayley, 1976) concluded as follows:

> ... one wonders whether the structure has not been built on too narrow a base. The amount of editorial material that can be isolated even by the most rigorous analysis is not large. Furthermore one is not confident that the author has altogether avoided those twin dangers of his method of analysis, excess of subtlety and excess of rigidity. He has undoubtedly produced an interesting piece of work, but this reviewer remains unconvinced by his thesis.

With this I can only concur and add that in my own view the same could equally be said of the theses of Würthwein and Langlamet.

I would argue that there are two major obstacles to the approach of these scholars. The first is that it starts from an unnecessary assumption. Langlamet's summary of the "problem", starting in particular from 1 Kings 1-2 (which is also Veijola's particular concern), is instructive (1976b:329-44). Aspects of the text which are "for" or "against" Solomon are listed and viewed as contradictions. A discussion follows as to whether it is possible to view both aspects as parts of a coherent vision of a single author. Langlamet admits that it is possible to so view them, by invoking, for example, the theological interpretation that sees in the story God's grace over against the frailty of our human condition; and he explicitly acknowledges that in its present form the story in 1 Kgs 1-2 may indeed offer such a vision. Nevertheless his discussion ends with the reassertion of a conviction of contradiction in the narrative (pp. 343-4):

> Let us admit that one and the same author could have presented the accession of Solomon as resulting at the same time from the free choice of Yhwh and from a "palace intrigue" worthy of Rebecca and Jacob (cf. Gen 27). But how is one to interpret the judgements, implicit or explicit, on the conduct of Adonijah (irreproachable or culpable?), the "promise" of David to Bathsheba (genuine or invented?), the executions ordered by Solomon (just or arbitrary?)? Would our theologian have been content to present these contradictory points of view without getting involved? – these contradictory points of view, which surely put in question the final victory of God's plan? It is clear that he has not done so: the actual narrative is no longer neutral; it is, when all is taken into account, pro-

> *Solomonic. This overall impression, however, does not manage to do away with*
> *(faire oublier) the tensions indicated above. None of the "solutions" proposed*
> *up to now has been able to resolve them in an integral way. If there exists a key*
> *to the enigma, it is necessary to look elsewhere.*

To this I would respond as follows.

(a) It is quite possible that an author might be content to leave us with a great deal of ambiguity in his presentation of characters even to the extent of leaving a large question mark hanging over the nature of God's activity (as elsewhere Ecclesiastes does so effectively).

(b) The present text (omitting with almost all commentators the obviously Deuteronomistic section in 2 Kings 2:2b-4,27) is only pro-Solomonic if one chooses to read it that way. As I try to show in Chapter Five this is not the only available reading of the present text.

(c) But why must we be looking for neat "solutions" which "do away with" the tensions? Why should the text be expected to be simply and neatly "pro" anyone? Do we seek to postulate editorial revisions of Shakespeare's *Henry IV* because it is exceedingly difficult to determine whether the plays are "for" or "against" Hal or Falstaff? An essential motivation of Langlamet's enterprise is mistaken. This text, which has for so long been viewed as an entity by scholars who have prosecuted the documentary theory with vigour, is only an enigma if one approaches it with the wrong questions and requires clear and unambiguous answers to the questions the text does indeed raise. In large part, then, this is a matter of genre or the expectation of the reader. Where the genre is political history or propaganda it is natural to expect something more definitive in the way of a message. Similarly when Langlamet is considering the hypothetical possibility of a coherent theological interpretation he would seem to be envisaging the text only in terms of a religious *tract*. Might not the generic model of *novel*, for example, have proved more accommodating to the "problems" of the text?

None of this, of course, proves conclusively that the solution whereby redaction is postulated is the wrong one. It only suggests that such a solution is not inevitable. There is a further consideration, and that is the matter raised by Brayley (above) concerning the criteria available for this kind of redactional hypothesis. First, appeal is made to the presence of doublets, tensions or contradictions in the plot, and the critic's ability to leave something out without affecting the essential story-line. My main criticism here is that evidence can only be accumulated under these heads by pressing, to limits which I regard as unacceptable, the logic or consistency expected of a given passage. Second, a particular segment having been deemed secondary, considerable use is made of correlating vocabulary as a criterion. That is to say, any passage which employs an item of the same vocabulary is in turn suspect as a redactional one. Once grounds, however slight, are found for rejecting passages like 2 Sam 16:31 or 1 Kings 1:46-8 (see Appendix A, below) it is relatively easy to show all other passages containing the language of faith and piety to be secondary. One ends with a massive, apparently interlocking (and so self-authenticating) set of redactional passages, which in fact rests on some, much fewer, particular, finely balanced judgements regarding niceties of style or plot construction and consistency. As observed above, I do not propose a major critique here, but present in the

Appendix A one or two particular cases in an attempt to indicate something of the kind of difficulty I see in this approach.

My general conclusion to this section, therefore, is that if the argument for redaction cannot be considered to have successfully isolated separate stages, each with its own particular political *Tendenz,* then the simple problem confronting the definition of the story's genre as political propaganda, viz. that the direction of the propaganda is unclear, remains a problem. Indeed there is a further problem which is equally formidable for most of the interpretations that have been advanced on the basis of the political document model, and that concerns the date of the text. This, however, is a subject to which I shall return shortly. At present I would conclude that there are sufficient difficulties inherent in this generic label to warrant looking for another.

To deny that the narrative is a document of political propaganda is not to deny any political interest within the narrative. To do so would be absurd. We are looking, however, for the broadest useful description of the work, its primary nature and purpose. Shakespeare's "historical" plays are clearly "political" in terms of subject-matter and themes explored, and few in an Elizabethan audience could have failed to appreciate the undercurrent of comment on contemporary political life and institutions; yet they are above all *plays,* works of art for the purpose of serious entertainment, and least of all are they "propaganda". Knights has commented (1959:29): "Indeed the distinguishing mark of Shakespeare's handling of political actions is the clarity with which he sees them, not in terms of 'politics' (that word which, perhaps as much as any, is responsible for simplification and distortion in our thinking) but in terms of their causes in human fears and desires and of particular human consequences" /9/. The colours of political propaganda are strident. The colours of this Shakespearean literature much too subtle. The same, I would argue, is true of our story of King David /10/.

WISDOM LITERATURE

A further generic model that has gained widespread acceptance for the story of King David in recent years has been that of wisdom literature /11/. This description owes much to the advocacy of Whybray who devoted the greater part of his book on the narrative to it (1968), and it received further support from Hermisson's essay (1971).

It is interesting to observe how the possibility of utilizing wisdom literature as a useful frame of reference comes to be raised. Having concluded (p.55) that the work is "primarily a political document" Whybray nevertheless feels that this description, though accounting for much of the content of the narrative, "is hardly sufficient to account for its literary character or its psychological interests" (p.56). (He has earlier shown a keen appreciation of the literary qualities of the narrative as a story and compared it to a novel). Having raised doubts as to the adequacy of the political description the question of date interposes: in order to account for the literary character "we must return to a more detailed consideration of the milieu in which the author lived". As Brueggemann has noted (1972a:5), the argument for wisdom literature starts from, and develops, von Rad's thesis of a Solomonic "enlightenment" and in broad outline resembles von Rad's analysis (1953) of the Joseph story as a product of tenth-century wisdom writing. Accordingly, by way of the hypothesis of a specially trained cultural elite surrounding David and Solomon /12/, we are brought rapidly by Whybray to the book of Proverbs, "our main source of information about this educational and scribal ideal".

There follows a comparison of the "Succession Narrative" and Proverbs, which leads to the claim (p. 71) that "on many fundamental matters . . . the Succession Narrative agrees closely with the scribal wisdom literature as represented by Proverbs rather than with the sacral tradition of Israel as reflected in — for example — the other Davidic stories in the Book of Samuel". This conclusion encourages the writer to press his case further, which he does, first, by examining further correspondences between the "Succession Narrative" and Israelite wisdom literature and, second, by a comparison with Egyptian political (and wisdom) literature. Whybray makes it clear that he is talking of wisdom literature primarily as *didactic* literature (i.e. meant to instruct, having the manner of a teacher): thus the author of the "Succession Narrative" was himself a teacher or educator, and the work was deliberately designed as teaching material /13/.

This hypothesis, that the narrative is didactic wisdom literature, has been subject to criticism by Crenshaw (1969), and in my view his fundamental argument, that the book fails to specify stylistic pecularities, themes or elements of subject matter, and ideological traits, that are found *primarily* in wisdom literature, is fair and decisive. Likewise, Hermisson's argument (1971), that the narrative is not a textbook *(Lehrbuch)* but history writing or exposition *(Geschichtsdarstellung)* in the context of wisdom thought *(im weisheitlichen Horizont),* is no less open to Crenshaw's basic criticism and does nothing to meet it /14/.

Most of the correspondences between the narrative and Proverbs are generally stated themes which might belong to almost any piece of literature giving an account of men's lives in almost any period of Israel's history. Crenshaw demonstrates this point by analysing in similar terms the prophetical legend in 1 Kgs 13. Similarly there is barely a theme listed by Whybray (or Hermisson, for that matter) which cannot be equally well "illustrated" (and in similar density) by material from, say, the patriarchal narratives or those stories in Samuel which Whybray considers not to belong to the "Succession Narrative". For example (space forbids a full list):

Patience and the control of temper: Jacob waits twenty years before taking action against Laban; David refuses to attack Saul.

Humility versus pride and ambition (also of central importance for Hermisson [pp. 138-41, quoting Prov 16:18]): Jacob humbles himself before Esau; the fall of Goliath.

The use of speech (the right word at the right time; cf. also Hermisson, pp. 141-43): Jacob securing the blessing of Isaac, or mollifying the anger of both Laban and Esau; David persuading Ahimelech to give him bread and a weapon, or convincing Achish of his loyalty.

Friendship, loyality and treachery (also Hermisson, 144-45): Abram and Pharaoh, Isaac and Abimelech, Jacob and Esau, the sons of Jacob and the men of Shechem, etc; David and Saul, David and Jonathan; Doeg and the priests of Nob, etc. /15/.

Moreover, Whybray's conclusions are open to criticism on their own terms. Take again that major conclusion on p. 71:

> ... on many fundamental matters... the Succession Narrative agrees closely with the
> scribal wisdom literature as represented by Proverbs rather than with the sacral tradition
> of Israel as reflected in – for example – the other Davidic stories in the Book of Samuel.

The "fundamental matters" used to differentiate the "Succession Narrative" and Proverbs from other literature are four in all: the importance attached to human wisdom and counsel; the acknowledgement nevertheless of the unseen, all-embracing purpose of God and of his retributive justice; the small attention paid to the cult; and the stress on the importance of ethical conduct, humility and private prayer. These are all clearly non-sacral emphases. Now the claimed correspondences between the two works only really gain force in the argument through the way they are contrasted with other material. The use of the term "sacral" used to describe all other "tradition" loads the comparison. Obviously, neither of these two works is "sacral" (concerned with sacred sites and rites); yet there is any amount of tradition in Genesis and 1 Samuel, for example, which might have been used by way of comparison and which is equally non-sacral in character. In fact the only comparison with *any* material that has been made in the section to which these concluding remarks belong has concerned not "many fundamental matters" but merely *one* of the four main points, viz. the attitude of the author towards the cult. Specifically (pp. 66-71) the "Succession Narrative" and Proverbs are singled out from the other stories about David by virtue of the relative attention paid to two aspects of cultic life, viz. the ark and the oracle – both of which are, in fact, mentioned (albeit briefly) in the "Succession Narrative" /16/ and neither of which plays any part at all in the bulk of the other stories about David (e.g. David and Goliath, 1 Sam 17; David and Michal, 1 Sam 18-19; David and Jonathan, 1 Sam 20; David sparing the life of Saul, 1 Sam 24 and 26; David and Abigail, 1 Sam 20; David and Achish, 1 Sam 27 and 29). As a basis for a significant comparison between Proverbs and the "Succession Narrative" on the one hand and other stories about David on the other these criteria seem a little insecure.

Criticism of this important conclusion in Whybray's argument may be taken further. One of the fundamental matters singled out is the stress in both Proverbs and the "Succession Narrative" on the importance of ethical conduct, humility and private prayer. But whether or not this is an accurate description of Proverbs, where is this *stress* in the "Succession Narrative"? What has actually been shown by Whybray (pp. 57-71) is that certain situations arise in the narrative that raise for the reader serious problems of moral evaluation (quite a different thing from the ethical imperatives, whether direct or indirect ["instruction" or "sentence"], that confront the reader at every turn in Proverbs), that humility is an important emotional ingredient (among others) in the story, and that there is *one* occasion when a character offers a private prayer (2 Sam 15:31).

A final criticism of Whybray's position concerns the suggestion on pp. 72-76 that there might be some parallels of function between the characters and situations of the "Succession Narrative" and the "dramatization of gnomic teaching" found in Proverbs (e.g. Prov 20:13, 20:4; 19:24 etc.; the description of the good wife, 31:10-31, or the "strange woman", 2:16-19; 5:3-8; 6:24-5, 32; 7:5; 25-7; the contrasting pictures of the woman of life and that of death, 1:20-33; chapter 8; the autobiographical recitation, 4:3-5; or the examples given by the teacher of his observations of others, 24:30-6; 7:6-23). Again this suggestion is hardly compelling. Formally speaking, none of this material in Proverbs is remotely like the "Succession Narrative" (cf. length, plot, named characters and dialogue). But the most pertinent difference is simply that the "dramatizations" of Proverbs all draw a clear *moral.* In most cases the teacher makes the lesson absolutely explicit (e.g. "And now, O sons, listen to me . . . let not your heart turn aside to her ways . . . ." [7:24-26]). This is obviously didactic literature. Yet if there is one thing the author of the "Succession Narrative" work never does it is explicitly to draw a moral (cf. Schulte, 1972:171).

THE NARRATIVE AND EGYPTIAN LITERATURE

A similar problem to that last mentioned besets the comparison with Egyptian literature which occupies Whybray's final chapter.

A characteristic *political* genre is the *Königsnovelle,* which however, is totally unlike the "Succession Narrative" in that it is essentially an elaborated and crude form of royal flattery. Hence Whybray himself concludes (p. 101) that the narrative "is obviously not itself a royal novel in the Egyptian sense: it corresponds with it neither in form nor in contents, and it is much longer".

But when we are directed towards literature that has a little more in common — he instances in particular the *Story of Sinuhe* — we find ourselves back where we started: for there is no more evidence that this story is in any important sense either didactic or political literature (or both) than there is in the case of the "Succession Narrative". While Whybray is well able to characterize it (p. 104) as having "great entertainment value" the evidence that it is wisdom (didactic) literature appears to consist largely of the fact that it is about a courtier and depicts, *inter alia,* a king who is fearsome, yet capable of great beneficence, courtly caution before this king, the themes of wealth, filial piety, old age and a good burial, and a central character who is a mixture of wisdom and folly (but is this not an over-simplification of the character?) and who suffers changes in fortune. It is simply not clear why these should be held to constitute the marks of didactic literature. To be sure, Peet (1929:40-1) does indeed claim that *Sinuhe* is "the complete fusion of the two genres [didactic literature and the short story] in a clever but artificial psychological story", but he offers no supporting evidence and neither in his preceding discussion nor anywhere else in his book (his separate section on "Wisdom Literature" does not mention *Sinuhe*) does he treat the narrative as anything other than the kind of short story which elsewhere (p. 27) he characterizes as "told for [its] own sake," "pure pastime, not propagandistic or aetiological in origin", "told...for the pure joy of story-telling" /17/.

Whybray's claim, following the suggestion of Posener (1956:87-115), that *Sinuhe* is also a work of political propaganda /18/, proceeds from little more than the fact that Sesostris, the Pharaoh, is presented in a favourable light. Posener himself (p. 115) is careful to qualify the extent of the link he sees between the story *(roman)* and royal politics:

> The picture which the story paints of the relaxed and happy situation, at the end of the reign of Sesostris 1, is all to the credit of this king. Despite this, and even though

the author devotes much space to the person of the pharaoh, one cannot say that it is
a matter, properly speaking, of a work of political propaganda.

A firmly negative response to the political propaganda suggestion is made by
Harris (1971:232).

Finally, we come to a comparison with the *Instruction of Amenemhet.* Yet once
again, as soon as we move back to literature that is more obviously didactic and
political we move away from the genre of the King David material: Whybray admits
(p. 111) that "Amenemhet seems to be in every way a totally different kind of work
from the Succession Narrative: it is short, it is autobiographical, it is not a novel, it
makes no psychological study of character, it does not express wisdom teaching
through narrative, but simply sets the two genres side by side". What then have the
two works in common? Virtually nothing, unless one is *already* convinced of the
preceding thesis about the "Succession Narrative". Thus it is claimed, for example,
that the author is, like the author of the "Succession Narrative", "a man who
combined the roles of educator, administrator and political propagandist", or that the
historical situations in which the two books were written (early in the reign of the
second king of a new dynasty) were identical.

None, therefore, of these comparisons with Egyptian literature adds significantly
to the case for describing our Hebrew narrative about King David as either didactic
writing or political propaganda. On the contrary, the closest parallel to the King
David story is to be found in a literary piece, the *Story of Sinuhe,* which may best be
described as a work of entertainment (Peet, 1929:40-1; Harris, 1971:232; cf. Whybray,
1968:104).

To conclude: there is little warrant for postulating wisdom or didactic literature
as the fundamental genre of the King David narrative. If the impact of the work upon
us has an aspect that might be termed "educational" this is only so, I would suggest,
in the sense that the reading and appreciation of any literary work of art, of quality,
may be termed an educational experience.

THE DATE OF THE NARRATIVE

The question of a Solomonic date for the narrative has appeared and reappeared
in this discussion of genre. It has clearly been of some importance for the understanding of the narrative. From the assumption about date stems a certain degree of
confidence about our knowledge of the narrative's particular cultural-political context
and of the relation between narrative and context. In fact almost every recent study
of note has linked an analysis of the narrative with a cultural or political description
of the tenth century B.C. and of the Solomonic period in particular. This dating is
almost universally accepted /19/. But what if the narrative were written in the time of,
say, Jehoshaphat or Uzziah or Hezekiah, or even during the exile? This would obviously
pose even further difficulties for most of the arguments about genre which we have
looked at.

The fact of the matter is, as Eissfeldt recognized (1965:140-1), that there is not a
shred of hard evidence to support this assumption that the author of the story wrote
as a contemporary or near-contemporary of the events described. Perhaps the most

commonly deployed argument is that the narrative contains a wealth of circumstantial detail, as though this, in the absence of external controls, somehow demonstrated a near-contemporary, or even "eye-witness", author. Thus Bewer (1962:30) writes: "All this [*sc.* the story] is told by a man who had been present in all these situations, with all the variety of graphic and intimate details that bears the stamp of veracity on its face" /20/. To the reader of, say, the *Iliad*, the *Chanson de Roland*, *Njálssaga*, or a modern historical novel, the lack of substance in this argument will be immediately apparent /21/.

Whybray's ascription of the work specifically to the *early* years of Solomon's reign has cogency, of course, only on the prior assumption of a Solomonic provenance of the work generally. Here he follows Rost in claiming that the author reveals no knowledge of the disruption of the kingdom; thus, it is argued, the work must be dated to the life-time of Solomon (p. 54 n. 70; Rost, 1926/1965:233; cf. Gray, 1970:18). But even if it were true that no such knowledge is revealed (and, as I argue further below, I doubt this very much), it is far from self-evident why this should be expected in a story that is not about the division of the kingdom and is set in a period long before this event.

An underlying reason why a Solomonic date has so readily been assumed by some recent writers may be that it fits the popular conception of the tenth century as a period of blossoming intellectual and literary life (the Solomonic Enlightenment). Alongside major developments in wisdom literature, the work of the Yahwist and the "Succession Narrative" have been important planks in this hypothesis (cf. Alt, 1951; von Rad, 1962:48-55; Richter, 1966b; Wolff, 1966; Scott, 1970; Brueggemann, 1972c : chapter 3).

But whether or not the period was actually one congenial to literary activity (it may well have been), the evidence for locating particular literary compositions in it is fragile, even where it is existent at all. First, the dating of "J" to the tenth century rests on no more solid ground than does the similar dating of the "Succession Narrative". There is nothing in the document, whatever its extent (and this is itself a question fraught with problems) /22/ that demands a *terminus ad quem* in the Solomonic period (cf. Eissfeldt, 1965:194; Fohrer, 1970:151-2; Wagner, 1972:122, 125-30). The move from the standard ninth-century date, itself based on little enough evidence, must be seen as essentially a matter of convenience in the interests of an hypothesis and not as a result of carefully evaluated evidence. Second, few scholars would wish to assign any particular and substantial piece of extant "wisdom" literature to the Solomonic period — an acknowledgement that there were other periods when literary activity flourished. Third, there has been a lack of serious consideration of such other periods in the exposition of this hypothesis of an "enlightenment" and the ascription of particular texts to this milieu.

This brings me back to my original question: what if the "Succession Narrative" were written at some other time, possibly several centuries after the event? If there is no internal or external evidence requiring a Solomonic date for the narrative, neither, I would argue, is there any inherent improbability in almost any date between Solomon's time and the exile. The only substantial objection I can see arising is the claim that the later the date the greater is likely to have been the influence of an idealized Davidic theology and the less a likelihood of the "realistic" presentation of the king that we actually find in the "Succession Narrative" (so, e.g. Kittel, 1896:47; Mauchline, 1971:240). This is a decisive argument for Rost (1926/1965:232-33): referring above all to the role of David in the Bathsheba episode he claims that "It is hardly to be supposed that a later writer would have dared to present David so starkly and without justification in this way". This is to assume, however, a monolithic view of Israelite literature. It is perfectly reasonable to postulate a multiplicity of traditions and ideologies existing side by side in a culture, perhaps sometimes in competition, over a long period of time /24/; and in this connection it is vitally important that we keep the Old Testament as a whole in its proper perspective – we have, of course, absolutely no means of knowing how representative it is of Israel's literary (and ideological) history. Furthermore, it remains the case as late as the sixth century that the Deuteronomistic Historian was happy enough to include the story, warts and all, in his work.

In fact, there are a number of particular indications of date in the text, several pointing to a post-tenth-century date, though in no case could there be claimed to be absolutely firm evidence (cf. Wellhausen, 1878:227-8; Kittel, 1898:47).

(a) In 12:20 David, after the death of the child of adultery, goes into the *house* of Yahweh (cf. "tent" in 1 Kgs 1:39, 2:28, 29, 30). This is most readily seen as a slip on the author's part, an anachronism which puts the date at least after the building of the temple (completed in Solomon's 11th year).

(b) On the other hand, the latest date is the end of the seventh century or the middle of the sixth, depending on one's view of the date of the composition of the Deuteronomistic History.

(c) In 2 Sam 13:18 where Tamar is thron out by Amnon after he has raped her, the text is probably best read, $w^{e\varsigma}\bar{a}le(y)h\bar{a}\ k^e t\bar{o}net\ passîm\ kî\ k\bar{e}n\ tilba\check{s}n\bar{a}\ b^e n\hat{o}t$-$hammelek\ habb^e t\hat{u}l\bar{o}t\ m\bar{e}^{\varsigma}\hat{o}l\bar{a}m$, "and she had on a long tunic, for that is how maiden princesses dressed *in olden days*" (NAB) – reading, with Wellhausen, $m\bar{e}^{\varsigma}\hat{o}l\bar{a}m$ (from of old, in olden days) instead of the extremely clumsy $m^{e\varsigma}\hat{\imath}l\hat{\imath}m$ (clothes) (see Driver, 1913b:300). This emendation is widely followed (cf. among recent English versions : RSV, JB, NAB), and to argue against it, as Hertzberg does (1964:321), that "a fashion for kings' daughters in Israel cannot have been all that old" hardly settles the question. Either Hertzberg is taking $m\bar{e}^{\varsigma}\hat{o}l\bar{a}m$ to mean literally "from eternity", which is unnecessary, or he is taking it in the sense of "in olden days, from of old" and assuming a Solomonic date for the text, in which case the fashion could only reach back a few generations at most and the expression $m\bar{e}^{\varsigma}\hat{o}l\bar{a}m$ would indeed be an odd one to use. My point, however, is that it is precisely the Solomonic date for the text that is in question and so cannot be allowed to determine whether the emendation should be accepted or not.

A different argument that would dispose of the evidence of $m\bar{e}^{\varsigma}\hat{o}l\bar{a}m$ would be to omit the whole sentence as a gloss, as does H. P. Smith (1899:330), for example, but only because he fails to appreciate the point of it in its context. It is not merely a piece of antiquarian information. Rather, as Ehrlich (1914:7) rightly noted, it prepares us for vs. 19 where Tamar tears the robe. The robe is of the kind worn by the maiden daughters of the king (and in *this* context $b^e t\hat{u}l\bar{a}h$ clearly has the connotation "virgin" – against Wenham, 1972:341-5) : the tearing of the robe is thus doubly symbolic of her loss of status.

Even if we were to retain the MT, or reject Wellhausen's emendation but omit $m^e c\hat{i}l\hat{i}m$ altogether as a gloss on $k^e t\bar{o}net\ pass\hat{i}m$, the rest of the sentence still remains a problem for an early date. The imperfect $tilba\check{s}n\bar{a}$ is most naturally taken as a past frequentative — "for thus the maiden princesses used to dress, were clothed" /25/ — and the very fact that the information is supplied at all in this way implies a time of composition when the fashion was largely unknown. The only way around this point, I think, is to argue that $tilba\check{s}n\bar{a}$ should be allowed a present sense and that the audience lay outside court circles.

For my part, I prefer to side with the great majority of modern versions and critics, and accept the emendation, with all that its acceptance implies for the date of the story.

(d)   18:18. After the account of Absalom's death we find: "Now Absalom in his lifetime had taken and set up for himself the pillar which is in the King's Valley, for he said, 'I have no son to keep my name in remembrance'; so he called the pillar after his own name, and it is called Absalom's monument to this day".

Some scholars find here an irresolvable conflict with 14:27 (did Absalom have sons or not?) and are inclined to see 18:18 as "earlier" or "original" (e.g. H. P. Smith, 1899:359; Kennedy, 1904:281; Mauchline, 1971:268). Hertzberg (1964:360) reasonably supposes that it was perhaps sorrow at the death of the sons that prompted the building of the monument. The narrator, of course, has a motive for not mentioning any such cause, for he is utilizing the story rather to highlight the prince's ambition, his desire for fame. The passage, therefore, may be regarded as original and again the implication is that some distance separates narrator and event /26/.

(e)   A scrutiny of critical comment on the parties involved in Absalom's rebellion quickly reveals a major division of opinion, depending partly on the meaning assigned at any given point in the text to such terms as "all Israel", "all the tribes of Israel", "Israel", "the men of Israel" and the "people" (or "army"): the issue here and elsewhere in the story is the relation of these terms to "Judah" and "the elders of Judah" /27/. The problem is that the narrator's usage appears to be inconsistent and is certainly confusing /28/. A tension exists between the depiction of events in terms of, on the one hand, the binary society (Israel and Judah) and, on the other, a concept of Israel or "all Israel" ("from Dan to Beersheba") which at times is reminiscent of the "all Israel" idealization in the Joshua narratives or Judges 19 and 20. I would argue that the simplest explanation lies in positing a late date for the text: the confusion is just what we should expect for someone writing long after the United Kingdom had ceased to be — someone who has but a hazy grasp of the political constitution of this kingdom and who is often unsure of which parties *precisely* were involved in the events which form the matrix of his story.

(f)   Finally, to anticipate the next chapter: I argue that the story shows clear signs of traditional composition and contains subject-matter and motifs that belong pre-eminently to the world of the story-teller. For the story to develop along these lines, at least a few generations are likely to have elapsed, perhaps many more.

SAGE ?

CONCLUSION

It is not my purpose here to press a case for any particular date or historical context for the narrative. I doubt that that could be done with the prospect of inspiring any more conviction than does the current uncritical acceptance of near-contemporary authorship. Rather I wish to stress how hypothetical is the nexus between the text and the generally accepted setting. And because it is hypothetical the effect is that the more the historical perspective becomes an integral part of our understanding of the text the greater the chance that that understanding may be grossly distorted. This is particularly the case where the "political propaganda" characterization is concerned.

I have examined prevailing views of the most appropriate genre-label for the narrative and exposed some of the weaknesses in the foundations of these views. In the next chapter I propose an alternative approach.

CHAPTER THREE
GENRE: AN ALTERNATIVE VIEW

Chapter Three
Genre: An Alternative View

NOVEL OR STORY

Much of Whybray's chapter on the character and purpose of the narrative is an examination of it as a novel (pp. 19-47); he analyses the work in terms of categories such as theme, structure, use of dialogue, characterization, and style. Indeed he arrives at the conclusion (p. 47) that "the work is a novel — albeit a historical one — rather than a work of history properly speaking" and he is prepared to offer the judgement that "No doubt purely literary and artistic aims and the desire to entertain the reader occupied an important place in the author's mind". As we have seen there is cause to doubt whether his subsequent qualification of this description in terms of political and didactic models is necessary.

Take that qualification away and his discussion remains an eloquent plea for classifying this narrative as a novel. I am constrained to ask, therefore, Why not let this, or some similar characterization, stand? Why should not literary and artistic aims and a desire to entertain the reader occupy not merely "an important place in the author's mind", but *the* important place? Why not accept the narrative as first and foremost a fine piece of story-telling and not as essentially something else?

As already observed, Luther (1906) saw this material primarily in terms of the *Novelle* or short story. Caspari (1909) also argued that the material has the style and character of a *Novelle* though he felt that it dealt with real historical events. Gressmann (1910), too, characterized the material as *novellistisch,* howbeit, in the case at least of 2 Sam 15-20, an *historische* rather than *literarische* (i.e. purely fictional) *Novelle.* Among more recent critics Jackson (1965) has accepted, with reservation, the characterization "historiography" but has nevertheless offered an account of the narrative primarily in terms of categories such as character, suspense, major and minor themes, scene and plot, all of which are more appropriate to a story like a novel than to a piece of history writing. A similar tension is found in Gray's discussion (1970:17-22). Rightly, in my view, he finds in this material "the substance of the novel" and also the style and "dramatic technicalities" of the "professional story-teller" or "narrative artist". Indeed he is prepared to recognize "dramatic interest" as the predominant compositional principle. Despite this he is unwilling to accept that "mere entertainment" can be the major purpose of the work and insists on defining its purpose in terms of historical as well as political and didactic categories.

My own suggestion, therefore, is hardly radical. It simply takes seriously as a major clue to the basic genre of the narrative the one aspect of the work that has commanded the most widespread agreement, namely its quality as a work of art and entertainment. The argument of the previous chapter showed the problems inherent in current classifications of the narrative as history writing, political propaganda or didactic literature. The case for viewing the narrative as a story in the manner of a modern novel or short story (*novella*) remains persuasive. My proposal is that the primary generic classification of the narrative should be as a story in the sense of a work of art and entertainment.

As already observed, Whybray and others have used the term "novel" in connection with our narrative and, to be sure, this term might appear to offer some advantages of precision over the rather loose term "story". We may certainly recognize in the narrative most of the ingredients of the novel that Whybray lists (p. 19): thematic and structural unity /1/; convincing and lively dialogue; credible characters, corresponding in their complexity to the experienced realities of human nature (though this is not true of all the characters); and a lively and flexible style, conveying to the reader mood, feelings, atmosphere, irony and humour.

Yet the term "novel" implies certain features of composition that I am less sure are appropriate in the case of the King David narrative. The term implies an essentially written as opposed to an oral genre, and it implies also a particularly high degree of autonomy of the author over his style and subject matter. Whybray, like von Rad (1944/1966), sets the narrative over against the "earlier sagas" and the "Yahwistic history" and speaks of it by contrast as a "free composition" ("the earliest work if its kind in Israelite literature", p. 19). As I shall soon argue, however, there are clues in the text which suggest that the narrative may be more of a traditional composition than is generally allowed and that it may not be so easily differentiated, generically speaking, from other prose stories, "legends" or "sagas", in the Old Testament. Accordingly I prefer not to describe the narrative as a novel, though it may usefully be compared to a novel in many respects. Yet to use the terms "legend" or "saga" at the present time is to court misunderstanding and entangle oneself in a form-critical, terminological dispute. The broader term "story", appropriately qualified, appears therefore to be the best available term. The primary generic classification of the narrative should be in terms of a story, told in a traditional vein, as a work of art and entertainment.

I must now substantiate my claim that there is a significant "traditional" aspect to the story.

TRADITIONAL STORY

Certain segments of the story show signs of having been patterned on traditional material. The patterning may be found in the details, including sometimes the specific linguistic expression of the constituent elements (content) of the segments concerned. It may also be found, in a more abstract way, at the level of structure, plot or shape (form), rather in the manner of a motif as one finds that term used in Stith Thompson's *Motif-Index*. It is sometimes a matter of both. In some cases the instances of the pattern relate to each other differentially in varying relations of form and content (which is not surprising since form and content are almost always inseparable).

In some cases the traditional (or conventional) nature of the material is to be inferred from the existence of similarly patterned material or motifs elsewhere in Old Testament narrative, in others from its existence in other story literature, and in yet others from a combination of both these circumstances.

A. TRADITIONAL MOTIFS

In this first section the argument for traditional composition in the narrative is drawn from my 1976a paper. The patterning mainly consists of abstract correspondences of form and content. For want of a better word I am inclined to term these patterns "motifs".

1. David and the Sons of Zeruiah

In a carefully contrived account of David's withdrawal from, and return to, Jerusalem in 2 Sam 15-16, 19-20 (cf. Jackson, 1965:194; Auzou, 1968:395; Flanagan 1972:177) we notice on both journeys an incident involving Abishai (16:5-13; 19:6-23). The stereotyped nature of the segments is clear enough. David is confronted by an avowed enemy. Abishai wishes to kill the man. David will have none of it and expresses a sense of dissociation or friction in terms that begin with the formula, "What have I to do with you, you sons of Zeruiah?". The man is then allowed to go his way.

If we turn back to 1 Sam 26 a similar pattern emerges. Joab's brother, referred to as "Abishai the son of Zeruiah", goes down with David to Saul's camp. David comes upon the sleeping Saul. Abishai wishes to kill him /2/. David refuses and they go their way. Although this time there is no explicit expression of friction it is clear that a tension exists — David and Abishai have completely different views on what is appropriate action in the circumstances. As Van Seters (1976b:24) has helpfully brought to my attention, this underlying pattern of tension persists even where there is a contrast of specific detail. Whereas in 1 Sam 26:6ff. the sanctity of the "Lord's anointed" is appealed to by David against Abishai as grounds for preventing a killing, in 2 Sam 19:21ff. the same notion is appealed to by Abishai as grounds for carrying out a killing.

Now it is noticeable in 16:10 and 19:23 that David does not address Abishai by his own personal name. Rather he is seen as representative of the "sons of Zeruiah" /3/. The implication is that there is a characteristic relationship of friction or tension between David and his nephews, the sons of Zeruiah; this kind of conflict might equally have been expected if it had been Joab (or Asahel) instead of Abishai who was involved /4/.

This brings us to the story of David and Joab in 2 Sam 3. Here the pattern is modified in one important respect: David is not in a position to prevent death (here that of Abner). Nevertheless his attitude is made clear to Joab: "It was told Joab.

'Abner the son of Ner [i.e. the enemy] came to the king, and he let him go, and he has gone in peace'" (3:23). Joab (or more precisely "Joab and Abishai") kills Abner (3:30). David's expression of dissociation then forms the basis of the rest of the chapter (note that Joab is made to eat humble pie) and his speech concludes, in terms which sum up the relationship (3:39), "These men, the sons of Zeruiah, are too hard for me".

The pattern surfaces again in the story of the death of Absalom in chapters 18 and 19. David orders Joab and Abishai (and Ittai) to "deal gently for my sake with the young man Absalom" (18:5; cf. vs. 12). Nevertheless when Joab confronts his (and David's) enemy, helpless in a tree, he kills him. David's reaction is to make it quite clear that he disapproves (18:32 – 19:5). In this case, however, there is a nice twist to the end. The roles of the chapter 3 incident are reversed: the sense of friction is expressed with vigour by Joab (vss. 6-8) and this time it is David who is obliged to back down. The wheel has come full circle.

Finally it is possible to detect vestiges of the same pattern of relationship in at least one other passage. In 21:15-17 /5/ we read of David fighting against the Philistines, growing weary, being rescued by Abishai, and being adjured by his men to go out to battle no longer. In terms of the stereotype we have David confronting an enemy and exhibiting "weakness", the son of Zeruiah as the man of action (who in this case, like Joab in chapters 3 and 19, actually kills the enemy) and there is an expression of friction, which, if the "men of David" are taken as including Abishai /6/, has its particular parallel in the end of the Absalom episode (19:6-8) where it is Joab who berates David rather than *vice versa* /7/.

While the pattern is found mostly within the story of King David (in Chapter Four, below, I argue for the inclusion of 2 Sam 2-4), it does occur elsewhere, which suggests that it may well be a traditional pattern, in this case part of the stock-in-trade of the narrator of stories of David and his men. Between them the passages just examined account for nearly all the stories (as distinct from mere mention) of Abishai, and for two of the eight stories of Joab, in Samuel and Kings. It would seem that the role of the sons of Zeruiah vis-à-vis David has in time been encapsulated in a memorable and easily deployed stereotype.

In terms of dramatic value this particular stereotype has a special piquancy. It is good story-telling material, not just because it deals with conflict over whether to kill or not to kill, but because it embodies a fascinating love-hate relationship between the characters. "What have I to do with you, you sons of Zeruiah?" asks David in exasperation. The answer, of course, is "everything", for they are his right hand men. Another answer might be that they are the sons of Zeruiah: that is to say, they are David's sister's sons (according to 1 Chron. 2:13-17); consequently they are bound in loyalty by ties of blood. In a sense, therefore, the matronymic is a constant reminder of this dramatic predicament /8/.

2. The Judgement-eliciting Parable

We now move to a case where the relation between the relevant passages is much more abstract or formal than in the previous case, and indeed the particular pattern of relation is one which Thompson cites in his *Index* of motifs (J80-99).

In 2 Sam 14 the woman of Tekoa tells David a fabricated story (parable) designed to elicit a particular response which then pre-empts his judgement on a matter concerning himself. The same technique is also used by the narrator in chapter 12, with Nathan's story of the rich man and the poor man's lamb. A third example occurs outside the King David story in a narrative in 1 Kgs 20 where one of the sons of the prophets tricks the king of Israel into self-condemnation by just such a parable /9/.

Simon (1967) terms the parable a "juridical parable" and stresses that the essence of the story is that it poses a "legal" issue and involves a judge *qua* judge passing sentence upon himself /10/. Thus he considers Isa. 5:3-4 to be "no more than a rhetorical-literary transformation of the actual appeal to the king or judges at the gate" /11/.

Now if Simon really is suggesting, as it would appear, that we have here a "literary genre" with a primary connection with a "legal" setting of kings and "judges at the gate", then one must observe that as such it can hardly have enjoyed much of a vogue. After all, it presupposes the litigant having a case against the king or judge together with a willingness to put them in the dock, as it were, by a deliberate deception — altogether, I should have thought, a rare and risky event in the ancient world, unless perhaps it were purely a prophetic genre for use in legal or royal situations. But then the woman of Tekoa is not a prophet /12/.

On the contrary I would argue that the legal element is merely an accident of these particular cases where the one to whom the parable is addressed happens to be a king with (implicit) judicial powers. Certainly this lends an added dramatic quality to the situation. But in terms of the function of the parable in these stories the role of the person to whom it is directed is irrelevant. The judgement may be any sort of judgement — moral, legal, or aesthetic, to note but three possibilities. All that is required is that the parable provide a sufficiently apt parallel to the addressee's situation that he makes the right judgement (i.e. one that suits the deceiver's purpose) and that when the key is provided ("*you* are the man") he cannot escape the force of its application to his own case.

The essential features of these particular parables are, first, the deception (as Simon rightly observes /13/): the parable is presented in such a way that its nature as parable is not apparent to the addressee; second, the aptness of the parallel /14/; and third, a judgement or evaluation by the addressee that suits the deceiver's purpose.

All these features invite the recognition that, as the parables stand, they are firmly rooted in their context. While Rofé (1974:153) may be right to say of the parable in general that it is "a story designed from its inception for its moral" this is only true for our parables in the limited sense that they are designed by a particular person in order that another particular person may draw a particular lesson ("moral") /15/. Apart from those persons these parables are meaningless.

Moreover, their significance in the context is fundamentally bound up with their success (the third feature). It is no accident that all these stories are stories of *successful* deceptions. If the addressee were to give the wrong answer to the parable (for example, if David had said to Nathan, "Well, I'm sorry for the poor man, but there may be more to this than meets the eye — take the case to the local examining magistrate") the parable would have been ludicrously pointless. That is to say, it is only the story of effective deception by parable that bears repeating.

My point then is this. Wherever else parables may occur (in wisdom literature, prophetic oracles or elsewhere) these particular ones are thoroughly at home in their narrative setting. And in this setting the parable functions as one element in a constellation of elements forming a narrative stereotype or motif — the imparting of self-knowledge by parable — which comes to concrete expression here in three distinct stories. The suitability of the motif for story-telling is obvious: it has, built in, the favourite ingredients of deception and irony, while an element of suspense, the risk of death, say, may also play some part, depending on the version. In addition, the construction of the parable is a challenge to the artistic skill of a narrator.

That the judgement-eliciting parable is, and has been, a popular motif of story of many kinds (folk tale, anecdote, *novella*) may be amply demonstrated from Thompson's *Motif-Index* (J 80-99) /16/.

Let me take one example from a French fifteenth century A.D. collection of *novelle* (Robbins, 1960:tale 10) which, when compared with our Old Testament examples, illustrates well the essential nature of the motif by reason of the very difference of its particular expression and moral tone, though it, too, like the Nathan-David story, involves a ruler and his adultery.

A young counsellor refuses to arrange extra-marital assignations for his newly married lord, a great nobleman of England. His master therefore sets about involving him in what is in this case not a spoken but an acted parable. Taking good care to disguise any connection between what he is about to do and the earlier refusal, he arranges for the young man to be fed no other food than his favourite — eel pie, no less. After initial delight the counsellor comes by degrees to protest strongly against the monotony: "By God, my lord, order them to bring me some other food to recover my appetite, otherwise I'll waste away". The nobleman then provides the key to the parable: "And don't you think that *I* might be bored?". The counsellor takes the point and the nobleman resumes his affairs.

In the story of King David, therefore, in these anecdotes of the judgement-eliciting parable, we have material (that is, the motif in question) that suits admirably an appreciation of the narrative as a story. And once more it is material that is likely to be traditional. Given its popularity in other literature, the occurrence in Kings and the fact that it is used twice in the King David story, the presumption must be, I think, that our narrator was not the first to deploy the motif in a Hebrew story.

Whether these particular versions of the motif are themselves traditional (in whole or part) is another matter. It is conceivable that these are merely Davidic versions of stories told of other prophets in confrontation with other kings (and not necessarily kings) — stories of a prophet or counsellor rebuking by this means a ruler for adultery, or of a courtier interceding thus on behalf of a ruler's son. The evidence for any final decision is lacking. Nevertheless there are some particular features in the story of the woman of Tekoa, quite apart from the use of the motif itself, that suggest a debt to tradition.

(i) The Woman Intercedes. In several respects the interview between David and the woman of Tekoa is reminiscent of the scene in 1 Sam 25 describing Abigail's intercession with David (Hoftijzer, 1970:424-7; cf. Budde, 1902:XVI; Segal, 1964-5: 326). Though I would not wish to press the matter too far, it seems to me that there are some indications here of traditional stereotyping, not only of the framework (the approach to the king, appropriate formulas of introduction, king's response) but also of the subject-matter (themes of revenge and bloodguilt in the context of a woman's intercession with the king) as well as some interesting verbal correspondences (cf. 1 Sam 25:23-4 and 2 Sam 14:4; 1 Sam 25:24 and 2 Sam 14:9; 1 Sam 15:24 and 2 Sam 14:9; 1 Sam 15:35 and 2 Sam 14:8).

(ii) The Fratricide. One further piece of evidence may be adduced for traditional composition in 2 Sam 14. As has been observed (Klaehn, 1914:39; Blenkinsopp, 1964: 449; 1966:51), the fictional tale told by the woman of Tekoa has a certain correspondence not only with the Absalom and Amnon incident which it is designed to parallel but also with the myth of Gen 4:1-16, the Cain and Abel story. The fratricide is in. danger of imminent death and needs the protection of a royal/divine decree; in both cases they are out "in the field" by themselves when the murder takes place; Cain is destined to be a "wanderer on the face of the earth", while to the woman there will be left no remnant "on the face of the earth".

3. The Woman who brings Death

It is remarkable how in the major episodes of the story of King David (David and Ishbosheth; David and Uriah; David and Absalom; David, Solomon and Adonijah) a woman is so often an important catalyst in the plot (Rizpah, Saul's concubine; Bathsheba; Tamar; Abishag, David's concubine). One is reminded of the key role of Potiphar's wife in the Joseph story.

Blenkinsopp (1966:52-6) detects in the Bathsheba story a motif of the woman who brings death /17/, observing that such a motif is common in ancient literature and that it is also to be found in the work of the "J" writer (this point is in line with the special interests of Blenkinsopp's paper). He notes (a) the case in Gen 38 of the marriage of Judah with the daughter of the Canaanite Shua (i.e. Bathshua; =? Bathsheba; cf. 1 Chron 3:5) which is followed by the violent death of the first two children born in their marriage; and (b) the classic case, at the beginning of the primeval history, of Eve, *the* woman who brings death.

But we may go further, to observe that Bathsheba is only one woman who brings death in the story of King David. Each of the women listed above is a catalyst in a story of death. The quarrel over Rizpah leads, indirectly but relentlessly, to the destruction of both Ishbosheth (the owner) and Abner (the claimant); the seduction of Bathsheba brings in its train the death of Uriah (the owner) and the illegitimate child (a token for David, the claimant?); the rape of Tamar leads to the death of Amnon (the claimant) and Absalom (her protector); and finally David's concubine Abishag, is the occasion of the deaths of Adonijah (the claimant) and Joab /18/.

It is also interesting to observe the regular occurrence of two deaths. This is also the pattern in the case of the Bathshua of Gen 38 and in a more obvious parallel to the motif in Genesis, viz. the story of Dinah (Gen 34), where both Hamor and Shechem meet their deaths through the woman /19/.

Such observations, therefore, lead to the suggestion that the material is built around a traditional folk motif.

4. The Woman and the Spies

The story of the lucky escape of Jonathan and Ahimaaz (2 Sam 17:17-20) is another segment in the narrative that brings one directly into the orbit of the teller of tales where stories of escape by deception are legion (cf. Thompson, 1955-8:K500-699). In this case there are sufficient shared features with the story of the spies at Jericho (Jos 2) to suggest again a particular traditional story pattern /20/. There are two spies in or at a city. The king of the city learns of their presence and sends men to find them. They are hidden in a house (under something) by a woman. The king's men come to the house and demand that the spies be given up. But the woman gives false directions, the pursuers go on their way, fail to find the spies, and return to the city. The spies escape.

There are, in addition, several further elements of detail that point to the stereotyped nature of the episodes.

It is curious that in 2 Sam 17 we read that "they came to the house of a *man* at Bahurim, who had a well in *his* courtyard; and they went down into it. And *the woman* took and spread a covering over the well's mouth". Not "the man's wife" or "his wife" but simply "the woman". And in any case why not the man himself? It is as though at this point the conventional pattern (seen elsewhere in the Rahab story) is asserting itself. The motif required is one of escape through being hidden by (an unknown?) *woman*.

It is also a curious fact that in neither case are we told that the pursuers searched the house. Rather the narrator is content for them to be given (false) directions by the woman. Yet this renders rather pointless the account of the hiding. In other words there are really two distinct motifs here, viz. escape by a cunning mode of hiding and escape through a confederate giving false directions; these motifs have not been combined in a completely successful way /21/. The fact that both stories offer us not only substantially the same two motifs (cf. the variety of suitable motifs in Thompson, 1955-8:K500-699: e.g. "disguise" instead of "hiding"), with merely differences of detail, but also the same somewhat unsuccessful manner of construction, argues strongly for their being derived from a common parent scene already in this basic form.

A further point worth noting is that in both cases the pursuers assume that the spies are (or have been) in this particular house. This is quite explicit in Jos 2:3 ("Bring forth the men that have come to you, who entered your house") and may be inferred in 2 Sam 17:20 ("Where are Ahimaaz and Jonathan?" And the woman said to them, "They have gone . . . "), where the directness and specificity of the pursuers' question (there is no explanatory preamble) and the manner of the woman's reply (she makes no attempt to deny that she has seen the spies) are not such as we might have expected were the narrator thinking of this as a random enquiry.

Now this knowledge on the part of the pursuers makes good sense in the Rahab story where the men go *first* to the woman's house: from the context it is clear that they are seen there and that this is reported to the king with the inference being drawn that they are spies (only the inference is given explicit expression in the actual narrative). In the case of Ahimaaz and Jonathan, however, they are seen at En-Rogel and flee from there to Bahurim, and it is at Bahurim that they seek and find refuge in the house. How then do the pursuers know about this particular house? We need at least some other indication of the two men having been spotted again in order that the pursuers' knowledge fit that narrative smoothly.

One reasonable explanation for the omission (though certainly not the only one) is that the pursuers' knowledge belongs to the motif and that the motif is more suitably decked out in Rahab's clothes, so to speak, than those of the woman of Bahurim. What has gone amiss in the King David version is that the narrator has introduced Bahurim (i.e. an additional venue) into the story, probably because it provides the fine irony that the scene of Shimei's cursing, only a few passages earlier (16:5-13), is now the place of refuge for David's spies who carry news that is crucial for his survival /22/.

Note finally that the false direction of the pursuit is connected in each case with water.

5. The Two Messengers

The critic who wishes to press this story of King David into simply historiographical, political or didactic moulds is faced with intractable material in the account of the bringing of the news of victory and of Absalom's death to David at Mahanaim (2 Sam 18). The account of the race is sheer entertainment. It adds no information of any importance for our understanding of the war and only indirectly has any bearing on the motives and roles of the leading characters. Nor does it *teach* us anything in particular; although it is possible that a didactic folk motif, viz. the round-about route may actually be the more straightforward (cf. Thompson, 1955-8:J2119.2.1 and 2; also J266), partly underlies the account of the race, this is no more than hinted at. Rather the tale of the race is essentially a tale of suspense which at the same time, by creating a "build-up" to David's reaction to the news of the battle, serves to heighten the emotional impact of his response as well as the irony in the ambivalence of his attitude to the victory /23/.

The suspense lies not just in our being given "ample time to ponder how David is likely to receive the report" (Ridout, 1971:97) but also how this is likely to affect the messenger — will he receive reward or might he, like the messengers of 2 Sam 1 and 4 /24/ be the object of violent displeasure (Gressmann, 1910:182; Budde, 1902:286; Hertzberg, 1964:360-1; McKane, 1963:266-7)? The ominous overtone emerges in the hint of understatement in Joab's words ("The king's son is dead . . . you will have no reward for the tidings") coupled with his extreme reluctance to let the young man run and the fact that it is a (mere, disposable?) Cushite who is despatched first. But it is probably not only the clues provided by the narrator himself that are meant to alert the reader to this undercurrent of risk. To an audience familiar with stories of kings, wars and courtly intrigue, the delicacy of the messenger's task and its risks and rewards would be a theme to which it would be immediately sensitive (cf. Thompson, 1955-8:J1675.2 [cf. J815], P14.9, R3) /25/. As it turns out the young Ahimaaz is more than equal to the task and manages to convey the news of victory yet equivocate on the potentially risky matter of Absalom's death /26/, while the narrator then dissipates the messenger-orientated tension in the introversion of David's emotional outburst, which then redirects the focus of the narrative.

The reception of the messenger is not the only element in the episode that is susceptible to interpretation as traditional story material. I have already indicated above the possibility of another motif (the round-about way may be the quickest) underlying part of the tale; similarly the eagerness of the young hero to be in the forefront of the action, against the advice of his older and wiser guardian, has a certain stereotyped quality that might suggest a traditional background (cf. Parry and Lord, 1953-4:1/273-4; 419 ([10] and [11]); 81-2). Moreover, there are particular descriptive features in the passage that show signs of stereotyping.

The report of a messenger's arrival is a favourite topic of elaboration in folk narrative (Chadwick, 1932-40:*passim*; Lord, 1960:80-1). Its dramatic potentialities are obvious: it provides a change of focus, a chance to express (if the narrator so desires) the expectations and attitudes of the receiving party, and, of course, can act as a retarding device (Ridout, 1971:100-1) drawing out the suspense. In the present case the elaboration in terms of a watchman scene is reminiscent of the scene in the story of Jehu (2 Kgs 9:17-20). In each case the watchman aloft has successive reports to make to the king and the movements of two messengers are the focus of attention. The identification of one of the arrivals forms the climax (and conclusion) of the watchman's part in the scene (though in 2 Kgs 9 the two messengers are not arriving, but sent out, in turn, to meet the arrivals):

"I think the running of the foremost is like the running of Ahimaaz,
son of Zadok" (18:27).
"And the driving is like the driving of Jehu, son of Nimshi" (2 Kgs 9:20).

18:27 contains also a formulaic reminder of another messenger scene in the story of King David. Just as the watchman's identification of Ahimaaz draws the comment from the king that "He is a good man ($^{\circ}y\check{s}$ *twb*) and comes with good news ($^{\circ}l$ *bswrh twbh ybw$^{\circ}$)*", so in 1 Kgs 1:42-3 the arrival of Jonathan the son of Abiathar with news for Adonijah prompts Adonijah to say, "Come in (b°) for you are a worthy man ($^{\circ}y\check{s}$ *ḥyl*) and bring good news (*twb tb\check{s}r*)". My concern is not with the rather curious notion involved (the correspondence of a man and his message — see McKane, 1963:267; Mauchline, 1971:288) but with its character as a cliché in such a scene.

6. The Letter of Death

The motif of a man carrying a written order for his own execution is widely attested in story the world over (Gunkel, 1921:132; Thompson, 1955-8:K978). Its inherent qualities of irony and suspense make it of the very stuff of story-telling. Indeed, like the use of the judgement-eliciting parable, one may be quite sure that it has thrived more in the telling than in the event. Although the account in 2 Samuel is the only occurrence we have in extant ancient Hebrew literature it is unlikely that the story of Uriah was the first or only time this motif was employed by Israelite narrators.

Accounting for the Patterns

Granted that the resemblances postulated above do indeed exist and are not trivial, there are two main arguments that might be raised against my suggestion that they illustrate the conventions of a tradition of story composition.

(a) The first argument is that some at least of the resemblances are coincidental — literary or historical accidents. Despite the folkloristic character of the scenes it remains possible that Uriah did carry the letter as recounted, that Nathan did reprove

David with just this parable and that there were two messengers despatched to David, the one overtaking the other in the way described. Strictly speaking this point is incontrovertible. My response would be to draw attention to (1) the accumulation of such motifs and (2) the story qualities of the individual passages and/or the contexts from which they are drawn (dominant interest in character, plot, dramatic suspense, etc.). If it were clearer that we were dealing with an historiographical genre reporting events at first or second hand, it would be easier to dismiss even the accumulation of such patterned or stereotyped material as a series of coincidences. As it is, the literary interests of the narrative suggest strongly that these are indeed literary conventions.

(b) The second objection to my argument is the one raised by Van Seters (1976b). Some of the resemblances (those where there is a high "content" factor as opposed to merely formal parallelism) are evidence, he argues, of direct literary dependence or even single authorship. To this I would respond as follows. (1) He would need to demonstrate clearly (and not just speculate about) the motivation for both the patterning and, in some cases, its specific variation. He signally fails to do so in regard to most of my evidence. As I have remarked elsewhere (1976:158-9), his inadequate treatment of this matter of the motivation of postulated cases of direct literary dependence or revision is one of several key failures in his argument (1975) concerning the growth of the Abraham stories in Genesis /27/. (2) The argument concerning single authorship is obviously of limited value, given the range of material discussed. In any case it raises large new questions about the original literary units of Samuel and Kings which would need to be settled before the argument could be pressed with the kind of confidence Van Seters employs.

Tradition

In the event Van Seters cannot account for the bulk of my evidence in terms of literary dependence and so he is prepared to speak of it in terms of "folkloristic motifs", howbeit in certain cases "minor" ones (1976b:27). He attempts, nevertheless, to dismiss this evidence of traditional composition as trivial.

(a) One argument depends on a manipulation of the meaning of the term "traditional".

In the present discussion and in previous papers I have been at pains to observe a distinction in my use of the terms "traditional" (implying a significant measure of conventional subject matter shared by an author, his contemporaries, and his predecessors) and the term "oral traditional" (where the mode of composition in which these conventions are found is specified clearly) (cf. Lord, 1974:201-5). The term "traditional" is used without prejudice to the further question of how the material might be related (whether directly, indirectly, or not at all) to an *oral* tradition. Much of Van Seters' criticism of my case conveniently ignores this distinction. Thus, while admitting that the judgement-eliciting parable "may be folkloristic in character and origin as far as its form is concerned", he writes that nevertheless "its use in the Court History is strictly literary. To follow Gunn's line of reasoning one would have to say that every piece of literature that contained even a popular story would have to be the product of oral story-telling, which is absurd" (1976b:26). His point, of course, depends on his presentation of the discussion as one about whether the material is oral or strictly literary (written) rather than whether or not it is traditional. In point of fact, however, I have nowhere argued either that the motif in question (judgement-eliciting parable) must be an oral one or that the narrative in which it is now embedded must be the direct product of oral story-telling.

Perhaps it is the use of the term "story-*telling*" (taken as indicating oral and not written composition) that has misled Van Seters, though the term has been used in the present discussion (a) in accordance with its regular use in the English language to denote both the writing and telling (in spoken words) of stories, /28/ and (b) in the context of a clear distinction drawn at various points between traditional and oral-traditional.

Somehow, indeed, Van Seters seems to have overlooked the conclusion to the paper he is criticizing on this score. I stated: (1976a:229):

Whether the stereotypes are oral as well as traditional is another matter. While it remains quite likely that they derive from oral tradition, even directly so . . . I cannot point, as I could [in an earlier paper (1974) – see below, on Oral-Traditional Composition] to a particular compositional technique that is so characteristically oral. Clearly motifs such as the judgement-eliciting parable and the Uriah letter may be firmly ensconced in a "written" literary tradition, as the extra-Biblical parallels show. But if there remains some difficulty in determining the precise relationship of the narrative to oral *tradition its debt to story-telling tradition should not be in doubt.*

Van Seters' point, then, does nothing to upset the argument for the traditional nature of the material in question. I shall turn to the issue of oral literature shortly.

(b) A second way in which the evidence of the folkloristic motifs may be minimized is to argue that in themselves they do not point to a body of tradition about David specifically. Thus Van Seters talks of the "constant reapplication of folklore motifs by story-tellers and literary artists to new persons, times and situations" (1976b:28). It is unlikely that he is thinking of the new persons, times and situations as actual historical ones. As the student of traditional literature well knows the adaptation of new persons and events to traditional story patterns or motifs can be a drastic process /29/. With cases such as the Uriah letter, the judgement-eliciting parable, the two messengers and the woman hiding the spies, one must either argue that the motif and historical fact happen to coincide in every case (I doubt that Van Seters has this in mind) or else admit that the incorporation of the motif is likely to have considerably transformed the depiction of the underlying historical event, in which case the resultant narrative will have become to that degree "traditional" and to that degree removed from any status as historical report or record.

Rather it seems that Van Seters must view the story as a creation of fiction, like a modern novel, with the author tempering his creation (*ex nihilo,* as it were) with elements of traditional material, motifs and techniques, at certain points. Now it has to be said that given the lack of demonstrably independent internal (i.e. Old Testament) corroboration of the main events of the narrative, and in the absence of external historical controls, it is impossible to contravert this hypothesis (which can in fact be applied to a great deal of the Old Testament). Nevertheless, I would argue, on the one hand, that there are still grounds on which a residuum of historicity can be postulated for the narrative (for example, the general coherence of this material with what precedes and follows in the Deuteronomistic History and the lack of evidence, from whatever source, conflicting with the broad outline of events as depicted in the King David story). On the other hand, we do have, elsewhere in the Old Testament, indications that other David material has come to us after a period of traditional composition and transmission, namely such variants as the killing of Goliath, David's entry into Saul's court, and David's sparing of Saul (1 Sam 24 and 26). Might it not merely be an editorial accident that we have few similar variants from the story of David as king? This state of affairs could be due simply to the conflation of a number of rather fragmentary sources to provide the story of his rise as against a heavy reliance upon one major and extended account to detail the subsequent period of his life. It is reasonable, therefore, to argue at the same time both for there to be genuine historical antecedents to the story and for it to have acquired non-historical characteristics through its transmission in tradition.

(c) An associated argument is the claim that despite the presence of traditional elements the genre as a whole is unexampled: "One cannot show any long tradition of such a story form either in the Old Testament itself or in ancient Near Eastern literature in general" (Van Seters, 1976b:22-3). But what can this mean? The Old Testament abounds in this kind of "historical" story and though our story of King David is undoubtedly more extensive and has a more complex plot than most (though compare the stories of Joseph and his family, Ruth, and Esther) these are differences of degree and not of kind. (Tolstoy's *War and Peace* is no less a novel than Steinbeck's *Of Mice and Men*). Nor is this kind of "historical" story absent from ancient Near Eastern literature in general (cf. for example, in Egypt, some of the stories in Petrie's collection of Egyptian tales [1895], including the tale of Sinuhe; also *ANET*, pp. 18-31).

B. ORAL-TRADITIONAL COMPOSITION

I have examined some criticisms directed against my claim to have discerned a significant degree of traditional composition in the narrative. Is it possible to say more and speak of an oral tradition in connection with the story?

I would argue that some evidence of patterned narrative composition in the Old Testament is indeed most readily explained as the product, direct or indirect, of an oral tradition. This is where instances of the pattern show close verbal correspondences, and yet at the same time a measure of dissimilarity (cf. Lord, 1974:206-10). Precisely such a relationship of similarity and difference, fixity and fluidity, in the stereotyped segments or building blocks of a narrative is a phenomenon familiar to the student of oral-traditional narrative, whether it be poetry or prose, including material not dissimilar to the predominant kind of "historical" tale found in the Old Testament. One finds considerable variety of types of stock description or incident (called variously by scholars, *topos,* typical scene, or theme, amongst other terms), with variation in length, function within the story, and relative fixity, depending upon different authors and different traditions. What I have particularly in mind as a possible model in the present case is a ready-made segment of narrative (usually a small ingredient of a plot or a descriptive elaboration) which may be repeated in different parts of the same story or in different stories, with a significant measure of verbal consistency. Thus different instances of the one typical scene will often show an intriguing blend of both similarity and difference even within the work of a single story-teller /30/. Each instance of a given patterned segment of this kind is likely to have been influenced by many others which its author has heard from other traditionists or composed and narrated himself, and will in turn influence others to come (in which case it may well be fruitless to try to trace an "original").

I have cited comparative evidence for this type of composition and discussed it more fully in my 1974a paper /31/. For present purposes I illustrate the argument with a selection from the evidence which bears directly on our story of King David.

1. The Gift of Provisions

An interesting parallel to 2 Sam 16:1 is found in 1 Sam 25:18. Both verses belong to a context where someone, attached to a potential enemy of David but acting independently of him, brings provisions to David as a conciliatory gesture. The people concerned are, respectively, Abigail the wife of Nabal, and Ziba the servant of Mephibosheth. In each case asses are used to transport the food and in each case it is specified that David's n^crym are to partake of the gift (1 Sam 25:21; 2 Sam 16:2).

Both lists begin with two hundred loaves *(lḥm)*. Abigail's gift then includes two skins of wine *(nbly yyn)*, five "sheep ready dressed" *(ṣᵓn ᶜśwywt)* and five measures of parched grain *(sᵓym qly)*. The 2 Sam 16 list does not include the sheep or parched grain but ends with a skin of wine. Both continue with one hundred bunches of raisins *(ṣmqym)*. Then where Abigail's list notes two hundred cakes of figs *(dblym)* Ziba's list has one hundred "summer fruit" *(qyṣ)*. It is very likely that these fruits are the same, viz. figs /32/. The quantity in 1 Sam 25, as with the wine, is double that in the other passage.

Leaving aside the two items in 1 Sam 25 with no equivalent in 2 Sam 16 (the sheep and the parched grain), we have a correspondence of content as follows (in order of items in 2 Sam 16) /33/:

2 Sam 16		1 Sam 25	
200	loaves	200	loaves
100	raisins	100	raisins
100	summer fruit (= figs?)	2 x 100	figs
1	wineskin	2 x 1	wineskin

There is even a certain correspondence of sequence disturbed only by the position of the wineskin(s), last in 2 Sam 16 but following the loaves in 1 Sam 25.

Presumably the tendency by commentators to ignore the parallels between the passages is based on the view that they are simply fortuitous, a coincidence of historical fact or narrative detail or perhaps a combination of both. This view, of course, must remain a possibility. It depends really upon how impressed one is with the parallels that have been drawn and inevitably there is at this point an element of subjectivity involved in one's decision.

On the other hand it must be borne in mind that it is not just a simple case of coincidence that is at issue. Not only is it a question of whether the particular foods involved are likely to have been included in any list of provisions /34/; it is also a matter of whether the quantities of the comparable items would be likely to be so similar — that is, precisely *two hundred* loaves, *one hundred* bunches of raisins, and, where there is a difference, for it to be constant, exactly *twice* the amount of wine and figs/summer fruit in 1 Sam 25 /35/. Furthermore there is the fact that the "coincidence" extends beyond the details of the list to the peculiar circumstances of the gift (described above, at the beginning of this section). Such an accumulation of coincidence carries with it a certain improbability.

A variation of the argument would be to concede a degree of stereotyping in the list but to consider whether in real life the offering of a gift in such special circumstances might have followed an established set of norms, including the items and quantities involved.

Against this argument is the fact that nowhere in either narrative is any indication given that the gifts are considered by the narrator or by any of the characters to be of any such distinctive type. Nor do the particular selections of food and drink receive special attention. Hertzberg's impression (1964:344-5) of the *ad hoc* nature of the selection in Ziba's case is certainly that gained from a reading of the Abigail episode.

Van Seters (1976a:149) has suggested that the similarities can be accounted for by postulating the literary dependence of 2 Sam 16 on 1 Sam 25. Precisely what explanation this provides is not clear. Perhaps he envisages a deliberate literary reference by the author of 2 Sam 16 to the other passage. But what would be the motivation for the reference and how do we account for its decidedly oblique nature? Would not a deliberate reference have been designed to be spotted as such? Why scramble the items at all? Why not give precisely the same list and make the reference a little more obvious? Or perhaps Van Seters envisages the stereotyped quality of the list to be the hallmark of a single author. The question remains, however, as to *why* the author should have standardized to this extent.

A simpler approach is to entertain the possibility already indicated, that such a list was a commonplace amongst story-tellers and that it is thus a piece of conventional narrative. This provides an explanation for the similarity irrespective of whether the passages derive from the same author or not.

2. The Battle

The brief description of the battle between David's and Absalom's armies, 2 Sam 18:6-7, fits a pattern of narration found elsewhere in the books of Samuel. To this particular pattern belongs also the account of the confrontation between the men of David and those of Ishbosheth, 2 Sam 2:17 (which, I argue in Chapter Four, also belongs to our story of King David /36/) as well as 1 Sam 4:10, from the story of the battle at Aphek and the death of Eli; 1 Sam 4:17, the report of that battle by the messenger who comes to Eli; 1 Sam 31:1, the defeat of Saul at Gilboa; 2 Sam 1:4, the description of that battle by the man who brings the news of David.

The passages divide into two segments. There is *first,* in those accounts which are not a messenger's report, a simple statement that the battle was joined, (= element 1), and *second,* in all passages, (a) an equally brief mention of the outcome in terms of the flight/defeat of one side (= element 2(a)), (b) a mention of casualties, usually described as large, on the side of the defeated, (= element 2(b)) and (c) an account of the death of a person or persons of importance usually on the defeated side (= element

2 (c)), an exception being 2 Sam 2 where it is Asahel, on the winning side, whose death is detailed /37/. At its most basic, this last element, (c), takes the form of a brief mention of the fact of the death, while in 1 Sam 31 this is followed by a more deatiled account, and in 2 Sam 2 and 18 the elaboration alone is given without any initial summary expression /38/.

In 1 Sam 4:10 a note about the ark comes between elements (b) and (c) and interrupts a simple three-part sequence here (cf. 1 Sam 4:17 where it follows (c)). On the other hand it does not disturb the basic analysis of the pattern: apart from the evidence of the other passages for the postulation of a "regular" sequence the context itself indicates clearly that the presence of the ark at the scene of hostilities was considered quite unusual in this period of Israel's history. It is probably fair, therefore, to characterize it as elaboration /39/.

2 Sam 2:17 varies the scheme somewhat, perhaps because of the distinctive way in which this battle opens. Whereas in 2 Sam 18:6-7, for example, the battle vignette is preceded directly by a sentence to the effect that the army went out against Israel /40/, in 2 Sam 2 such verbs of movement are found rather earlier, in vss. 12 and 13; moreover there is here what can only be a deliberate ambivalence: the obvious hostility of *wyṣ³ lqr³t* (2 Sam 18:6) in such a context gives way to *yṣ³w wypgšwm* /2:13/. Whether or not a battle will ensue is thus yet uncertain.

The account then details the peculiar contest between the two groups of twelve. But with the men falling dead together we are already dealing with element 2(b) where the details of the severity of the encounter are given. Hence in vs. 17 the standard pattern is picked up with an element 2(b) clause ("And *the battle was very fierce* that day"), yet one which at the same time, through the subtle use of the language, incorporates a standard element 1 expression indicating formally the onset of the battle (= 2 Sam 18:6: "And *the battle took place*):

1/2(b)   <u>*wṯhy hmlḥmh qšh ᶜd m³d bywm hhw³*</u>
            <u>and there took place a battle, a very fierce one,</u> that day

Element 2(a) then follows naturally, whether considered as normal sequence or a simple case of reverse sequence: "and Abner and the men of Israel *were defeated* by the servants of David".

As far as the linguistic affinities between the various instances of the pattern are concerned, they are fairly complex, as may be seen in the accompanying table of the central portion set out by elements /41/.

These passages, then, are closely linked and the pattern that emerges is basically a tight one. The constituent elements are limited in number, a firm core is present in each case, even the sequence is constant except where special factors have necessitated a change (2 Sam 2:17), and there are some close linguistic affinities.

But this is not all. In two cases, 1 Sam 4:17 and 2 Sam 1:4, the pattern overlaps with another, quite different, set of parallels.

2(a)

ישראל	וינגף		1	4:10
לאהליו	איש	וינסו		
ישראל לפני פלשתים	נס			4:17
ישראל מפני פלשתים	אנשי	וינסו		31:1
מן ‧המלחמה	העם	נס	2	1:4
ישראל לפני עבדי ד'	א' ואנשי	וינגף		2:17
עם ישראל לפני עבדי ד'	שם	וינגפו		18:7

2(b)

מאד	גדולה	המכה	ותהי	1	4:10
ויפל מישראל שלשים אלף רגלי					
היתה בעם	גדולה	מגפה	וגם	4:17
בהר הגלבע		חללים	ויפלו	31:1
נפל מן העם וימתו	הרבה		וגם	2	1:4
המלחמה קשה עד מאד ביום ההוא			ותהי	2:17
ביום ההוא עשרים אלף	שם המגפה גדולה		ותהי	18:7

2(c)

בני עלי מתו		ושני		1	4:11
חפני ופנחס					
בניך מתו	שני		וגם	4:17
חפני ופנחס					
ואת בניו	וידבקו פלשתים את שאול			31:2
פלשתים את י' ואת א' ואת מ' בני שאול	ויכו			1:4
שאול ויהונתן בנו מתו			וגם	2	1:4

Table 1.   The Battle pattern——elements 2(a)(b)(c)

2(a)

		And	[every] man	Israel	was defeated	to his tent /42/.
1	4:10	And		Israel	was defeated	to his tent /42/.
		and	[every] man		fled	before the P's.
	4:17	And		Israel has fled		before the P's.
	31:1		the men of Israel		has fled	from the battle.
2	1:4	The army				
	2:17	And A. and the men of Israel			were defeated	before the servants of D.
	18:7	And the army	of Israel		was defeated there	before the servants of D.

2(b)

1	4:10	And there was	very great slaughter and there fell	of Israel	30,000 foot-soldiers.
	4:17	And also	great carnage	has there been among the army.
	31:1	And they fell,	the slain,	on Mt. Gilboa.
2	1:4	And also	many	fell	of the army and died.
	2:17	And there was	a very fierce battle	on that day.
	18:7	And there was there	great carnage	on that day 20,000 men.

2(c) /43/

1	4:11		And the two sons of E.	died,
			H. and P.	
	4:17	And also	your two sons	are dead,
			H. and P.	
	31:2	And the P's overtook	S.	and his sons,
		and the P's struck down	J. and A. and M.	the sons of S.
2	1:4	And also	S. and J.	his son	are dead.

Table 2.   The Battle pattern—elements 2(a)(b)(c)

3. The News of Defeat

1 Sam 4:12-7 and 2 Sam 1:2-4 both tell of the bringing of news of the defeat of Israel before the Philistines /44/.

A man comes from the defeated army:

2 Sam 1	1 Sam 4
והנה איש בא מן המחנה מעם שאול	וירץ איש בנימין מהמערכה ויבא שלה ביום ההוא
And behold, a man came from the camp, from Saul.	And a man of Benjamin ran from the battle-line, and he came to Shiloh that day.

He bears the signs of disaster /45/:

ובגדיו קרעים ואדמה על ראשו ויהי בבאו ...	ומדיו קרעים ואדמה על ראשו ויבוא ...
And his garments were torn and there was earth on his head, and when he came . . .	And his clothes were torn and there was earth on his head, and he came . . .

In 2 Sam 1 he goes straight to David, whereas in the other passage there is some elaboration and heightening of tension at this point — it is only indirectly that he reaches Eli, the key figure in the scene. David's first words to the messenger are to ask whence he has come. In 1 Sam 4, however, probably because Eli has just been described as being blind, it is left to the messenger himself to announce his presence and say whence he has come:

ויאמר אליו	ויאמר האיש אל עלי אנכי הבא מן המחנה (²) ואני מן המערכה נסתי היום
ממחנה ישראל נמלטתי	
And he said to him, "I have escaped from the camp of Israel".	And the man said to Eli, "I am he who has come from the camp /46/, and I have fled from the battle-line today".

David and Eli then ask the same question:

ויאמר אליו דוד מה היה הדבר הגד נא לי	ויאמר מה היה הדבר בני
And David said to him, "What thing has happened? Tell me".	And he said, "What thing has happened, my son?".

Each messenger then replies (a) that the army has fled, (b) that there has been great loss of life, and (c) that two people of great importance to the listener are dead (note the details of the language in the table set out above).

This last pattern, of course, brings us back to the Battle passages, for it is the core of the more specialized battle pattern that we have just previously been eaxmining. (Whether the singling out of *two* people in each of these particular cases is more than coincidental is hard to judge.)

Here the parallel ends. 1 Sam 4 adds that the ark has been captured. Following the messenger's report Eli falls back dead. The episode in 2 Sam 1 also finishes with a death, though this time it is that of the messenger.

The pattern as a whole is obviously somewhat looser than the previous one. Certain clusters of elements which are given a fairly standardized expression are linked by the broad direction of the narrative moving from depiction of the messenger to the end of his recitation. It is a looser set of parallels certainly, but remarkable for all that.

Accounting for the Patterns

In accounting for the patterning there are, as in the case of the Gift of Provisions, two main possibilities to be considered. First, is it possible that the similarities noted among the passages are simply fortuitous (cf. Löhr, 1898:121)? After all, one could argue that given a large enough number of short accounts of battles, some are bound to coincide to some extent. It is hard to dismiss this possibility out of hand. Nevertheless one can weigh some of the factors involved and remain sceptical.

The parallels between these battle scenes not only involve subject-matter in common but an economy of subject-matter. It is not only a matter of what is said but of what is not said. One can imagine a great many features of a battle that might have claimed the narrator's attention but which receive no mention at all /47/. Moreover, the rather terse sequence, in markedly circumscribed language, occurs in the face of some important variables, viz. the relative length and particular details of the stories in which it occurs /48/.

It is noticeable also that in 1 Sam 31 the pattern in what seems to be its basic form (with virtually a single clause sufficing for each element), while remaining an integral part of the narrative as a whole, rather spoils its flow since it anticipates the more detailed (and aesthetically more satisfying) account of the death of Saul and his sons which immediately follows upon it /49/. In other words, it could be argued that element (c) in its simplest form is narrated in 1 Sam 31 *despite* the subsequent development of the passage, just because it *is* part of a regularly employed sequence /50/.

The extension of the parallels into the "Bringing of News" scene naturally compounds the difficulty in accepting simple coincidence as an explanation of the similarities. For despite a general looseness in the parallel as a whole, there are some remarkable points of close linguistic and elemental correspondence quite apart from the actual report of the battle.

The second consideration is whether the resemblances are due in any way to direct literary dependence. Since in at least one case the set of similarities may well cross an authorship boundary (1 Sam 3 1/2 Sam 1) /51/, it is likely to be more than a matter of the literary idiosyncracies of an individual author, though even that would constitute only a partial answer. Rather the literary critic is likely to press for an explanation involving the deliberate assimilation of one passage to another: either an author has modelled one passage on another, perhaps in order to evoke certain connotations, or an editor has glossed one passage by another, perhaps in order to fill in details or else to create a specific reference /52/.

Probably the greatest single stumbling block to any such explanation is the complexity of the linguistic affinities of the battle scenes. (It is significant that Van Seters [1976a:145-8] in his criticism of my [1974] analysis of this material makes no attempt to meet this crucial point). A glance at the table setting out elements 2(a), (b) and (c) is sufficient to give a reasonably accurate impression of the multiplicity of lines of both correspondence and difference. A systematic check, passage by passage and element by element, simply confirms the impression: it is virtually impossible to discern any consistency in the way one passage relates to any other or others in this respect. There is too much variation from one point of comparison to another. Even where one might have expected the closest parallels, in the case of 1 Sam 4:10 and 4:17, it is hard to say that there is a closer relationship between these two than between, say, 1 Sam 4:10 and 2 Sam 18:6-7 (except for element 2(c)) or between 1 Sam 4:17 and 2 Sam 1:4. Perhaps 2 Sam 2:17 and 2 Sam 18:6-7 may be singled out since they do appear to share several points of detail which are rather distinctive /53/, but even so each contains elements or parts of elements which are closer to other passages.

If further doubt remains about the probability here of direct literary assimilation one has only to attempt to account for the numerous small differences in the language of parallel elements to dispel it. Such an exercise simply ends in a degree of arbitrariness that is unacceptable.

The similarities, then, are in some sense the product of artifice and yet probably not of direct literary assimilation or adaptation. Certainly the simplest explanation is to postulate that we are, indeed, dealing with material that is, in some measure, conventionally patterned.

Several further observations are in order now.

(a) First, we are dealing with passages of narrative, each of which is a subsidiary segment or constituent part of a larger story. In fact, in the cases we have looked at it is hard to detach any of them without doing violence to the larger story, for they are part and parcel of it. This is particularly well illustrated in 1 Sam 4, where both patterns are part of a movement culminating in the death of Eli, with the core of the battle account occurring again in the messenger's report to Eli. Here the information conveyed to the old man, via the pattern, is essential to the story. Again, therefore, it is very difficult to see either pattern in terms, say, of an editor's gloss. They are part of the *basic* shaping of the story as we have it.

(b) The term "story" is highly appropriate for all the larger contexts to which the passages belong: the dramatic account of the death of Eli (1 Sam 4), the miserable fate of Saul (1 Sam 31), David's shrewd, flamboyant gesture of respect to the dead Saul (2 Sam 1), the creation of a blood feud between Abner and the sons of Zeruiah (2 Sam 2), and the crucial testing of David before his friends and attendants at the news of the death of Absalom (2 Sam 18), the last two, of course, coming from our story of King David.

On the face of it there is little here that one could reasonably describe as "annalistic" in tone, despite Van Seters' repeated urging (1976a), certainly not if the Assyrian and Neo-Babylonian (or even Hittite) annals are anything to go by /54/. The stories in which our patterns are located are not dreary records, mechanically rehearsing king-centred clichés. They touch the human condition, indeed are directed

to the common man in a way that is rarely found in the annals of kings. The account
of the suppression of Absalom's rebellion has several distinct movements, but they
drive relentlessly towards that cry: "Would that I had died instead of you, O Absalom,
my son, my son!". The king ceases to be king. From this point on he is simply and
essentially man. In the same manner, the blind Eli sits alone. The bringing of the news,
that he too has lost his sons, is prolonged. The shout in the town, to Eli, is full of
ambiguity. Even in this simple story there is an element of universality that is surely
integral to the point of the narrative.

The range of characters (what annalist would have paused thus over the details of
the death of young Asahel, swift of foot as the wild gazelle?), the frequent use of
direct speech in genuine dialogue, the circumstantial detail in 2 Sam 2:23, for example,
all these point in the same direction — this material is the stuff of the story-teller,
whatever its historical status and whatever its redactional history. All this makes it
very difficult to be persuaded by Van Seters' assertion that we have here the scribal
conventions of an annalist or chronicler.

(c) Finally, it is significant that a second stereotype has emerged in close
association with one of the instances of the "Battle" pattern. It is, I would argue,
only a token of the extent to which recurrent patterns are probably a factor in the
composition of these stories, given the extremely limited amount of comparable
story material that is available for analysis in the Old Testament.

Oral Tradition

As previously noted, the argument for oral composition in Judges as well as
Samuel is pursued further in my 1974a paper. Further cautious explorations of
"parallel scenes" in Old Testament texts have been made by Culley (1976a) and I
find myself largely in agreement with his conclusions (pp. 64-7). The blocks of
material he examines are generally more abstractly related than mine, often
constituting plots in themselves. By and large they lack the tight linguistic
correspondences that are a crucial feature for my argument and are to that extent
not directly comparable. Nevertheless many of his scenes may readily be accounted
for in terms of stock or traditional material along the lines expected in orally composed
prose. There are, of course, problems, particularly because of the limited amount of
text available for analysis. It is rarely possible to rule out entirely the possibility of
literary imitation in a written (scribal) tradition as an explanation of the relationship,
though in some cases I think Culley is perhaps over-generous in allowing this
possibility as a particularly likely one. Especially useful is his exploration of the
middle ground, the possibility that what we have in the Old Testament at many points
may be a "transitional" text. Such a text would derive from what had become a
wholly or largely written tradition but it would use modes of composition which were
an extension of the modes earlier developed and established in an oral tradition.

In the light of his discussion I am encouraged to stand by my argument in
the 1974a paper that we do have some small clues pointing to specifically oral
composition in a number of specific cases. On the other hand it is only too clear that
the available evidence, like that discussed by Culley, is strictly limited, and that even
if we may be reasonably sure that the passages examined reflect an originally oral
mode of composition, the question of how precisely the stories to which they belong,

taken as wholes, are related to oral tradition must still be an open one. A given text could be a direct transcript by dictation from oral tradition; it could be the free composition of a literate author. who was familiar with the style and content of oral-traditional narrative, and who had heard the story in oral tradition; it could be the product of a literate author dependent in part on oral tradition for content and style and in part on the use of archival material; or it could be the end of a line of composition by literate authors which began with oral-traditional narrative being committed to writing and which developed into a written tradition still influenced by traditional content and modes of expression (as I suspect was the case with the Icelandic "family sagas" /55/). These are only some of the possibilities. I doubt, however, if evidence sufficient to give more precision is, or is likely to be, available, since as Culley would agree (1976a:66-7) there is little reason to suppose that the texts produced under the circumstances just indicated would necessarily differ in ways that would provide evidence clear enough for us to discriminate between them (short of our identifying actual written sources).

So even if the argument of my 1974a paper be accepted it does little more than indicate that somewhere behind the story of King David (or parts of it) lies a tradition of oral narrative composition. Nevertheless this would be some specific evidence of oral origins in an area where otherwise only broad generalizations about the most likely mode of composition and transmission of stories are available as evidence. Not that even such generalizations are without value. Like many before me I would argue that in its formative stages Israel's "historical" stories were most likely to have been composed and transmitted orally. The picture of rural family and tribal life in the patriarchal and early settlement periods, and the pattern of archaeological evidence for writing in Palestine and the uses to which it was put, both suggest this as a reasonable postulate /56/. The evidence discussed earlier in this chapter shows that material in our story of King David is related to traditions of Hebrew story-telling that we glimpse elsewhere in narratives from Genesis to Judges /57/. If so, it probably shares with them their debt to oral tradition.

A further small point in favour of my thesis is of a quite different kind, namely the balanced, almost rhythmic, nature of the prose. This characteristic made it relatively easy for Bruno (1935) to postulate, albeit unnecessarily, a poetic original. E. F. Campbell (1976:5), observing this style of "artistic prose" also in a number of other Old Testament narratives, (for example, the stories of Joseph, Judah and Tamar, Eglon and Ehud, Ruth) suggests that the rhythmic elements were probably partially mnemonic in purpose. Another striking factor. seen at best in a scene such as David's flight from Jerusalem, is the fondness for the infinitive absolute, a feature which contributes strikingly to the flow of the story and one which might well be linked with an essentially oral art form.

Are there any features of the text which might militate *against* my case? The form critics, such as Gressmann (1910), who distinguished between the *Sagen* (legends) of Judges or even 1 Samuel, and the *Geschichtsschreibung* (history writing) of 2 Samuel, argued from the sophistication and elaboration of the story. But sophistication (by our standards) or skill, whether in plot construction, use of language, rhetorical devices or characterization, tell us nothing about the compositional character, written or oral, traditional or otherwise, of a narrative. There are simplistic story-tellers in oral traditions, and there are sophisticated ones, just as there are naive and complex traditions as such. Similarly the length of a story is irrelevant as a criterion. Oral-traditional narrative can sustain multi-scene and complex plots no less than written literature, especially in the work of narrators of talent; and the story of King David is no run-of-the-mill story. Moreover, when comparing this narrative with others in the Old Testament that have been thought to be derived from oral tradition it is as well, once again, to be aware of the many different forms in which oral material can reach written form. One may consider, for example, whether individual stories of patriarchs or judges were deliberately abbreviated for, or by, the recorder in order to facilitate the compilation of material on a broad scale, such as the recording of a whole "cycle" of stories (Gunn, 1974b:516; Wilcoxen, 1974:65; cf. Rofé, 1970:432).

The question of sophistication or creativity in oral-traditional texts is one that has caused great confusion. It is well known that Milman Parry, on discovering the oral-formulaic nature of the Homeric texts, argued that it must have been impossible for Homer to do anything more than manipulate already existing material (formulas and "themes" or stock scenes) (cf. 1930:146-7; 1932:15). But this was not a position to which he held rigidly and subsequent research on both Homer and the Serbo-Croatian heroic narrative, which provided the verification of Parry's basic thesis about the traditional nature of the Homeric texts, has led many scholars further away from the view that oral-traditional style cannot tolerate a creative narrator (cf. A. Parry, 1971:xlvii-lxii; Holoka, 1973).

The point can also be made from less well observed prose traditions and generalized for our purposes. There are varieties of oral tradition as there are varieties of narrator within a given tradition /58/. It is a "tradition" because of a relatively high level of redundancy in conventional content together with the employment of long-standing conventional techniques of composition /59/. Within a given tradition one may find narrators whose art consists of little more than a facility for memorizing and transmitting in near-verbatim form the art of their mentors; or one may find narrators who employ traditional techniques of composition and traditional story-content to individual effect, by appropriate expansion and contraction of constitutent segments, novel jutaposition of elements, elaboration of plot, descriptive embellish-ment or indeed the paring of descriptive embellishment, re-motivation of characters, and the adaptation or reformulation of the linguistic expression of traditional descriptive elements. Clearly, too, the content of an oral tradition may change with the incorporation of new characters and events. Thus it makes sense to talk of Homer as an artist of genius working within, most probably, a living oral tradition; it makes sense to contrast the artistry of the Yugoslav narrator, Salih Ugljanin, with the much poorer performance of his compatriot Sulejman Fortić, both of them certainly oral-traditional composers (Parry and Lord, 1953-4); and it makes sense to explore the skill and sensitivity of the author of the King David story while at the same time drawing attention to traditional aspects of his composition. "Creative" and "traditional" are not incompatible terms when one is exploring oral-traditional narrative composition.

It is failure to grasp this point that leads Van Seters (1976a:152) to find my postulation of a significant traditional dimension to the story of King David at odds with my analysis of it (1975, and see further below, Chapter Five) as a sophisticated and carefully constructed composition. The description of a narrative as "traditional" does not imply that the author has *no* personal control over his material or is totally unable or unwilling to innovate; rather it indicates that the composer works with influences or constraints regarding style and content which are relatively greater than is generally the case with modern novel writing (a possible exception would be the "pulp" novel).

CONCLUDING OBSERVATIONS

There is evidence in the story of King David that significant elements in it have been derived from an existing story-telling tradition. Given that our extant sample of ancient Israelite story-material is so small, it is reasonable to assume that in fact the debt of the King David story to tradition probably exceeds considerably what is immediately demonstrable. Accordingly we may properly speak of the story as a traditional story. I have argued, furthermore, that this story probably stands not far from an oral stage of transmission, though its precise relation to oral story-telling is impossible to determine.

A few observations remain to be made. The purpose of the story, I have argued, is entertainment. Old Testament scholars, when they can bring themselves to admit that entertainment might have had something to do with the composition of this particular piece of literature, are apt to qualify "entertainment" with the adjective "mere". I prefer the adjective "serious". Matthew Arnold (1895) used the phrase "high seriousness" to describe the artistry of the finest poets – a seriousness born of artistic excellence, absolute sincerity and an ability to tap significant veins of truth about humankind. Such seriousness is characteristic of the art of the King David story as it is of the entertainment which this story undoubtedly provides. As with art, entertainment can mean different things. There is entertainment designed for simple amusement, to fill an idle hour and be forgotten and there is entertainment which demands the active engagement of those being entertained, which challenges their intellect, their emotions, their understanding of people, of society and of themselves. It is in this latter sense that I would speak of our narrative as a work of art and *serious* entertainment.

But if the purpose of the story is serious entertainment, there is no clear indication that the author regarded the work as one of fiction. Rather the likelihood, given that his story is about a former king and a civil war, among other public events, is that the author believed himself to be recounting in essence what actually happened, whether or not it *was* precisely what happened. Certainly the story is narrated with a firm feeling for actuality (or potential actuality) and in its realism it reminds one of the Icelandic "family sagas" (so also Schulz, 1923:177; Chadwick, 1932-40:II 636-7). With the Icelandic stories a similar problem arises: there is good reason to believe that the genre was treated by authors and audience as though it yielded what we might call "historical" truth, yet scholars are able to detect demonstrably fictitious or highly conventional elements in the stories. The solution is not to describe the sagas as either fictitious "novels" or historical records of the utmost reliability handed down verbatim over generations, but to understand that stories based on historical incidents can be subject to reshaping in tradition while yet retaining for teller and audience the character of "truth" (Steblin-Kamensky, 1973; cf. Parry and Lord, 1953: I 239, 356). Clearly, therefore, my description of the story of King David as a story told for the purpose of serious entertainment must include the likelihood that the retailing of "historical" information was considered a normal ingredient of such entertainment. How accurate that information might have been we are unable any longer to determine with any precision, lacking, as we do, any significant external controls.

What of the life setting of such a story? Who might the author have been? This must remain a matter for speculation only, as it has always been, no matter what view has been taken of the narrative. It is possible that the story might have emanated from court circles, perhaps as the work of a professional or semi-professional raconteur. The *mazkîr* is one named official whose function might have included the recounting of the stories of former times /60/. The Chadwicks (1932-40: II 403) make the interesting suggestion of a link with the harem, and this speculation, to my mind, remains well within the bounds of possibility /61/. On the other hand, the court, or even exclusively upper-class life, is by no means the only possible location for such a composition, even if it is perhaps easier to imagine court or scribal centre (assuming the existence of a scribal school) as providing the incentive and facilities for the recording of oral-traditional story-telling. Certainly an audience for such a story may be envisaged in both court or countryside alike.

Some may object that such a conclusion about the life-setting of the work is far from positive. I believe, however, that it is better to recognize the limits of the evidence than to pursue a "positive" conclusion which would be, in point of fact, merely yet another speculation.

CHAPTER FOUR
THE BOUNDARIES
OF THE STORY

Chapter Four
The Boundaries of the Story

It has long been accepted that the narrative contained in 2 Sam 9-20 + 1 Kgs 1-2 is largely a coherent unit composed by a single author (cf. Wellhausen, 1878:224-6; Fohrer, 1970:222). Notable exceptions were Gressmann (1910) and Caspari (1909, 1926), who argued instead for a series of independent short stories within this material but who did not succeed in displacing the unitary view (see, however, Flanagan, 1972). Otherwise, until recently, the only major disagreements over the material within these boundaries have concerned 2 Sam 10-12 and 1 Kgs 2 /1/. (a) With regard to 2 Sam 10-12 some scholars have taken 10:1-11:1.+ 12:26-31, or some part thereof, as a separate (annalistic) source incorporated into the work to provide a framework for the Bathsheba episode, and there has also been disagreement over the originality of the Nathan oracle in chapter 12. (b) Apart from a widely recognized Deuteronomistic addition in 1 Kgs 2:2b-4, 27, and the annalistic note in vss. 10-11, a variety of other, much less obvious, interpolations has been postulated. The most recent development has been one already discussed (Chapter Two), namely the emergence of a series of studies postulating a much greater degree of redactional interference throughout the length and breadth of the text (Würthwein, 1974; Veijola, 1975; Langlamet, 1976ab). As previously indicated, however, I find too many difficulties in the way of accepting these arguments in favour of extensive redactional manipulation, and in my judgement similar difficulties face another, more limited, redactional hypothesis for 1 Kgs 1-2 proposed recently by Mettinger (1976:27-32). Accordingly I still follow Whybray (1968:8-9) and the broad consensus in treating only vss. 2b-4, 10-11, and 27 as redactional in 1 Kgs 2. As for the other commonly debated areas, I follow Rost's analysis of 2 Sam 10 (1926/1966:184-91) and suggest that vss. 6b-19 were not originally part of our story, but find the continuation of 10:6a in 11:1 rather than in 11.2; amd while it is more than likely that the pronouncements by Nathan against David in 2 Sam 12 have been reworked (probably at the stage of incorporating the King David story into the history as a whole) I doubt that the extent of the reworking can be defined with any certainty.

But these are all familiar and much discussed positions. What concerns me in this chapter is rather the matter of the limits or boundaries of the story in a more radical sense. By and large 2 Sam 9-20 together with 1 Kgs 1-2 has been accepted as a coherent unit. Arguments concerning style, outlook (world-view) and theme, story-line (plot) or interlocking subject matter, have all played a part in producing this consensus. But while there is general agreement that 1 Kgs 2 marks the *end* of the narrative (Schulte, 1972:169) /2/ there exists considerable uncertainty about the point at which the document begins (Wellhausen, 1878:230; Eissfeldt, 1965:137; Whybray, 1968:8; Schulte, 1972:138-9).

My purpose in the present chapter, therefore, is to examine again this question of the beginning of the story, and to argue that the bulk of 2 Sam 2-4, and probably 5:1-3, should also be included in the narrative, as has been argued by Schulte (1972: 138-80) and Segal (1964-5:323-4) /3/.

A. THE BEGINNING OF THE STORY: 2 SAM 2-4

2 Sam 9 is widely adopted, at least for practical purposes, as a starting point for the narrative as a whole. Apart from similarities of style with the succeeding chapters it is closely linked with 2 Sam 15-20 by the Mephibosheth sub-plot (Carlson, 1964: 131; Segal, 1964-5:319). On the other hand, the previous chapter, 8, with its mechanical, annalistic rehearsal of David's victories and its lack, for example, of dialogue or focus upon character, has no significant connection whatsoever with what follows /4/. Yet, as I have already indicated, it is hard to find a scholar who is prepared to defend chapter 9 as a certain (or even satisfactory) beginning to the story that follows: it starts abruptly and with a question that seems to imply some previously narrated event. Its adoption as a beginning is largely the result of failure to come to a consensus on an alternative. It is, so to speak, a lowest common denominator.

Rost, (1926/1965), in his influential study of the narrative, could only suggest (pp. 212-6) on this point, and then almost solely on "thematic" grounds (on which see further below) that the Michal episode in 2 Sam 6:20-23, and perhaps an original dynastic oracle in 2 Sam 7 (vss. 11b, 16), preceded 2 Sam 9 and had been woven into the ark narrative (6:1-19, following 1 Sam 4-6) /5/. But he admitted that this material was fragmentary, and he was certainly unwilling to press the connection of chapter 7 with chapters 9-20 (see especially p.215), which is hardly surprising since it is quite the weakest part of his argument /6/.

The thematic connection that is claimed between these verses in chapter 7 (the separation of which within the chapter is itself highly debatable) /7/ and the "Succession Narrative" proper is that the promise of a Davidic dynasty is then follow- ed by the vicissitudes of David's actual reign: the tension is resolved by Solomon's enthronement and "the problem of the succession to the throne [is] solved" (von Rad, 1944/1966:202; cf. Rost, pp.213-4).

This is to confuse two related yet distinct questions, viz. (a) "Will David be succeeded on the throne by *any* of his own sons?" and (b) "*Which* of David's sons will succeed him?". The question "Who shall sit on the throne of David?" (1 Kgs 1:13) which Rost employs to state his theme of "succession" is clearly equivalent in 1 Kgs 1 to "Which of David's sons shall succeed him?". And inasmuch as a "succession" theme is present in 2 Sam 9-20 it must also be stated in the latter form, at least in the bulk of the narrative (that concerning Adonijah and Absalom): that the throne will go to someone *other* than a Davidide is a possibility that arises only tengentially through the distinctly minor characters, Mephibosheth and Sheba.

Accordingly, the promise in chapter 7 which ensures David of a dynasty is simply irrelevant as a source of dramatic tension in the following stories about David and his sons. Rost's attempt to single out a verse and a half and join it to a large connected narrative beginning some chapters later, on the ground of a thematic link as fragile as this one, must be rejected as totally unsatisfactory.

Recently Ridout (1971: especially chapter V) has re-opened the question of chapter 7 and pressed for the inclusion of the whole of the chapter (with the exception of vss. 12b-13a and possibly also vs. 16) as the introduction to the narrative. But while many of his observations are valuable for the study of the *redactional* compilation of 2 Samuel, I find it impossible to accept that these chapters originally had any intimate connection with each other, if for no other reason than that they are fundamentally different in character and in the stance of the author: the one (chapter 7) is ideologically obvious and tediously repetitive; the other (2 Sam 9-20 etc.) a subtle story told in a compelling manner /8/.

To come back to Rost's other suggestion, concerning chapter 6 and the ark story; it must be replied that it is in no way clear why the author should have wanted to begin his own story with the ark narrative, a story that has nothing to do with the "succession" theme which is elsewhere so important for Rost's argument, has no obvious link with the content of 2 Sam 9-20 and 1 Kgs 1-2, apart from the mention of the ark in 15:24-9, and, as Rost himself urges (e.g. pp.218-24), is of a markedly different literary style and general outlook. The suggestion, therefore, does little if anything to resolve the problem of a beginning to the narrative. If the Michal story in chapter 6 originally belonged to the King David story and not to the ark story it is highly unlikely that its present location was the work of the author of the King David story (Mowinckel, 1963:10). This leaves us with the fragment of a story (Michal in chapter 6) which again, like 2 Sam 7, has on the "succession" argument no primary thematic connection with the bulk of 2 Sam 9-20 and 1 Kgs 1-2 /9/.

If chapters 8, 7 and 6 offer no satisfactory solution to the problem of a beginning for the story, no more does chapter 5. Again like chapter 8 (though it has not quite the same secular, annalistic flavour) and unlike the story of King David it is essentially a disjointed compilation of separate incidents or notices, sparsely narrated and with little interest in, or observation of, the participants as *people*. Also unlike the story of King David there is no development of plot or tension, dialogue is desultory, and the rather simple minded religious focus of the anecdotes about David and the Philistines (consulting the oracle and receiving a direct reply; the idols of the Philistines; expressions such as "David did as Yahweh commanded him") has no parallel in the other material.

With chapters 2-4. on the other hand, the picture is quite different. Here we have, at least from 2:8 or 2:12, what is generally recognized as a long, coherent, and flowing story of how David came to be in a position to receive the crown of Israel, with only a few passages (e.g. 3:2-5) that might be considered extraneous (Wellhausen, 1878:222; H. P. Smith, 1899:267-8; Budde, 1902:207-8; Nowack, 1902:XIX-XX; Gressmann, 1910:126-33; Hölscher, 1952:374; Carlson, 1964:41, 49-51; Schulte, 1972:140-2, 165-6; *contra*, Cook, 1899:147-50; Rost, 1926/1965:238). Moreover, it appears to have many of the literary qualities of 2 Sam 9-20 and I Kgs 1-2: it is relatively extensive and elaborated, its primary focus is upon the characters involved and their inter-relations (Luther, 1906:194-5), and it makes superb use of direct speech /10/. I suggest, therefore, that there is a *prima facie* case for considering this material further.

B. NARRATIVE THREAD

One possible line of enquiry explored by Rost (pp.192-3) starts from a consideration of 2 Sam 9:1: "And David said, 'Is there still anyone left of the house of Saul that I may deal loyally with him for Jonathan's sake?'" Does this presuppose the story of the Gibeonites' revenge, now in 2 Sam 21?

A common answer to this question is that this or some other version of this story *is* presupposed (so, e.g., de Vaux, 1961:178; Hertzberg, 1964:299, 381). Some scholars would further claim that at one stage in the history of the book 21:1-14 actually preceded chapter 9 (so, for example, Budde, 1902:244, 304-6; Schulz, 1923: 6; Carlson, 1964:198-203; Auzou, 1968:364) /11/. On the other hand, few have been prepared to argue that this episode formed an original part of the "Succession Narrative" itself /12/. It appears to differ in its religious outlook and, as it stands, is clearly linked through the plague motif with the story of David's census, which only takes us away from chapter 9 and the following episodes rather than forming a connection with it. Such was Rost's conclusion and this is my own view (so also Whybray, 1968:8; cf. Wellhausen, 1878:224, 228-9; Ridout, 1971:41 n.1, 163 n.1) /13/.

A much simpler solution is to link 9:1 with the end of chapter 4 and hence with the large narrative of chapters 2-4. What 9:1 basically requires as an antecedent is an account of the death of any surviving Saulides of public or political standing (i.e. any whom, in terms of the narrative, David would be expected to know about; cf. Kennedy, 1904:234). The narrative of chapters 2-4 appears to take it for granted that Ishbosheth is in fact the last such Saulide /14/. With the story of Ishbosheth's death, therefore, we have precisely the situation presupposed by 9:1 (Segal, 1918-9:54-5; cf. Nübel, 1959:72).

One advantage of this hypothesis is that it accounts simply and naturally for 4:4 being where it is /15/. The author is anxious to foreshadow the forthcoming episode (chapter 9); at the same time it enables him to fill in some of the background of the new character (Mephibosheth), thus removing some contraints on his construction of the scene in chapter 9.

The other obvious link of plot between chapters 2-4 and 9-20 + 1 Kgs 1-2 comes in 1 Kgs 2 in the account of Joab's death (Segal, 1964-5:324; Schulte, 1972:142). In David's instructions to Solomon (2:5-9) and in the ensuing account of Solomon's implementation of the instructions (2:28-46) every character and every incident mentioned is found in the body of the "Succession Narrative" as it is commonly demarcated, *except* the killing of Abner (2:5,32) /16/. This, therefore, must count as a particularly strong piece of evidence in favour of the inclusion of 2 Sam 2-4 within the boundaries of the narrative.

The mention of Abner raises a further point. With 2 Sam 2-4 the reader of the books of Samuel must notice at least one significant change in the subject matter, a change which concerns the characters in the stories. Previously, the focus has been directly upon David and Saul; now, although the action has a profound bearing on David and in that sense he remains the focal point, David actually stands on the circumference of much of the action. On the other hand, Joab and Abner, men who have played only minor roles in the stories in 1 Samuel become leading figures. The whole circle of people involved in the narrative also broadens (Schulte, 1972:140-8). This state of affairs is precisely parallel to what we find in 2 Sam 9-20, the respective roles of David and Joab, in particular, being strikingly similar.

If, then, we add 2 Sam 2-4 to the rest of the narrative the resultant story is a coherent one of how David gained the throne of all Israel, of how he then nearly lost it, and of how he finally relinquished it: it is a story of accession, rebellion and succession /17/. This coherence is more fully explored in Chapter Five, below.

On the negative side I see only two serious objections to the suggested link. In chapter 4 David is based in Hebron, while in chapter 9, if vs. 13 is not a gloss (as suggested by H. P. Smith, 1899:311-2; Pfeiffer, 1937:315; Hertzberg, 1964:301; Flanagan, 1971:49; cf. Titkin, 1922:50), he is apparently living in Jerusalem, and this is certainly the case from chapter 11 onwards /18/. Furthermore, from chapter 10 onwards it gradually emerges that David is now king of "all Israel" and not just Judah as is the case in chapters 2-4. These difficulties, however, are not insuperable as I shall now attempt to show.

2 Sam 9-20 + 1 Kgs 1-2 itself falls into quite distinct blocks of material (for example, chapters 11-12, 13-14, 15-20, 1 Kgs 1-2) and at least in the case of 1 Kgs 1-2 there appears to be a radical break in time between it and the preceding narrative. Moreover, it cannot be said that the narrator has taken much trouble to bridge the gap (compare the careful statements of the lapse of time in 2 Sam 13-20, viz. 13:23, 38; 14:28; 15:7 (reading ʾrbᶜ [šn(y)m] with LXX); so also Whybray, 1968:30) /19/.

Nor is the setting of the action in 2 Sam 9 or 10-12 in the least important for the story, and only after the account of Absalom's rebellion is well under way does it play a role of any significance in the narrative. All we might expect, therefore, is the briefest indication of the change of scene. This raises two possibilities.

(a) We know that the whole complex in which the story is now embedded (1 and 2 Samuel) has undergone a redactional process: it is quite possible, therefore, that the inclusion in the complex of the story of the taking of Jerusalem (5:6-9) has lead to the omission from the King David story of a brief clause, now redundant, to the same effect. (All it would require is something like "And it came to pass when David dwelt in Jerusalem" or "After David had taken Jerusalem").

(b) It is noticeable that, until the last verse of chapter 9, the story of Mephibosheth's reception makes no mention of a particular city; the reiterated phrase is simply "you shall eat at my table always", not as we might perhaps have expected if the scene were set in Jerusalem, "you shall eat at my table in Jerusalem always". It is only with vs. 13, which together with vs. 12 has sometimes been seen, on other grounds, as a gloss (noted above), that we are told "and Mephibosheth dwelt in Jerusalem". The option is open to accept vs. 13 as a gloss, and to connect chapter 9 initially (primarily?) with chapters 2-4 rather than 10ff., assuming its precise setting (which, I stress again, is of no significance to the story: the point is that Mephibosheth was where David was) to be still Hebron. Thus the next major episode, the account of

David's adultery and the murder of Uriah, begins (10:1) with a formule *(wyhy* ʾ*ḥry kn)* which marks a major division, just as it does later at the beginning of the *next* major episode, in 13:1.

Following Rost's analysis (pp. 184-91) of chapter 10 I would then suggest omitting vss. 6b-19 as not originally from the "Succession Narrative" (so also Flanagan, 1971:50; cf. 1972:175-6), but unlike him, I would find the continuation of 10:6a in 11:1ff., instead of 11:2ff. /20/. The verse is closely linked, ironically (Ridout, 1971: 152-3), with what follows and it provides, as Ridout (p. 65) observes, "the *datum* which makes possible David's cohabitation with the wife of Uriah" (see also Budde, 1902:250; cf. Carlson, 1964:146-8). Setting the scene for the main episode, therefore, is a brief prelude (the quarrel with the Ammonites) which ends (11:1) with just the kind of simple indication that the setting is now Jerusalem that we were looking for: "And David was dwelling in Jerusalem" *(wdwd ywšb byrwšlm* : normally taken as "But David remained in Jerusalem [cf. RSV]: on my interpretation the clause obviously serves a double function).

Finally, the change in David's status that we find in chapter 13 onwards (i.e. he is now king of all Israel) need be no problem. It may simply be a matter of cultural background: we may quite reasonably assume that by doing no more than indicate that the scene had in fact changed, that David was now dwelling in Jerusalem, the author could be sure that his audience or readers would be in possession of the wider significance of that move. Nevertheless, this is not the only way in which this particular objection may be met. The question of David as king of all Israel prompts a closer look at the precise boundaries of the story in chapters 2-4.

C. THE PRECISE BOUNDARIES OF THE DAVID–ISHBOSHETH STORY

The Ending

Does the episode relating to the death of Ishbosheth end not with the burial (4: 12) but with an account of the crowning of David as king over all Israel as Schulte suggests (1972:165-6; cf., e.g., H. P. Smith, 1899:286; Nowack, 1902:xx; Gressmann, 1910:131-3)? She takes the passage 5:1-3 as a conflation of two sources (so, e.g., H. P. Smith, 1899:286; Kittel, 1896:46; Budde, 1902:218; Mauchline, 1971: 215; Flanagan, 1971:47), one of which she sees as the concluding account of the Ishbosheth story, the other as the continuation of a David History running through 1 Samuel and found also in 2 Sam 1 (:1b-4, 11-12 + ? 19-27) and 2:1-7 (see pp. 105-180) /21/.

Whatever the precise merits or otherwise of Schulte's analysis it does demonstrate that the story of David, Abner and Ishbosheth in chapters 2-4 can be removed from its immediate context (with which it is only loosely associated) and linked with the major episodes in the succeeding chapters, without disturbing any of the main threads of the *preceding* narratives /22/. That is to say, while to link chapters 2-4 with 9-20 may cut across many conventional source-divisions of this part of 2 Samuel, it does so in a way that allows relatively simple modification of most of these analyses /23/.

2 Sam 5:1-3

The status of Schulte's particular argument concerning 5:1-3 is more difficult to assess (the details are on pp. 165-6).

Whereas most commentators who have seen a doublet here have simply divided vss. 1-2 from vs. 3, Schulte takes vss. 1, 2a and 3b ("and they anointed David king over all Israel") as the continuation of the David/Saul history (i.e. it links with 2 Sam 2:1-7), 3a as the conclusion to the story in chapters 3-4 (cf. the "elders of Israel" in 3:17 and the "covenant making" in 3:21), and vs. 2b as a Deuteronomistic gloss (cf. 1 Sam 25:30).

Against this I would argue, first, that the passage is one of those where undoubted repetition cannot with complete confidence be cited as evidence for source division, since the repetition may equally well be understood as a deliberate rhetorical device (Carlson, 1964:55); second, that in particular, Schulte's analysis (a) requires the arbitrary discarding of the phrase, *gm ᵓtmwl gm šlšwm,* in vs. 2a, as a gloss from 3:17, and (b) fails to observe that the speech in vss. 1b-2 has more in common with 3:17-18 than this phrase alone. This latter point (b) is of some significance for any hypothesis concerning the composition of 2 Samuel and therefore warrants some attention. The speech in question (5:1b-2) has a certain structural parallel with 3:17-18:

(1)   In times past (*gm / ᵓ/tmwl gm šlšwm:* occurs only here and in the parallel passage, 1 Chron 11:2)

        (i) you have been seeking David as king   (3:17)

        (ii) you (David) were in effect king ("it was you who led out and brought in Israel")   (5:2)

(2)   Yahweh said to ⎰ David:
                   ⎱ you (David):

        (i) by the hand *(yd)* of my servant David, I will save my people Israel, from the hand of the Philistines, and from the hand of all their enemies.   (3:18)

        (ii) *you* shall shepherd my people Israel, and *you* shall be prince *(ngyd)* over Israel.   (5:2)

The close affinity of these two speeches is further underscored when their relationship to several other passages in Samuel is seen.

2 Sam 19:10-11:

    And all the people were at strife throughout *all the tribes of Israel,* saying:
    "The king delivered us from the hand (kp) of our enemies,
    and saved us from the hand (kp) of the Philistines;
    but now he has fled out of the land from Absalom.
    And Absalom, *whom we anointed over us* is dead in battle . . . "
+ vss. 12-13:

    And king David sent this message to Zadok and Abiathar the priests:
    "Say to the elders of Judah . . . You are my kinsmen, you are my bone
    and flesh . . . " (*ᶜṣm + bśr*: in Samuel only here and 5:1 /24/).

1 Sam 9:16 (Yahweh to Samuel, concerning Saul):
"*. . . and you shall anoint him to be prince (ngyd) over my people Israel,*
and he shall save my people from the hand (yd) of the Philistines . . . "
+ 10:1 (LXX : see Driver, 1913b:77-8; Mettinger, 1976:66-7)
(Samuel to Saul):
"Has not Yahweh *anointed you to be prince (ngyd) over his people Israel?*
And you shall reign over the people of Yahweh, and you will save them
from the hand (yd?) of their enemies round about . . . "

2 Sam 19:10ff. is linked with both 3:17-18 (David will save the people from the hand
(but note *kp*, not *yd*, in 19:10) of the Philistines/enemies; and there is consultation
with the "elders") and 5:1-3 ("all the tribes of Israel"; "your bone and flesh";
"anoint" as king); and all three passages find at least partial parallels in 1 Sam 9:16 +
10:1.

It would seem to me, therefore, that this rather complex inter-relationship of
the passages must make any attempt to describe a redactional history here hazardous.

Nevertheless, there are several points which may be borne in mind if an attempt
is made to explore the relationship:

(1)   In contrast to the other passages, 2 Sam 19:10ff. contains no hint of
Yahweh's presence or motivating power behind the king's deliverance (in 2 Sam 19:10
the people say, "the king delivered us . . . "; 2 Sam 3:18: "Yahweh said to David,
'By the hand of my servant David, *I* will save *my* people . . .'"; 2 Sam 5:2:"and
Yahweh said to you, 'You shall shepherd *my* people . . .'").

(2)   2 Sam 19:10 has *kp* for "hand" and not *yd* as in 2 Sam 3:18; 1 Sam 9:16
and 10:1 (probably).

(3)   The line about deliverance in 19:10 has a different balance from that in
3:17 and strikingly so from those in 1 Sam 9:16 and 10:1, which have no poetic
structure at all.

(4)   In 19:10ff. David's claim to a "bone and flesh" relationship with Judah
(and Amasa) seems clearly to be in contradiction to any relationship he has with
Israel; yet in 5:1 it is the northern tribes who make this claim.

(5)   3:17-19 sits a little awkwardly in its present context and makes Abner's
conversations with David in vss. 20-21 seem out of place (H. P. Smith, 1899:278;
Nowack, 1902:XXXIII; Flanagan, 1971:46). Moreover, the information in 4:1 that
when Ishbosheth heard the news of Abner's death his courage failed and *all Israel
was dismayed* hardly seems to suggest that Israel was eagerly seeking to switch
allegiance to David (Veijola, 1975:61).

(6)   It has been argued by some that the passages in 1 Sam 9 and 10 come from
a redactional stage in the formation of the material of these chapters (see further
Miller, 1974; Mettinger, 1976:65-7).

All these observations prompt the following tentative suggestions:
(1)   Schulte's division of 5:1-3 is unsatisfactory in the light of 3:17-19, let alone
the other parallels.
(2)   3:17-19 may not originally have belonged in its present context; on the

other hand it seems closely connected with 5:1-3. There is some ground, therefore, for suggesting that neither passage may originally have belonged to the main narrative of chapters 2-4.

(3) Furthermore, given several significant points of distinction between these passages (and those in 1 Sam 9 and 10) on the one hand and 2 Sam 19:10ff. on the other, it is conceivable that the composition of 3:17-19 and 5:1-3, especially the latter (with "all the tribes of Israel"; "bone and flesh"), has been partially influenced by the account of the negotiations between David and the people in 19:10ff. (where the "bone and flesh" motif appears to be more securely anchored in the story) (cf. Veijola, 1975:62 n.96).

(4) If the passages in 1 Sam 9 and 10 are indeed the result of a redactional overlay, it is possible in view of the affinities between these passages and 3:17-19 + 5:1-3 (but note the more prosaic structure of the passages in 1 Samuel) that the same redactor is at work, his object being perhaps to show the central role of Yahweh in the designation (and in Saul's case, rejection) of the king.

There is some ground, therefore, for linking 3:17-19 and 5:1-3 with 2:1-7 (+ 3: 1-6?) and for taking this material as either the continuation of an original source narrating David's rise to power to be found also in 1 Samuel and perhaps in 2 Sam 1 (cf. Mettinger, 1976:44-7) /25/ or for seeing it as a redactional overlay tying the particular story of David and Ishbosheth into a broad history of Saul and David that is presented with a certain theological *Tendenz*.

On the other hand, it must be clear that the foregoing argument is far from definitive and can be advanced on a tentative basis only. Moreover it seems to me that the judgement that locates the ending of the episode in the coronation segment is substantially correct: the story from the first struggle between Ishbosheth's and David's men onwards is wholly directed towards, and has its point in, Ishbosheth's downfall and David's gain of his throne.

This leaves three possibilities: (a) Schulte is right after all; (b) Schulte is right to locate the ending in 5:1-3 but her analysis is wrong and the conventional one should be followed; (c) the passage as it stands is redactional, as I have suggested, but it replaces, or is a careful reshaping of, the wording of an original ending. In the light of the foregoing discussion this last naturally commends itself to me.

There remains, however, a further complication for this assessment of 3:17-19 and 5:1-3. This concerns the possibility of a link between 5:1-3 and the Michal story in chapter 6.

It has for some time been customary for scholars, though by no means for all, to distinguish, as Rost did, between two separate traditions in chapter 6, viz. the story of the ark and that of Michal's childlessness (Rost, pp. 150, 212-15; von Rad, 1944/ 1966:176-7; Hertzberg, 1964:277; Maier, 1965:61; Flanagan, 1971:48; cf. A. F. Campbell, 1975:144, 168). The Michal story is usually traced in vss. 16 and 20b-23; but if we are to work on the basis of this hypothesis of two integrated traditions a more refined analysis may be made as follows:

Vs. 20a certainly belongs to the ark narrative, providing a neat *inclusio*. The episode opens with the blessing of Obed-Edom and his household, and ends with the blessing of David's household. Vs. 16b ("and she saw King David leaping and *dancing before Yahweh*") requires vs. 14 ("and David *danced before Yahweh with all his might*") and this in turn appears to demand vs. 5 ("And David and all the house of Israel were *making merry before Yahweh with all their might* with songs [reading *bkl ʿz (w) bšyrym*; cf. vs. 14 and 1 Chron 13:8 and see Driver, 1913b:266; Titkin, 46] and lyres and harps . . . "). The exclusion of these verses (5 and 14a) leaves the thread of the ark narrative undisturbed. On the other hand we now have a separate and coherent story of David and all Israel making merry "before Yahweh", of David in particular dancing and leaping "before Yahweh" with all his might, of Michal despising him (for "showing off" *[glh]* – not necessarily "uncovering himself" literally) /26/, and of David insisting that it was done in honour of Yahweh ("and I will make merry before Yahweh").

In this material about Michal the only clue to the story's original context is to be found in vs. 16a ("And the ark of Yahweh came into the city of David" /27/), a clause that could well be either redactional /28/ linking the two narratives, or belong to the ark narrative itself. If so, the only remaining connection between the two blocks of material is that each entails a situation of rejoicing "before Yahweh". We may fairly consider, therefore, whether the present context of the Michal story is not an artificial one.

This brings us back to 5:1-3, the coronation of David at Hebron "before Yahweh" (vs. 3). Here too we expect a scene of rejoicing just as we find if we turn back to the story of Saul's coronation in 1 Sam 11:15 /29/:

> So all the people went to Gilgal, and there they made Saul
> king *before Yahweh* in Gilgal. There they sacrificed peace
> offerings *before Yahweh*, and there *Saul and all the men of
> Israel rejoiced greatly*.

Moreover, in David's speech to Michal (vs. 21: "It was before Yahweh, who chose me above your father, and above all his house, to appoint me as *prince [ngyd] over Israel, the people of Yahweh*") we find direct echoes of the language of the promise in 5:2.

My suggestion, therefore, is that the Michal story of chapter 6 may originally have belonged after 5:1-3, but has been re-located in the ark story as part of a process of focussing the whole complex of material in 2 Sam 1-8 upon chapters 6 and 7. David's greatest moment of rejoicing is to be found in his bringing of Yahweh's ark to the great cult centre, Jerusalem, an act which leads in turn to Yahweh's promise of dynastic security.

The complication for the analysis of the David-Ishbosheth story in chapters 2-4 and the relationship of these chapters to 5:1-3 lies in the fact that if the Michal story of chapter 6 really belongs with 5:1-3, as I have indicated may be the case, then it certainly seems to presuppose knowledge of some such story as 3:12-16 (i.e. the bringing of Michal to David). It thereby must count as evidence for the inclusion of 5:1-3 (or something very like it), and thence 3:17-19, in the main narrative about David and Ishbosheth /30/.

Again, however, it is as well to be cautious about any conclusions. The relationship between the Michal material in chapters 3 and 6 may be accounted for in other ways. For example, the apparent dependence of the one episode (chapter 6) upon the other (chapter 3) may be explained, just as I suggested might be the case with 5:1-3 in relation to 19:10ff., by regarding the chapter 6 material as secondary to that in chapter 3, and thus from a stage of redaction when the main narrative of chapters 2-4 was subjected to expansion and integration into a larger complex. Such an hypothesis would fit with that of Schmidt (1970:58-102) concerning the place of the Samuel oracles in the story of Saul's rise to kingship in 1 Samuel 9 and 10 (followed by Miller, 1974:157-8; see also Schulte, 1972:108-9; Carlson, 1964:52-5). Yet it must also be said that any such hypothesis involves a large measure of speculation. Perhaps the most that can be said with any certainty about the redactional history of all this material is that it is probably complex and it has led to some degree of interweaving of component sections.

In the face of these uncertainties and complications, therefore, it would appear best to accept an original connection between 5:1-3 and the preceding narrative without being prepared to specify precisely what form that connection took, and to allow (without wishing to press the issue) that the coronation scene itself may well have concluded with the incident involving Michal which is now woven into chapter 6.

The Beginning

I now pose the question whether the story that begins in 2:8 or 2:12 (Schulte, 1972:165) may with certainty be accounted the beginning of the whole narrative with which we are concerned. While I believe (with Schulte) that it constitutes a far more satisfactory beginning than does chapter 9, let alone the Michal story in chapter 6 (Rost), it remains possible that it was itself preceded by earlier episodes in the present books of Samuel.

The immediately preceding segment recounting the coronation at Hebron is uncharacteristically (for our narrative) sparse — unless it presupposes a more broadly spun tale of the events leading up to it, as, for example, the story of David, Saul and the Philistines in 1 Samuel — and the oracular consultation (2:1) is atypical of the "Succession Narrative" or, as I would prefer to call it, the "Story of King David" (including now 2:8 to 4:12 or 5:3) but typical of some narratives in 1 Samuel (for example, chapters 22, 23 and 30). In addition, 2:4-7 presupposes 1 Sam 31:8-13 and seems thus to be firmly linked to the Saul narratives of 1 Samuel, whereas the story leading up to the coronation of David as king of Israel appears to make a fresh beginning.

On the other hand, Carlson (1964:51) rightly notices "a striking correspondence between [the] account of the murder of Ishbosheth and that in chapter 1 of David's treatment of the killer of Saul. The agreement is further accentuated by the fact that both murders are carried out by foreigners, an Amalekite and two Beerothites respectively". Furthermore, similarities of style, language and compositional skill might suggest a reconsideration of chapters such as 1 Sam 25 (David and Abigail), 20 (David and Jonathan and the arrows) and perhaps to a lesser extent 24 and 26 (Saul at the mercy of David) /31/.

With this material, however, we again come face to face with major questions about the composition of 1 Samuel. Despite many recent studies (above, n. 23) — or, perhaps I should say, in view of them — I am not convinced that we are much nearer to untangling the "probably insoluble skein of problems" (Blenkinsopp,

1964:424) involved in the composition of this book. It may well be that there are certain links of style and even theme with some of this material; it may be that some of it is indeed the work of the author of our story of King David; but it is not easy to detach, from this tangle of traditions, an integrated unit that fulfils our criteria and can be linked smoothly in terms of plot with our story. My own exploratory analysis has suggested strongly to me that more problems are created than are solved. Accordingly I leave it to some other critic to demonstrate otherwise. With 2 Sam 2:8 or 2:12 to 5:3, on the other hand (as I have already argued), we have material that can be detached from its matrix without undue dislocation of existing theories of composition. The only real difficulty that arises concerns 5:1-3 which clearly is important to any "story of David's rise" (unless this finished with the crowning in Hebron). This passage, however, may well be a point of overlap between the two stories; and, as indicated above, the evidence seems to suggest that the passage as it stands has been subject to editorial revision.

In the meantime, therefore, I am content to argue that the bulk of 2 Sam 2:8 or 2:12 to 5:3 should be considered as belonging to the King David story, providing in fact the direct antecedent to chapter 9 (or almost so – I also argued for the probable inclusion of the Michal scene in chapter 6), and furnishing a much more satisfactory beginning to the narrative than either chapter 9 or chapter 6.

I now propose to provide some further backing for this suggestion through an examination, first, of the style of these chapters (2 Sam 2-4) and second, of their thematic relationship to 2 Sam 9-20 + 1 Kgs 1-2.

D. STYLE

A major aspect of Rost's definition of the "Succession Narrative" was his argument for the stylistic unity and distinctiveness of these chapters when compared with other material in Samuel (see especially pp.218-26; cf. Whybray, 1968:45-7). In the main I thoroughly agree with his designation of stylistic characteristics and his delineation of significant differences in the material he dealt with (mostly the ark narrative in 1 Sam 4-6, and 2 Sam 6, 7 and 8), but when one examines closely his treatment of the chapters in 2 Samuel prior to chapter 6 it is fairly clear from its brevity that he had already decided the question of the extent of the narrative on the basis of the "succession" *Leitmotif* which had led him to chapter 6.

While he goes to considerable length to illustrate the undoubted stylistic differences between the "Succession Narrative" and the ark narratives his comparison with the material in the earlier chapters of 2 Samuel is cursory (Blenkinsopp, 1966: 46) and is confined to a comparison with what he deems, with no supporting argument, to belong to an early source giving an account of David's reign, viz. 1 Sam 23:1-13. 27:1-28:2; 29:1-30:26; 2 Sam 1:1; 2:4a; 3:20-9; 3:31-7; 4:1a, 5-12; 5:3, 17-25 (+ chapter 8?).

This idiosyncratic analysis is far from self-evident (see the studies cited in n.23; also the charts in Löhr, 1898:XXXIV-LXVIII, and Nowack, 1902:XXX-XXXIV) and in my view, as will be apparent from my observations above, lumps together material that is as different as chalk and cheese. For example, on the one hand we have the narrative which concerns us here, the skilfully developed story of 2 Sam 2-4 (from which Rost arbitrarily selects bits and pieces), and the sparsely narrated notices of the fighting with the Philistines in 2 Sam 5:17-25 (and similarly the capture of Jerusalem, 5:5-9) /32/ which are best compared with the stories in 21:15ff. and 23:8 ff. (and cf. chapter 8 and 10:15-19) which Rost takes for granted, rightly in my view, as not belonging to the "Succession Narrative". Given the presence of this latter type of narrative in his source one is hardly surprised to find him concluding (e.g. p. 239) that the source lacks the breadth of style so characteristic of the "Succession Narrative" proper.

In effect, then, it is fair to say that Rost's study of the "Succession Narrative" lacks any proper comparison with the extended narrative of chapters 2-4. In the present section I shall examine this material and show that it is stylistically homogeneous with chapters 9-20 + 1 Kgs 1-2 /33/.

Inclusio

In his characterization of the style of the "Succession Narrative" Rost (p. 221) particularly singles out the abundance of what he terms *Ploke* (ring composition or *inclusio*; see also Schulte, pp. 139, 31 n.61; and esp. Ridout, pp. 36-47, and cf. pp. 47-74) and notes the relative frequency of similes, rare in the Hebrew prose of the Old Testament.

In chapters 2-4 we come across both simile (cf. Schulte, p. 142, arguing the same case) and *inclusio* with the Abner story barely begun. The simile : Asahel was as swift of foot as the wild gazelle (2:18). The *inclusio* (there are two together in fact):

	And there *went out*
(1)	Abner the son of Ner and the servants of Ishbosheth the son
vss.	of Saul, from Mahanaim to Gibeon;
12-13	And Joab the son of Zeruiah and the servants of David
	went out.

(2)	And they met /34/ at the pool of Gibeon *together (yḥdw)*
vss.	. . . (details of contest)
13-16	And they fell *together (yḥdw)* /35/.

While 2:18 is, as it happens, the only simile in chapters 2-4, the use of *inclusio* in these three chapters is striking, particularly in the speeches. Rost and Ridout between them list sixteen examples in the whole of 2 Sam 9-20 + 1 Kgs 1-2 (though there are more examples than they cite). That it is possible to find at least ten cases of this stylistic device in the story of David, Abner and Ishbosheth suggests that in this respect the two blocks of narrative are highly comparable. As with the cases cited by Rost and Ridout those in chapters 2-4 vary from the quite simple and rather mechanical to the highly subtle; sometimes only a few clauses separate the ring elements, sometimes a number of verses. Further details are given below in Appendix B /36/.

Other Forms of Repetition

Ridout's analysis (Chapters II and III) makes clear that several other forms of repetition play an important role in the "Succession Narrative" author's technique of composition /37/ : (1) the repetition of words, phrases, or even sentences or groups of sentences as key motifs or for emphasis (see also Whybray, 1968:26); (2) *chiasmus;* (3) repetition as a means of linking successive episodes, by significant phrases (etc.) appearing at identical places in each segment. Again parallels abound in chapters 2-4.

(1) Ridout's analysis (pp. 97-102) of the function of *bśr* (9 times) and *rws* (12 times; observed also by Rost, p. 226) in the messenger episode of 2 Sam 18:19-31, or of *ʾḥ* (11 times) and *ʾḥwt* (8 times) in the Tamar story in 2 Sam 13:1-22, can be matched, for example, in the story of pursuit (going "after" someone) in 2 Sam 3:19-30 by the persistent and subtle, and, in the death scene in vs. 23, ironic, variations on *ʾḥr* (14 times): for example, *rdp ʾḥry; nṭh/swr mʾḥry; bʾḥry ḥḥnyt* ("with the butt of his spear" – see Driver, 1913b:243; cf. Titkin, 41); *mʾḥryw* ("from his back"); and even *bʾḥrwnh* ("in the end").

Also noticeable in this story is the way in which the death scene moves rhythmically to a climax through the reiteration of the phrase "turn aside", expressed in a variety of ways /38/, roughly speaking diminishing in length as the climax is approached so that what starts (vs. 19) as "and as he went he turned *(nṭh)* neither to the right hand nor to the left from following Abner" ends (vs. 23) incisively as "but he refused to turn aside *(swr)*" /39/. The insistence on the phrase serves not only to control the rhythm and pace of the narrative, it is obviously hermeneutically significant; it draws attention to the fact that Asahel quite deliberately took on Abner, so that even if there is an element of deception in Abner's mode of killing him it is made crystal clear to the reader that Abner was pressed into taking this action. We are immediately reminded of the similar technique in the Uriah story (with the key phrase "to go down to his house", in 2 Sam 11:6-13) or in the story in 2 Sam 9 of Mephibosheth's reception at court (cf. "to deal loyally with" and "to eat bread at the king's table always"), both discussed by Ridout (pp. 102-7 and 109, 117-18; cf. Rost, p. 226).

Nor is this the only case of key-word repetition in 2 Sam 2-4. Another excellent example occurs in the account of Abner's death ("and he sent him off and he went in peace") in 3:20-7 which is linked with the repetition of *šlḥ* throughout the whole episode. Notice also the ironic play on "know/not know" (four times) in vss. 25-6.

(2) One of the several examples of *chiasmus* in chapters 2-4 (see further, Appendix B), is the speech of David to Abner (3:13) /40/:

"Good, I will make a covenant with you; but one thing I require of you, namely:

a	You shall not see my face
b	unless you bring *(bwʾ)*
c	Michal the daughter of Saul /41/
b'	when you come *(bwʾ)*
a'	to see my face.

(3) Ridout (pp. 74-87) discusses several cases where repetitions appear at identical places in succeeding narrative units and serve to relate the episodes together as part of a larger unity; sometimes the repetition is at the beginning *(anaphora)*,

sometimes at the end *(epiphora)* /42/.

A clear case of *anaphora*, may be found in 4:5-12 (vss. 5 and 7):

> 5.　And they *went (hlk)*, the sons of Rimmon . . .
> and they *came (bwᵓ), about the heat of the day,*
> *to the house of Ishbosheth . . .*
> 　　　　(+ account of the death of Ishbosheth).
> 7.　And they *went (hlk)* by way of the Arabah,
> *all night, and brought (bwᵓ)* the head of Ishbosheth
> *to David at Hebron . . .*
> 　　　　(+ account of death of sons of Rimmon).

On a larger canvas a concluding notice of burial links the three major episodes in chapters 2-4:

> 2:32 And they took up Asahel and buried him in the tomb of his
> 　　　　father, which was at Bethlehem.
> 3:32 They buried Abner at Hebron.
> 4:12 And they took the head of Ishbosheth and buried it in the
> 　　　　tomb of Abner at Hebron.

Again the irony (or is it pathos here?) so typical of the narrator in chapters 9-20 + 1 Kgs 1-2 (see further Chapter Five, below; and cf. Ridout, Chapters III and IV) ought not to be missed, and indeed the repetition draws attention to it. Asahel is buried in the family tomb. By contrast, Abner is laid to rest in the heart of his opponent's territory (one might say that his hand came to be with David [3:12] rather more permanently than he bargained for) while poor Ishbosheth, the pawn in the whole story, is interred not only in his rival's capital but in the tomb of the very man who betrayed him.

Vocabulary and Phraseology

　Finally in connection with an argument from style it is worth comparing the vocabulary stock of the two complexes as well as particular phrases or formulas that might be distinctive (see also Segal, 1964-5:324).

　(1)　A comparison of vocabulary shows considerable homogeneity. I reproduce in Appendix B, below, some of the more striking items; this list may be compared with Rost's treatment (pp. 130-8) of the vocabulary stock of the ark narrative in comparison with 2 Sam 9-20 + 1 Kgs 1-2.

　(2)　Phrases, expressions and larger units:

　(a)　2 Sam 4:9; 1 Kgs 1:29.
　　　　"As Yahweh lives, who has redeemed my life *(pdh ᵓt npšy)* from all adversity".
　　　　These are the only occurrences of the expression in the OT. The

phrase *pdh npš* is found apart from here in Job 33:28; Ps 34:23; 49:16; 55:19; 71:23.

(b)   2 Sam 3:39; 16:10; 19:23 (the speaker is David).
      "I am this day weak, though anointed *king;* and these men, the *sons of Zeruiah, are too hard for me"*.   (3:39)
      "What have I to do with you, you sons of Zeruiah? If he curses because Yahweh has said to him 'Curse David', who then shall say, 'Why have you done so? '"*.   (16:10)
      "What have I to do with you, you sons of Zeruiah, that you should *this day* be as an *adversary to me?* Shall any man be put to death in Israel *this day?* For do I not know that *I am this day king* over Israel?"*.   (19:23)

(c)   2 Sam 2:23; 3:27; 4:6 /43/; 20:10.
      ḥmš meaning (?) "belly" only occurs in the Old Testament in these passages, and then only in a single formula with *nkh*:
      wykhw b . . . ʾl hḥmš . . . wymt   (2:23; 20:10)
      wykhw šm   hḥmš   wymt   (3:27)
      wykhw   ʾl hḥmš (cf. vs.7: *ymthw*)   (4:6)

(d)   2 Sam 2:28; 18:16; 20:1-2; 20:22.
      The expression "to blow the trumpet" *(tqᶜ bšpr)* is used only here in the Old Testament in connection with the withdrawal of troops. In three of the cases (2:28; 18:16; 20:22), moreover, it is Joab who is the subject of the verb.

(e)   The scene in 2:23-32, the death of Asahel, is closely paralleled by 20:10-22, the death of Sheba. I argue elsewhere (1974: 303-11; cf. the criticisms of Van Seters, 1976a:147-8, and a response, Gunn, 1976b:157-9) that the correspondences between the episodes are probably due in general to their being patterned on a conventional (traditional) narrative model. At the same time the use of some of the particular linguistic items (e.g. *ḥmš* and *tqᶜ bšpr)* suggests the possibility of identical authorship /44/.

Foreshadowing

Another device employed with great skill in 2 Sam 9-20 + 1 Kgs 1-2 is that of foreshadowing (Rost, pp. 226-31, esp. 230; Whybray, 1968:25-31). A particularly fine example in chapters 2-4 occurs in the remark made by Abner to Asahel as the culminating point in his attempt to dissuade him from his pursuit: "Why should I strike you to the ground?" And he adds, with superb understatement as it transpires, "How then would I lift up my face to your brother Joab?" The author then cleverly allows the point to lie dormant; its force only hits us much later when we suddenly find Abner dead at the hands of Joab (3:27). In that scene, moreover, we are not allowed to know for certain Joab's intentions in calling back Abner until the actual deed is done – yet all the time we possess, from the previous episode, the clue to the inevitable outcome /45/. A further case of foreshadowing, taking chapters 2-4 as part of the story of King David, would be the mention of Mephibosheth in 4:4 (discussed earlier in this chapter), though this example is executed with much less skill.

Conclusion
        To sum up, the evidence suggests quite clearly that had Rost properly considered the major narrative in chapters 2-4 he would have been obliged to conclude that it shares those features of style that he (and others) have seen as characteristic of the "Succession Narrative" and on that account cannot be differentiated from it.

E. THEME

        The argument of the preceding sections brings us hard up against the major aspect of Rost's analysis, namely his argument (see especially p. 217) that the "theme" *(Thema)* of the whole work is posed in the question in 1 Kgs 1, "Who shall sit upon the throne of David?" To borrow Whybray's words (p. 21), the narrative "shows how, by the steady elimination of the alternative possibilities, it came about that it was Solomon who succeeded his father on the throne of Israel". Clearly if this is indeed *the* over-arching theme then 2 Sam 2-4 has only the most tangential association with it; the best we could say is that it shows how David came in the first place to have a throne on which to be succeeded. In my view, however, the centrality and significance of this theme of Solomonic succession has been considerably overstated /46/.

Methodology
        First, there is a methodological difficulty in too great a reliance on the thematic method of defining the boundaries of a narrative such as this, since it entails a large risk that the crucial definition of the theme will be arrived at *before* the boundaries of the material are known. This is in fact what happens in Rost's analysis. Yet strictly speaking (though one cannot be rigid in this matter) the reverse procedure ought to be followed. How can a critic be to any degree certain that he has accurately characterized the theme of a piece of literature, at any time a delicate and intricate business, unless he knows what that piece of literature consists of?

The "Succession" Theme
        Even so, the link between the bulk of Rost's narrative and this theme of "succession" is at best fragile.
        Although I cannot wholly accept Flanagan's thesis (1972) that the Bathsheba incident in chapters 11-12 and the account of Solomon's succession in 1 Kgs 1-2 were later redactional additions to 2 Sam 9-10, 13-20 (see my n. 19), his focus upon the nature of the individual episodes in the narrative is salutary. It is hard to deny that the bulk of the story (i.e. without the Bathsheba and Solomon episodes) is more readily described as concerned with "the difficulties and challenges that David faced in maintaining his control over the kingdom of Judah and Israel" (Flanagan, 1972: 177) than with the matter of "succession" as such. The central feature of the material

is "the most severe threat to his sovereignty," the rebellion of his own son, Absalom. Underlining this theme of "rebellion" is, of course, the Sheba episode which finally punctuates the whole Absalom story with a last momentary focus upon fragile loyalties and the tenuous nature of David's hold on the throne. If there is any sense in which this segment may be claimed to be designed to show how it was that Solomon came to be king it is exceedingly remote (see also Jackson, 1965:194). This incident (and also the Mephibosheth sub-plot) only comes into focus as "succession" material by allowing the interpretation to slide from one distinct understanding of this theme ("Which son shall rule?") to another ("Will David establish a dynasty at all?") as we saw earlier in the case of 2 Sam 7 /47/.

Likewise, it is difficult to argue that the *essence* of the Bathsheba episode in chapters 11 and 12 lies in its connection with the theme of (Solomonic) succession found in some later sections of the story. By virtue of its mention of the birth of Solomon it does have this connection but it has a far more important connection with the rest of the narrative than this. As is widely recognized (for example, M. Smith, 1951; von Rad, 1944/1966:196; Hertzberg, 1964:313-14, 322, 377-8; Whybray, 1968:23-4, 37; Auzou, 1968:379-80; Gray, 1970:19), it is spelt out in Nathan's words of condemnation to David: "Now therefore, the sword shall never depart from your house" (12:10), and "Behold, I will raise up evil against you out of your own house; and I will take your wives before your eyes, and give them to your neighbour, and he shall lie with your wives in the sight of the sun" (12:11; cf. especially 16:20-2) /48/.

There is a pattern of behaviour here that is repeated in the following episodes and we are invited to see it as somehow causally connected with what happens in chapter 11. As such it leads us directly to the rape of Tamar, the murder of Amnon and the resulting estrangement between David and Absalom, which in turn introduces the account of the lifting up of Absalom's sword against his father. And the whole story ends with Solomon re-living the circumstances of his own birth: his accession is marked by intrigue, deceit and murder (within his own house, moreover — the victims are his brother and cousin) which he employs as the best means of protecting his own interests, just as David had done in the matter of Bathsheba (see further below, Chapter Five).

I would argue, therefore, that the primary connection between the Bathsheba story (chapters 11-12) and the story of Absalom (chapters 13-20) is not to do with "succession": rather the first episode establishes an ironic connection, through the theme of rebellion, between David's public and private life. Similarly with 1 Kgs 1-2, the most important connection with 2 Sam 11-12 is not the fact that the key figure in a kind of elimination game ("Succession") is introduced there — this could have been done quite briefly with much less embarrassment to all concerned /49/, but that the pattern of circumstances surrounding Solomon's birth provides a measure of the circumstances of his succession which brings our focus back from Solomon and affairs of state to David and his private life.

This brings me to my major criticism. To claim that the theme of the narrative is the question, "Who shall *succeed* David?", is in fact to shift our focus away from its natural centre of interest throughout the whole story. It is to suggest that ultimately it is Solomon who is the protagonist, since the whole story apparently bears on *his* accession, and that "deuteragonists" are the sons Michal did not have,

Mephibosheth, the illegitimate child of Bathsheba, Amnon, Absalom, Shimei, Sheba and Adonijah (see Whybray, 1968:21, on the "succession" theme). On the contrary, this is above all else a story about *David* and not any successor or potential successor. It is David who stands in or behind every scene and David around whom every episode ultimately revolves /50/.

Nor, I would maintain, is the final episode any different. The story reaches its climax not with the establishment of the kingdom in Solomon's hands, as Rost and many have claimed (pp. 195-7, 230; cf. Whybray, pp. 21-3, 29; Gray, 1970:16; Ridout, 1971:217) /51/, but with the death of David and the circumstances of that death (I develop this point in Chapter Five).

By contrast Solomon is one of the less substantial figures in the story, since like Amnon or Adonijah he exists only in relation to a very limited segment of the narrative. "[He] can hardly be said to be more than a minor character", notes Whybray (p. 39) /52/. For a story which is meant to reach its climax in the fact that it is he who succeeds David this is a curious state of affairs. After the brief notice of his birth in chapter 12 we do not even find him lurking in the wings as the drama progresses. He simply drops out of sight /53/ and until Kgs 1 the story-teller does *nothing* to bring him into focus even in the background of events. This is of the utmost significance.

Following Rost, Whybray (p. 22) claims that after 2 Sam 12 the narrative "is devoted to the rival candidates for the throne, Solomon's half-brothers Amnon, Absalom and Adonijah, and their elimination, leaving the field clear for the triumph of Solomon at the very end", or again (pp. 20-1; cf. Auzou, 1968:364) that the narrative "shows how, by the steady elimination of the alternative possibilities, it came about that it was Solomon who succeeded his father on the throne of Israel".

The narrative itself, however, hardly goes out of its way to convey such an impression: we get little if any hint that we are to view either Amnon or Absalom as *Solomon's* rivals, nor that what is taking place in chapters 13-20 is a steady movement bringing us significantly nearer to the point where only Adonijah (" the remaining rival candidate") will stand between Solomon and the throne. Solomon's ranking amongst the many sons of David is never mentioned in the Absalom story /54/; nor for that matter is the ranking of any other son with the possible exception of Amnon (LXX at 16:21 notes that Amnon was the "first-born").

Any indication, therefore, of a line of succession ("the alternative possibilities" to Solomon) *with or without Solomon,* can barely be said to exist in these chapters. It is not until 1 Kgs 1-2, when the theme of succession does at last emerge prominently (cf. M. Smith, 1951), that Solomon and his candidature comes into view, but even here we never learn how many sons other than Adonijah stood between Solomon and the throne. The narrator is only interested in making it clear that Solomon was *not* expected to rule. Adonijah was not only an older brother but possibly the eldest for he was popularly expected to be king (1 Kgs 1:6; 2:15, 22).

Thus in terms of the narrative itself Solomon arrives quite unexpectedly on the scene.

So to reiterate my earlier point: in the bulk of the story Solomon has virtually no literary presence whatsoever. Nor, I may now add, is there in the story itself any noticeable formulation of the theme of "succession" such as might convey a clear sense of significant development or direction in the narrative or constitute the primary source of any dramatic tension.

This is not to deny that there is any such theme at all. On the contrary: a certain progressive element in the elimination of elder sons is undoubtedly there in the story, particularly when one looks back from the perspective of 1 Kgs 1, where Adonijah is mentioned as born "next after Absalom". Moreover it is reasonable to suppose that, to some extent, the author might have deliberately counted upon his audience's knowledge of the fact that it was Solomon who eventually succeeded. Rather it is to argue strongly that this is but one theme in the story, linking *at a subordinate level* one series of episodes.

There is a need, therefore, to look again at the question of theme and coherence in the narrative as a whole and certainly it may no longer be claimed that Rost's argument from the "succession" theme to the definition of the boundaries of the story is in any sense truly definitive /55/.

F. CONCLUSION

On grounds of both plot (narrative thread) and style, 2 Sam 2-4 (2:8 or 2:12 to 4:12 or more likely 5:3) may be connected with chapters 9-20 + 1 Kgs 1-2. This provides a more satisfactory beginning to the narrative than does chapter 9 (or 6). Rost's thematic argument, that the story is primarily a "succession" history, is methodologically secondary to the above considerations and in any case is itself open to a number of serious objections; at most a succession theme may be shown to be a subsidiary one providing a limited level of connection between certain parts of the narrative.

In the following chapter I explore an alternative interpretation of the story of King David, some indication of which I have already given in the present chapter. I assume the inclusion of 2 Sam 2:8 or 2:12 to 5:3 and the "Michal" section of chapter 6, and would suggest that my account of the coherence of the resultant narrative itself constitutes additional justification for this inclusion.

CHAPTER FIVE

AN INTERPRETATION
OF THE STORY

Chapter Five
An Interpretation of the Story

INTRODUCTION

An interpretative essay such as the one that follows is likely to provoke questions about method. How, for example, do we decide that one reading of the story in terms of a given statement of theme is more persuasive than another? Or, for that matter, is only one reading of the text valid and/or intended?

I doubt that the answer to the first question is to be found by intensifying the search for "extrinsic" evidence, by pursuing, for example, the original social setting or audience of the story. On the contrary, to do so is to cultivate the law of diminishing returns. While such studies may yet conceivably be productive in the case of some Old Testament literature there is little sign that they are likely to be so in the present case. Where is new and substantive evidence for a refined sociology of ancient Israelite story-telling likely to come from, short of major new archaeological discoveries of texts? Recourse to the texts themselves for further detailed "information" is to encourage speculation and risk circularity in argument. It may seem eminently reasonable to wonder how, without further elucidation of the original audience(s) of the story, we can know that it (or they) interpreted the story as I am suggesting we interpret it. The answer must be that we are not in the ideal situation that such a question presupposes. The fact of the matter is that it is precisely the audience that is unknown to us, and despite any amount of guessing, likely to remain so. Indeed my argument, in Chapter Two above, was that interpretation of this narrative has been put in a straitjacket by a preoccupation with a particular *supposed* audience and a particular *supposed* historical and cultural context. What we can be *sure* of is that we have here a piece of ancient Israelite literature, written for Israelites (we know not whom) sometime in the period of three of four hundred years after the death of David.

Certainly we must be aware of some of the cultural differences between our own world and that of those Israelites – such awareness is taken for granted in a scholarly context. We should also be aware of the similarities between our own condition and that of those other human beings despite their remove in time from us. In this case it seems to me that it is reasonable to ask the reader to face the proffered interpretation directly and to judge it on its own merits in the context of his or her own understanding of what it might have been like to be an Israelite in the first half of the first millennium. Is the interpretation sufficiently well delineated? Does it strain the *prima facie* meaning of the text? Is it a coherent and comprehensive interpretation? Does it remain doggedly with one on a re-reading of the story? Does it, in short, illuminate or enrich one's reading of the text?

A further point concerns the question of the relationship between different readings of the story. Is only one reading valid and/or intended? My answer would be "no" on both scores. It is a truism to say that a piece of criticism can never replace a work of art. It bears repeating. The interpretation is only a guide book, a conducted tour; it is not the thing itself. Its attempt to delineate significant meanings in the work can only be a matter of approximation. Meanings also exist at various levels in a piece of literature (hence, for example the range of critical terms such as plot, motif, theme, structure). Accordingly there may be room for various methods of approximation as well as for interpretations at various levels. On the other hand, to be equally valid these interpretations would presumably need to be mutually compatible.

The matter of "levels" is also directly related to the question of "intention". Without access to the author we cannot be certain that he may not have intended his work to convey multiple meanings (cf. Clines, 1976a:484-8; 1976b:60). In any case, whatever his conscious intention, we who live in a post-Freudian era can appreciate the possibility of meanings emerging from unconscious intention. Nor is it necessary to stick with the author. It is the work that confronts us, not the author. The critic is in business to read words, not minds. And if the work is to have meaning it must be meaning for us who live in the twentieth century. That means, though the historicist-purist may not like it, that the business of critical interpretation may be a somewhat messy compromise.

In the end the test of the value of the interpretation is whether it enables the reader to see the text in ways that are new to him or her. Do the critic's guidelines uncover patterns of meaning which open the text to a deeper or more comprehensive reading? Do they lead to an appreciation of the way in which the work is an integrated whole? I reiterate: the process of literary criticism is essentially an empirical one. The reader tests the theory by "trying it on for size" in his or her reading. The interpretation in this chapter is offered in this spirit of empirical enquiry.

DAVID AND THE KINGDOM: THE PRIVATE AND THE POLITICAL

Perhaps the simplest account of the story is in terms of the kingdom.

The scene is set by the story of how David came to be crowned king of all Israel. His achievement is then underlined with an exploration of his relationship (of superiority) to the dispossessed house of Saul (Michal and Mephibosheth), together with an account of the Ammonite war, in which he confidently utilizes the resources of his kingdom to extend its boundaries. The scene setting is now complete.

The Ammonite war provides an ironical frame-work for an episode, the story of David and Bathsheba, which on the face of it has little to do with the kingdom, but which turns out to be pivotal in the story as a whole. It provides the complication that sets the plot in motion. First it culminates in the birth of the future heir to the kingdom (inaugurating a "succession" theme), and so prepares for the final episode of struggle for the throne (1 Kings 1-2); it also, as Nathan's prophecy makes clear, triggers a sequence of (providential?) events of which the central is Absalom's rebellion.

David thus loses his kingdon. The closing scenes of chapters 19 and 20 then show a rather tentative restoration, which prepares us for the final episode. David effectively relinquishes the kingdom to Solomon and Solomon makes it secure for himself.

In sum, it is possible to describe the story as one of accession, rebellion and succession. It is a story about David as king.

Yet this analysis clearly leaves out of account a major aspect of the story. It might well be said that, despite its public and political implications, the key episode in chapters 11-12 is about a private matter — about how David came to gain a wife (and a son). The way in which he does this is then almost caricatured in the subsequent events within his own family. The child of adultery dies. One of his sons rapes one of his daughters. That son is killed by another son. This son seizes his father's throne, "goes in to" his concubines, wages war on his father, and is killed, in turn, by his father's right-hand man. The way is then left open for two more sons to compete for the throne, to quarrel over their father's bed-fellow (Abishag) and for one finally to murder the other in order to make secure his position. The pattern of intrigue, sex and violence in the Bathsheba episode is played out at length in the subsequent story within David's own family. The story of David then, is also a story about David the man, about David and his family, about David's own personal or private life.

The story of David as king itself divides into two major themes. The first concerns David's acquisition and tenure of the kingdom, and so finds expression in the stories of the accession and later of Absalom's and Sheba's rebellions. The second concerns David as the founder of a dynasty, and is to be traced in the birth of Solomon, the elimination of prospective heirs and the struggle between the factions of Solomon and Adonijah. Similarly the story of David and his family readily falls within the scope of two major themes. The first concerns David in a sexual role and most obviously comes to expression in the story of Bathsheba (or later in the seizure of his concubines). The second concerns David in his role as father, and so is realized in his relationship to and dealings with Amnon and Absalom, and, in the struggle for succession, with Adonijah and Solomon.

The foregoing observations give us the following scheme:

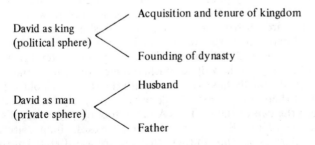

Fig. 1: basic themes.

Now there is an obvious point of connection between the political and private spheres and that is in the themes of David as father and David as dynastic founder. Both themes are concerned with David and his sons in the matter of succession which, as already indicated, has often been regarded as *the* theme of the whole story (at least from chapter 9 onwards). We might therefore add to our analysis:

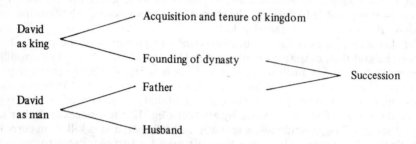

Fig. 2A: partial analysis of the interrelation of major themes. The political and personal themes are linked by the (sub-)theme of Succession.

Yet even this analysis is too simplistic. The theme of the founding of a dynasty really revolves around two distinct questions: (1) Will *any* of David's sons succeed him as king of all Israel? (a question posed by the challenge of Mephibosheth [according to Ziba] and by that of Sheba) and (2) *Which* of David's sons will succeed him? (as it is raised by the elimination of sons and echoed in the refrain of 1 Kgs 1 as to "who should sit on the throne" of David). But the former question (Will any of David's sons succeed him?) can be seen to be merely a qualified way of uttering a broader one, Will David *remain* on the throne of all Israel (so that he has a throne to bequeath to a son)? As such it clearly belongs also to the theme of acquisition and *tenure,* alongside the rebellion of Absalom. Accordingly we need to 'unpack' our major themes a little in order to show this interrelationship.

If then we turn to the personal themes, a similar interconnection is apparent. Absalom expresses his usurpation of his father's role not only by taking into his own hands the decision concerning Amnon's punishment for the rape of Tamar (usurpation of paternal authority) but also by publicly going in to his father's concubines (usurpation of his sexual role). Similarly Amnon's own action is redolent with aspects of both themes. The narrator stresses the family relationship among all the participants in the scene and underscores the way in which David, the head of the family, is by-passed: Amnon turns to David's brother for advice, while later Tamar's own comment ("Speak to the king; for he will not withhold me from you" – note that the use of "king" here additionally links the scene with the theme of political rebellion) makes it clear that there was no insuperable bar to a properly authorized sexual relationship between the two of them. Thus Amnon, too, by-passes David's paternal authority. At the same time his crime in a sense rehearses the immediately preceding story (David and Bathsheba) though there the violence was directed against a third party, here against the sexual partner herself. Thus we are again confronted with the theme of David's sexuality.

The themes converge again in the story of Abishag. There is a touch of pathos in the way the sexual theme is introduced: a young maiden of great beauty, sought out of all Israel to lie with the king, not in order to give him pleasure (or children) but simply to keep him warm. Indeed the king "knew her not" (*could* not?). It is a far cry from the man who had sought out that other great beauty, Bathsheba, to lie with him. The hint of sexual impotence establishes the tone of the political scene to follow: as I argue below, the narrator offers us the possibility of seeing David's response to the conspiracy of Nathan and Bathsheba as one of equal impotence. As if to echo his loss of sexual power the kingdom too slips from (is taken from?) his grasp. Nor does Abishag's involvement end here. With the father barely dead his two sons are quarrelling over his bed-fellow — clearly no impotence theirs! Who will take his father's place in that bed? Perhaps Adonijah's inability to suppress his desire (so impolitic) for this woman is the last faint echo of David's former sexual aggression. If so, it is also a final supreme irony that she is asked for, not seized, and that this asking is the occasion for the asker's death /2/. Adonijah must now ask his younger brother for permission to marry, for kingship has also bestowed on Solomon the authority of the father. The upshot is a Solomon secure also in his position as inheritor of his father's sexual power. He succeeds where Absalom so nearly did before him. Here also, then, we find the themes of paternity and sexuality (as well as of kingship — in terms of rebellion and succession) linked.

In diagrammatic form this interrelation of themes could be expressed now as follows:

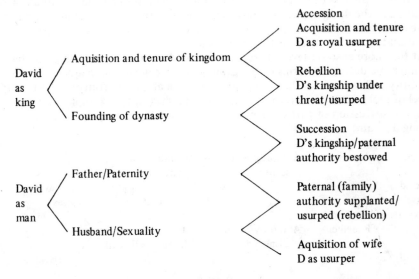

Fig. 2B: fuller analysis of the interrelation of themes. Read (for example): rebellion is one expression of the important theme of David's acquisition and tenure of the kingdom. Will he *lose* the kingdom (for example, to Absalom)? It may also be related to the other major "kingship" theme, that concerning the founding of the dynasty. Will *any* of David's sons inherit all Israel?

(The possibility of a negative answer is raised, for example, by Mephibosheth
[according to Ziba] and by Sheba).
Note: the "political" themes are mirrored by equivalent "private" themes;
this correspondence is best seen when all are defined in terms of status or
authority. See further Fig. 3.

Nor does the interrelation of themes stop here. It is not only in the case of
succession that there is significant connection between the political and personal
themes.

It is interesting to observe how David's acquisition of his kingdom and consolid-
ation of power provides a backdrop to his acquisition of a new wife. Ishbosheth thus
pre-figures Uriah. The taking of Bathsheba is complemented by the taking of Rabbah
(2 Sam 12). As king, David is a "new man", as we are reminded initially by the
presence of a rival king, Ishbosheth, and later (2 Sam 9) by the presence of a son of
Jonathan (Mephibosheth) and later still (2 Sam 16) by the alleged hope for restoration
of that same son, by the curses of Shimei, and (2 Sam 20) by the secessionist cry of
Sheba. He is also a "new man" for Bathsheba. Accession or the securing of royal
tenure can be seen therefore as the political expression of a theme of acquisition (or,
from the other point of view, usurpation) which finds personal expression in the
gaining/usurping of a wife.

Likewise the political theme of rebellion (as in the cases of Absalom and Sheba)
mirrors that of the loss of paternal authority (as in the cases of Amnon, Absalom and
Adonijah) and the displacement of status whether as father or "husband" (as happens
with Absalom and Solomon). Again the loss may be seen in terms of usurpation, in
this case usurpation by others at David's expense.

At this more abstract level, therefore, we could say that we find three themes
which might be defined in terms of the gaining, displacement and bequeathal of status
or authority. These themes then come to expression at a more concrete level (nearer
the level of plot) in specific political or personal forms (as, for example, accession
rebellion or succession of particular persons). This analysis is expressed in the
following diagram:

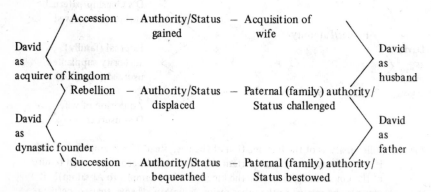

Fig. 3: analysis of the interrelation of themes, complementary to Fig. 2B. The

"political" and "private" themes are shown as equivalent expressions of deeper themes concerned with authority or status.

Read (for example): "Authority/Status displaced" is expressed in the political theme of rebellion, which in turn may give expression to the theme of the acquisition and tenure of the kingdom ("David as acquirer of kingdom") and/or of the founding of a dynasty ("David as dynastic founder"); this same "deep" theme is also expressed in the private theme of paternal (family) authority or status challenged, which in turn may give expression to the theme of the father/paternity and/or that of the husband/sexuality.

Interconnection between the political and private themes also exists at the more concrete level, as in the case of succession where David's roles as father and dynastic founder are obviously inextricably linked. Similar interplay is to be seen in the other themes.

Thus clearly Amnon's disregard for his father's authority is also disregard for that of the king. The action is an outrage against the law of the land as well as against the decencies and unity of the family. Moreover it would seem that David's reluctance to deal with it stems in large part from his conception of his role as father (I follow the LXX in 13:21: "When King David heard of all these things, he was very angry. But he did not trouble his son, Amnon, because he loved him, for he was his first born"). But this particular interconnection of private and political worlds does not end here. Before long this reluctance to judge is being recapitulated in the lead-up to Absalom's rebellion (16:1-6). "There is no man deputed by the king to hear you", says Absalom to prospective litigants. "Oh that I were judge in the land! Then every man with a suit or cause might come to me, and I would give him justice". Whether the claim is true or not in this case (see further, below) we have seen evidence of David's neglect of his responsibilities earlier in the story. Thus his weak response to Amnon's domestic rebellion is linked ironically with this further rebellion of son and subject, which now has a major political dimension. Again the outcome of the rebellion is complicated by David's twin roles: "Deal gently for my sake with the young man Absalom", he says (2 Sam 18:5). When the Cushite announces a king's victory (2 Sam 18:32), "May the enemies of my lord the king, and all who rise up against you for evil, be like that young man", David laments a father's loss: "Would that I had died instead of you, O Absalom, my son, my son".

In the final episode (1 Kgs 1-2) the theme of challenge to status, in the political form of rebellion, reappears with Adonijah's self-exaltation. "I will be king", he says, as he takes on the trappings of kingship. Like Absalom before him he gets for himself "chariots and horsemen and fifty men to run before him" (1 Kings 1:5; cf. 2 Sam 15:1). In case the parallel is not already ominously apparent the narrator underscores it: "He was also a very handsome man" (cf. "Now in all Israel there was no one so much to be praised for his beauty as Absalom" — 2 Sam 14:25); and he was born next after Absalom" — which last clause neatly adds the theme of succession to that of rebellion. (This complicates the "message": Adonijah is in fact the heir presumptive, as even Bathsheba, Solomon's mother, does not deny — 1 Kings 2:15. Perhaps in that case he might quite properly say, "I will be king"). We note, however, that in the midst of the vignette the paternal theme has reappeared. No matter whether the political threat is real or imagined, it is clear that David will make no move himself to determine which is the case, not because of political impotence but because his hands are tied by his role as father. Of Adonijah we are told: "His father had never at any time displeased him by asking 'Why have you done thus and so?'". David's reluctance to act against Amnon and likewise his acquiescence in the murder of that son by his eventual reception of Adonijah at court come strongly to mind.

In another case, that of Michal, the accession and sexuality themes are inseparably bound together. She is potentially both a sexual partner and a means of royal legitimation. Her failure in the one regard (she bears no child) entails David's failure in the other. There is to be no child who might have been that political convenience, a son of both houses.

One further point that might best be made here. It is not only with David that political and personal interests provide convenient points of reference for an exploration of the text. It is somewhat similar with Joab, perhaps the next main character in the story to David. Where he most comes into the foreground his actions inevitably raise questions of motivation, if for no other reason than that they cut across David's own plans or disposition of affairs. I shall not elaborate this point here, since it will emerge in the discussion to follow, except to say that each case readily resolves itself into a matter of whether Joab is acting out of personal interests, on the one hand, or in the interests of the state, as he sees these, on the other. As observed earlier (Chapter Three) his relationship to David is itself encapsulated ironically in the formula, "What have I to do with you, you sons of Zeruiah?", where the answer is "everything" — Joab is both friend and blood relation, as well as David's party manager, his right-hand man in the running of the state. What makes the portrayal of the character so interesting is that, even more than with David, the narrator rarely allows us to determine for certain which sphere of interest is dominant at any time. The effect is to suggest that perhaps for Joab political and personal interests are more often closely married. In that case he is a splendid foil for David whose story is one of the struggle to reconcile such interests.

Such thematic observations may be multiplied and explored in much greater detail. To some extent this is done in the following section (Giving and Grasping). For the present, however, I trust that enough has been said to warrant taking at least the broad lines of the analysis as a helpful way of charting an important set of meanings in the story. It is a story about David and his kingdom, which explores the complex interaction, generating a sequence of tensions, between the political and private (especially family) worlds of David.

DAVID AND THE KINGDOM: GIVING AND GRASPING

This brief examination of the political and private or personal dimensions of the story led at one point to the postulation of some "deep" themes: the gaining, displacement and bestowal of authority or status. Carrying the process of abstraction a little further, it is clear that what these three themes have in common, apart from the status aspect (which becomes concrete in political and personal terms), is the activity of giving or taking. This may appear to be a trivial observation, since giving and taking must belong in some degree to most, if not all, stories of human interaction. However I would argue that in the present narrative it is pervasive to the extent of constituting an important underlying theme. "The king and the private individual" (whether as father or husband) defines the subjects of thematic interest, "giving and grasping" defines their mode of treatment. It is not only David's gaining, losing or bestowing status, and the complicating interconnection of his political and private roles, that is of interest. The manner in which he gains, loses or bestows status is highly significant. Thus it can be argued that it is when David's mode of action is most attuned to giving that he is most successful. His grasping (especially in the Bathsheba scene), on the other hand, brings in its train a series of disasters in both political and private spheres.

In terms of this analysis the story can be described as follows: the king who is content to be given the kingdom (2 Sam 2-5) nevertheless seizes with violence the woman of his desire (Bathsheba). The theme of seizure then erupts in the rape of Tamar, the taking of Amnon's life and the rebellion of Absalom. With the loss of his throne, however, we see again momentarily the radical, magnanimous David who will allow the matter of the kingdom to rest in the hands of others (2 Sam 15-18). His fortunes accordingly improve and he is restored, but the restoration is itself marked by compromise — David will not allow Sheba the freedom to opt out. The final episode (1 Kings 1-2) then shows the death of the king in the context of political intrigue where the theme of grasping predominates, expressed in terms of David as well as of others (notably Solomon). The kingdom is effectively taken from David. Ironically the agent of seizure is Bathsheba, the benefactor her son.

I shall now attempt to expand and justify this analysis, starting at the beginning of the story, with 2 Sam 2.

The Scene is Set: 2 Sam 2-5, 9, 10

2 Sam 2-4 pivots on the question of David as alternative ruler of Israel to the house of Saul. Where Abner is cheated in his attempt "to bring over all Israel" to David (3:12, 21), the sons of Rimmon succeed, if only indirectly: whether or not the beginning of chapter 5 (vss. 1-3) belongs in precisely its present form, it is quite clear that the gift of Ishbosheth's head is at the same time the gift of the kingdom.

There is thus a curious ambivalence about David's response to this action of Baanah and Rechab. On the one hand there is something appealing in his refusal to countenance the violence done to his rival; we are reminded of David's relationship with Saul in 1 Sam 24 and 26 (cf. also 2 Sam 1). This focusses our attention on the remarkable fact that David, despite his obvious position of power, has made absolutely no attempt to seize by force the throne of Israel. Indeed it is noticeable in the plot that all the key initiatives are taken by characters other than David, namely Abner, Joab and the sons of Rimmon /3/.

On the other hand, David's role is not entirely passive. It remains the case that the gift of the head is extraordinarily convenient: as we have seen in the negotiations with Abner (3:12-3, 21) and as we shall see in the final segment (5:1-3) David is far from being averse to the thought of gaining the kingdom. Indeed there is more than a hint of a public relations exercise in his dramatic despatch of the bringers of the gift, just as there is in his elaborate dissociation from the killing of Abner. Does he protest too much? Perhaps his anger against Joab is directed not simply against an "evildoer" but against the man who had to all extents and purposes put an end to hopes of a straightforward transference of power to himself.

The stark contrast he draws between Abner, the "prince" and "great man", and Joab, the "evildoer" and "wicked" man before whom Abner had fallen, prompts some reflection. Has this really been a story of greatness and wickedness? After all, Abner *had* killed Joab's brother and himself recognized (2:22) that this was a serious matter bearing directly upon Joab. Moreover, whereas from David's point of view Abner may well have gone from Hebron "in peace", as the narrator is at pains to observe (3:21, 22, 23), things may have looked different to Joab who appears on the scene in the context of war (3:22; cf. 3:1, 6) which was also the context in which we had last seen him (chapter 2) where, of course, he was to be found fighting David's battles and against Abner no less. And whether or not his words to David in 3:25 ("You know that Abner the son of Ner came to deceive you, and to know your going out and your coming in") indicate a motive playing a genuine part in his killing of the enemy captain, the fact that they could be uttered at all confirms this impression that the context may still be seen as that of war. Perhaps, then, from Joab's perspective the incident is merely an extension of the battle at Gibeon. And would David have complained had Joab killed Abner on the hill of Ammah?

As for Abner, even if we decide that pique and a keen sense of Ishbosheth's ingratitude /4/ is Abner's predominant motivation for his conspiracy we are still left with his claim (3:9-10; cf. 3:17-9, 5:1-3) that Yahweh had promised David the throne of all Israel. On the other hand, in the broader context of the previous defeat and its indication of David's growing strength (cf. also 3:1) we may fairly wonder whether the quarrel is merely a pretext. Is Abner deserting a sinking ship? Is this talk of loyalty and ingratitude merely a cover for his own skin-saving disloyalty? Are we then to echo with unreserved enthusiasm David's view of Abner (or is this merely for public consumption?), that "a prince and a great man has fallen this day in Israel?".

Against a simple scheme of contrasting worthiness and wickedness, therefore, the narrator has set other perspectives which put the characters in shades of grey rather than black and white: there are elements of self-interest and deceit as well as of loyalty and self-restraint in this narrative. Far from being polar opposites, as David's speech might suggest, Joab and Abner share much in common for both belong, *par excellence*, to the grey world of power politics, expediency, and the ruthless initiative: they are the party managers. The only difference is that Joab happens to be on the winning side.

David, for his part, also has some share in this world. Nevertheless, it remains the case that his restraint in the matter of gaining the kingdom is remarkable. It is something which cannot easily be assimilated to a doctrine of political expediency. David is prepared to risk allowing the kingdom to be the gift of others. It is this that singles him out qualitatively from the others.

The gift of Saul's kingdom to David is followed by David's gift of Saul's land and servants to Mephibosheth, Saul's grandson, as a token of his loyalty *(hsd)* towards Jonathan. At least that is ostensibly what it is about. Yet again there are indications in the text that suggest another possible perspective. The gesture is perhaps less magnanimous than David suggests: it is not merely without cost to himself (since he is giving away someone else's land and labour) but it is also likely to result in a healthy subsidy for the court (cf. 9:9-10) /5/ and (as often noted by commentators) it will enable him to keep this last scion of the house of Saul under perpetual surveillance. There is then a delicate irony in the possibility that in 16:1-4 Ziba's gesture of generosity to the dispossessed David may be no less devious than David's to the dispossessed Mephibosheth /6/. Characteristically, however, the narrator refuses to allow us the luxury of making simple judgements. We are left with a perception of the ambivalence of events /7/.

The gift to Mephibosheth is followed by the offering of consolation to Hanun (and notice again the parellel motif of *ḥsd*). This, however, is rebuffed and war ensures. The reaction of Hanun's courtiers to David's offer of friendship echoes directly the reaction of Joab to Abner's visit in chapter 3:

> But the princes of the Ammonites said to Hanun their lord, "Do you think, because David has sent comforters to you, that he is honouring your father? Has not David sent his servants to you to search the city and to spy it out and to overthrow it?" (10:3).

> Then Joab went to the king and said, "What have you done? Behold, Abner came to you; why is it that you have sent him away, so that he is gone? You know that Abner the son of Ner came to deceive you, and to know your going out and your coming in, and to know all that you are doing" (3:24-5).

In the political world of Joab and the courtiers suspicion is the order of the day. An unsolicited offer of friendship belongs to unreality. Reality is the aggressive extension of self-interest, whether political or personal, or preferably both.

Complication: 2 Sam 11-12

The Ammonite incident establishes the tone as well as the setting of the following crucial episode, the story of David, Uriah and Bathsheba. The direction of the plot, then, is from gift offered and received, through gift rebuffed, to the polar opposite of giving, grasping by force. However precisely one interprets Nathan's parable in relation to its setting (cf. Simon, 1967; Delekat, 1967:32-3; Hoftijzer, 1970; Seebass, 1974) it is absolutely plain that it encapsulates the essence of David's dealing with Bathsheba; the episode is the story of the rich man who *took* the poor man's lamb. The ironic contrast with 2 Sam 2-5 is marked: the king who was content to be given his kingdom must seize by force (against Uriah if not Bathsheba) a wife. From Nathan's perspective the issue is clear. It was Yahweh who gave the kingdom. Yahweh in turn will not then let his king's act of violent taking pass without consequences for his kingdom (12:8-11) /8/.

The immediate token of the consequences is the taking away (forcibly, as it were) of the child of adultery. But the real issue will lie in the events of the succeeding chapters, with the onset of a pattern of events that continually harks back to the theme of "seizure" in this episode.

Now it is tempting to find here a straightforward scheme of retribution in line with an unqualified condemnation of David by the author. Certainly the ironic treatment of David in connection with the death of Uriah is the most scathing in the whole narrative (see further Ridout, 1971:63-73, 102-7, 152-8; Delekat, 1967:26); yet a clear-cut perspective is blurred by several factors.

First, the stunning simplicity of David's response to Nathan — "I have sinned against Yahweh" — functions powerfully to reinstate him in the reader's estimation; and indeed Nathan's reply — "Yahweh also has put away your sin" — reinforces this emotional trend. Dramatically this sets up a certain tension with the long term outworking of the pattern of violence.

Something similar is effected by the way the episode ends. David is able, but with apparent impunity now, to do precisely what he had done to set the story in motion; he can have sexual intercourse with Bathsheba, the woman of his desire (11:4; 12:24). The outcome is the birth of Solomon, of whom we are told, "Yahweh loved him" — clearly, for as every reader knows, this child eventually becomes king. From the perspective of the end of the episode (which projects to the end of the whole story) Uriah becomes merely a disposable pawn.

But what then of Yahweh's role in the whole process? Delekat's observation (1967:32-3; but cf. Seebass, 1974:206 n.6), that one way of "casting" Nathan's parable is to give *Yahweh* the role of the rich man, in which case David is the guest and Uriah the lamb (both of whom are killed), offers an ironic viewpoint that ties in here. It is all very well Yahweh being "displeased", for ultimately he must bear some measure of responsibility; David is the one whom he has chosen and protected, and will continue to protect (17:14). Moreover, from at least one point of view Yahweh in effect blesses David's action in the course of time through Solomon's good fortune. On the other hand, as I shall presently argue, Solomon also stands at the centre of the final outworking of the pattern of seizure and violence within David's house (and bearing directly on the kingdom) which is set in motion by the present episode. Thus the tension between forgiveness (blessing) and retribution is never finally resolved. The narrator's treatment of Yahweh as a character in the story retains a measure of ambivalence if not an undercurrent of irony /9/.

An appropriate link between the Bathsheba episode and the major ones to follow is provided by the resolution to the account of the Ammonite war (12:26-31), which provides not only an ironic comment on David as king (who has to be summoned by his general to "capture" the city; cf. similarly 11:1 where we are told that "at the time when kings go forth to battle" David sent Joab to beseige Rabbah while he remained at Jerusalem) /10/ but also a striking symbol of what has gone before and the scene that immediately follows. The assault and capture of the city gives way to seizure and rape of Tamar, and that in turn to the taking of Amnon's life.

Transition: 2 Sam 13

Clearly we are expected to see in chapter 13 a recapitulation of what had gone before in chapter 11. David had seen a beautiful woman, had taken her and lain with her; then, in order to prevent discovery through the birth of an obviously illegitimate child, he had attempted to trick the husband into a false paternity and, failing this, had finally engaged in an intrigue which led to Uriah's death. Amnon, David's son,

a Sexual affair

desires a beautiful girl, he conspires to trick her into a position where he can seize and lie with her, but is in turn conspired against and murdered. David finds, coming to expression within his own family, the elements of his own earlier experience. The family relations are stressed: "son", "brother", "sister", are repeated throughout the episode (even to the point of Amnon's summons, "Come lie with me, *my sister*"). This is all bound up with David's private world. His sin has come home to roost. Indeed he also participates (albeit unwittingly − or is there room for doubt in the matter of Amnon's death?) in the new deeds: it is he who sends Tamar to Amnon and it is he who assents to Amnon's fatal visit to Baal-Hazor.

Moreover, there has been a transformation of the deed. It is striking how the emotions and actions of chapter 13 are heightened compared with those of chapters 11 and 12. David's dealings with Bathsheba have a curiously matter-of-fact character:

> ... he saw from the roof a woman bathing; and the woman was very beautiful. And David sent and enquired about the woman .... So David sent messengers and took her; and she came to him, and he lay with her .... Then she returned to her house. And the woman conceived and she sent and told David, "I am with child". So David sent word to Joab .... When the wife of Uriah heard that Uriah her husband was dead she made lamentation for her husband. And when the mourning was over David sent and brought her to his house and she became his wife and bore him a son .... On the seventh day the child died .... Then David comforted his wife Bathsheba and went in to her and lay with her; and she bore a son ....

There is nothing here about David's emotions, nothing about "love" or other feeling for Bathsheba, only that he comforted her after the death of the child of adultery. That she was anything more than a "beautiful woman" for him is never made clear. It is, after all, only with the news of the child's conception that he makes any move concerning Uriah and only when his stratagem has failed and his own position looks like being seriously compromised that he decides to remove the husband so as to legitimize his relationship with the woman. It has all the appearance of a casual affair, a king's whim. Likewise we hear nothing of Bathsheba's response. Certainly David is the king, but we are told of no protest against his initial approach, nor of any enduring hostility.

The contrast with the Amnon and Tamar episode could not be more marked:

> Now Absalom, David's son, had a beautiful sister, whose name was Tamar, and after a time Amnon, David's son, loved her. And Amnon was so tormented that he made himself ill because of his sister Tamar .... And when she brought [the cakes] near to him to eat, he took hold of her *[ḥzq]* and said to her "Come, lie with me, my sister". She answered him, "No, my brother, do not force me *[ᶜnh]*; for such a thing is not done in Israel ...." But he would not listen to her; and being stronger than her *[ḥzq]* he forced her *[ᶜnh]* and lay with her. Then Amnon hated her with very great hatred; so that the hatred with which he hated her was greater than the love with which he had loved her. And Amnon said to her, "Arise, be gone". But she said to him, "No, my brother, for this wrong in sending me away is greater than the other which you did to me". But he would not listen to her .... "Put this woman

out of my presence, and bolt the door after her" . . . . And Tamar put ashes on
her head, and rent the long robe she wore; and she laid her hand on her head,
and went away, crying aloud as she went . . . . So Tamar dwelt, a desolate woman,
in her brother Absalom's house.

There is excess of love at the beginning, excess of hate at the end. The violent
fluctuation is conveyed superbly in the dialogue. "Come, lie with me, *my sister*"
gives place to "Put *this woman [ꜣet-zo ꜣt]* out of my presence". At each point Tamar
resists: she is willing neither to lie with him, nor having been compelled to do so,
simply to go away. When she does go it is in deep lamentation and she dwells,
desolate *[šōmēmāh]*, thereafter. Set in relief by all this is the central point: whereas
David, we are told, "takes" Bathsheba *(lqḥ* — 11:4) Amnon "seizes", "overpowers"
(ḥzq) and "forces" or "humiliates" *(ᶜnh)* Tamar.

Even David's calculated disposal of Uriah — "Set Uriah in the forefront of the
hardest fighting, and then draw back from him, that he may be struck down and die"
— has an element of forbearance in it. The killing, however engineered, is left finally
to the chance of an enemy arrow. With Amnon's murder nothing is left to chance —
"When I say to you, 'Strike Amnon', then kill him" (13:28).

Thus, especially in the sexual theme, the mode of "taking" is carefully
differentiated. We are not forced to dissociate entirely from David; Amnon's eventual
death, on the other hand, causes little regret. Yet the broad connection between the
two episodes (Bathsheba and Tamar) remains plain to be seen, even if it is not quite so
obvious how precisely the one can be the *consequence* of the other.

There is a nice irony in Joab's initiation of the move to secure Absalom's return.
It would seem to be perhaps the one and only time that he acts from simple generosity:
"Now Joab the son of Zeruiah perceived that the king's heart went out to Absalom".
If there is a political motive, or self-interest, in the action, it is not apparent. Yet it is
to prove disastrous for the state and, in the aftermath of the war, for Joab's personal
status. Nor is this the only irony of the episode. The process of reconciliation gains
speed at the last only through Absalom's recourse to violence as a means of securing
attention.

In chapter 14 the pace has slackened after the hectic events of chapter 13. The
narrator spends a whole chapter showing how the reconciliation was painfully effected.
Then comes a sudden change of pace. In the space of about ten verses we are
confronted with the results of this reluctant reconciliation — rebellion. Another major
episode is set in motion.

Further Complication: 2 Sam 14-17
Although the initial scene between Absalom and the men of Israel is ostensibly
Absalom's it very much constitutes a question about, if not a comment on, David.

Absalom's return to Jerusalem has moved to a climax with the prince demanding
access to the king. His concern to be re-admitted to his father's presence is moving:

Why have I come from Geshur? It would be better for me to be there still. Now,
therefore, let me see the face of the king; and if there is guilt in me, let him kill
me. /11/

And the force of the appeal is underlined with brilliant simplicity in the narration of its impact on David /12/ : "Then Joab went to the king and told him; and he summoned Absalom". What other could David have done or said in the face of such a cry. The reader is likely to find himself emotionally reinstating the prince; and to lose sight of the aggression of the field-burning incident or the acute problem raised by "if there is guilt in me" /13/ is easy. Such features in the narrative only come back into focus with the ensuing scene which effects a sudden shift in perspective: we find Absalom engaged in conspiratorial activity against his father.

Yet in turn the rapidity with which we find ourselves reading that "the conspiracy gew strong, and the people with Absalom kept increasing. And a messenger came to David, saying, 'The hearts of the men of Israel have gone after Absalom'" (15:12-3) prompts reflection. What kind of conspiracy is this that could so rapidly gain popular support? Just what was David doing all this time? Is it possible that the king who sent others to fight his wars for him — while he abused his privilege as king — had also failed to provide properly for the administration of justice in the land?

We are not allowed a final answer to our query; any judgement we make about the conspiracy must always contend with the fact that it contains one significant variable in the foreground. But while we are invited to see the rebellion as in some way consequential upon the Bathsheba/Uriah outrage (e.g. as the sin of the father working itself out in the son) the extent of our sympathy for him at this further deprivation is subject to the suspicion that we may indeed be culpable in the present instance as in the former one.

If the nuances of the scene tease us, the main direction of the story is clear: the strongly adverse sequence of events initiated in the Bathsheba episode culminates now in rebellion. The theme of giving, transformed in that episode into a theme of grasping, comes fully to expression here in its original, political form: Absalom "steals the hearts of the men of Israel" and their gift of the kingdom to David is revoked (15:1-13). The kingdom is now taken from him.

The rebellion puts David back where he started. This reverse, however, has a curiously positive effect. From the Bathsheba episode up to this point the king has stood largely in the background, brushed in with only the lightest of strokes. Now his presence is strongly felt again, but it is not the presence of the grasping "rich man" of the Bathsheba story, it is much more that of the man who was content to be given the kingdom. If now the kingdom is taken from him David is prepared to let it go without a struggle. Once again we find a certain ambivalence in the portrayal of the character. David's relinquishing of power has a comic and critical aspect. Yet it is also a source of appeal and energy: some of his best moments occur in the narrative of the progression from Jerusalem to the Jordan — moments characterized by his readiness to allow the matter of the throne to rest ultimately in the hands of others /14/.

From the critical (comic) perspective we observe that his only response to threat is flight; indeed, barely has the retreat begun before we find him in conversation with a powerful mercenary captain, referring to Absalom as "the king" (cf. Schulz, 1920: 184-5; Ridout, 1971:159-60) and, of all things, urging this ally of potentially vital importance to desert him. Yet while from the perspective of the kingly hero the parody is clear enough, from that of the anti-hero it is a matter of freedom. Ittai is

made no unwilling captive to a contract. Instead the open-handed gift of total liberty
from any bond of loyalty brings an equal and opposite response of total commitment
to just such a bond. Ittai will be his lord's servant in life or death: "As Yahweh lives,
and as my lord the king lives, wherever my lord the king shall be, whether for death
or for life, there also will your servant be". In this commitment lies already germinated
the seeds of David's restoration. Ittai refuses to acquiesce to any simple logic of
realism (after all David has left the royal city and both it and the trappings of kingship
are indeed Absalom's for the taking): David is still his lord the *king* (Ridout, 1971:159)
and in the event Ittai will play an important role in effecting the transformation of
this designation from ideal to actuality again.

　　At several other points in the episode a similar pattern emerges: David is prepared
to allow that the kingdom is not his to grasp or cling to but lies in the hands of others
to give /15/. Confronted with the question whether the ark should go on with him or
remain in Jerusalem, he answers that it should remain (15:25-6): "If I find favour in
the eyes of Yahweh, he will bring me back . . . but if he says, 'I have no pleasure in
you', behold, here I am, let him do to me what seems good to him". Shimei advances
just this latter perspective (16:8): "Yahweh has given the kingdom into the hand of
your son, Absalom. See, your ruin is on you; for you are a man of blood". Abishai's
violent response — "Why should this dead dog curse my lord the king? Let me go
over and take off his head" — establishes the norm. Against this is set David's
remarkable restraint — "Let him alone and let him curse" — at the heart of which is
a strong sense of his being in the hands of Yahweh, whether for good or ill.

　　There is, then, an underlying parallel between David here, where he no longer
holds the kingdom, and in the opening episode of the story, where Israel is not yet
his. From the comic perspective, there as here things "happen" to him /16/. Although
Abner's conspiracy to secure for him the throne of Israel goes badly awry, a fortuitous
consequence of this mishap leaves David with the throne in effect secured and without
his hardly having lifted a finger to further this end himself. Likewise, in the present
case of Absalom's rebellion, David's restoration is due in the first instance, at least, to
two factors which lie beyond his control — the persuasiveness of Hushai, and the
victory of the army (including Ittai who, as we have seen, is there on his own initiative),
which pointedly does *not* include David himself. Even the fact that it is at least *his*
decision that puts Hushai in a position to work his verbal magic on Absalom is undercut by the fact that it is Hushai who initially comes to meet David (the gift of Yahweh?
not David who sends for Hushai /17/.

　　Seen from another viewpoint, however, none of this is fundamentally an accident
but stems from a life-style, howbeit at odds with the norm, which is basically
envigorating: there as here, he refuses to grasp violently what is not yet (or any longer)
his, he is prepared to let the initiative pass beyond his control. In other words, to
return to our theme, he recognizes, however momentarily, that the kingdom is the
gift of others. If, as Shimei urges, "Yahweh has given the kingdom into the hands of
Absalom", so be it, says David.

Resolution/Transition: 2 Sam 18-20
　　Thus the tide turns for David. But unlike the opening episode there can be this
time no simple resolution. The parties to any possible resolution are too compromised

by their involvement in the past events: nothing can be quite the same again. The David who at the first, however ostentatiously, could mourn the dead Abner and cut down the killers of his rival, Ishbosheth, now finds the scenario more complicated — he must now choke back his grief at the death of his own son and endure the scathing rebuke of the very man who had sped Absalom on his way to Sheol.

The scene is rightly a famous one. Here comes to a head the conflict between king and father. As Brueggemann has argued (1969:484-91; 1972c:29-38; 1974:181) it is when David stands in opposition to the norm that his appeal is greatest. Here his initial refusal to behave as a *king* at the news of the death of Absalom the rebel, generates something of that appeal.

The presentation is complex. David's behaviour draws the bitter criticism by Joab: "You have today covered with shame the faces of all your servants . . . because you love those who hate you and hate those who love you" (19:6-7). On the other hand, as Delekat observes (1967:30), drawing attention to the Sermon on the Mount:

> *Joab's principle, "you should love your friends and hate your enemies", is a human commonplace, but David's feeble resistance to this law is the resistance of* true *humanity, which feels itself trapped in this law.*

In other words Joab's attack carries force and conviction; yet the very terms in which it is expressed effect, however momentarily, a shift in perspective which forces admiration instead of condemnation for the man who could so step outside the confines of convention, here the boundaries of political necessity.

And the ambivalence accurately reflects the quality of the immediately preceding scene. David's reaction to the news of Absalom's death is possibly the most remarked-upon passage in the whole narrative. Yet to define it in terms either of the genuine humanity of the king or of his self-indulgence (as is often done) is to underrate the author's skill. The passage functions in both ways. The negative function needs no elaboration. Joab's speech does that admirably. But there *is* something positive here. There is genuine grief. The narrator breaks his habit (Schulz, 1923:197-9) and confronts us directly with the inner emotion of the man: "and the king was deeply moved" /18/. And genuine grief has a magnetic attraction: the reader is cold indeed who can eliminate sympathy from his own reaction to David in this passage. In its positive function, therefore, the passage elicits our identification with the king as man at his most elemental.

With his appearance at the gate to review the troops, however, we see that it is Joab's perspective, the norms of political necessity, that has won the day. The king reviews the troops in celebration of the victory and thus succumbs to the norm. As Jackson comments (1965:194), David is at the end reduced "to a shell of a man". In terms of the kingdom it is obvious, moreover, that it is the victory in battle that has become the most important factor in the shaping of events. Any gift is now secondary. Likewise the fact that David has been deposed cannot simple be glossed over.

The prelude to restoration is thus a passage (19:10-11; EVV:9-10) that exudes compromise and irresolution. Then follow negotiations and more compromise — the buying of support through the appointment of Amasa over the army — before the return proper can begin.

The fragility of the renewed gift is heavily underlined. Despite a momentary

glimpse of the radical David (again with Abishai and Shimei) it comes as no surprise
to find that the scene of return culminates in the quarrel of the men of Israel –
"Why have our brothers the men of Judah *stolen* you away?" – and the withdrawal
of their support from the king: "We have no portion in David, and we have no
inheritance in the son of Jesse" /19/.

The last scene in the story of the rebellion thus provides at best an uneasy
resolution. David, given back the kingdom, immediately initiates violent action
against the ringleader of those (many) who had chosen to have no part in the giving
/20/. In the plot within the plot Joab echoes his erstwhile master's action: he
eliminates his rival, Amasa, and with him another potential source of danger to the
political *status quo*. We need not speculate too much about the precise reasons for
Amasa's crucial delay. What little is said about Amasa both here and elsewhere in
the story suggest that the elements of disployalty, treachery and incompetence
belong to the configuration of this particular cameo /21/.

The tone of the narrative in this last scene is remarkably flat: there is little in
the presentation of the characters (David, Joab, Amasa, Sheba) to engage us strongly
for or against them. Though the echo of the violence and grasping that emerged in
the Bathsheba episode at the beginning of the reign is clear enough there is a
difference. Here is not the kind of act that might finally elicit an acknowledgement
of sin; it is simply what might be expected, indeed required, of a king in such a
situation. Here is neither the appealing dissociation from convention of the king who
was content to receive, nor the boldly despotic attitude of the adulterer and murderer,
merely the initiation of a rather shabby act of political expediency. This sets the tone
of the final episode in the story, Solomon's accession and the death of David.

Final Outcome: 1 Kgs 1-2

The pivotal action in the final episode, the giving away of the kingdom, may
assume from one position the appearance of being the act of a man who can recognize
his inability to cope any longer (David is now very old) and can by choice relinquish
his hold over something that he can no longer claim with responsibility to be his.
But this view struggles to hold its own. The predominant perspectives are negative.

One moment when we do, momentarily at least, recapture an echo of a former
spirit in the king is when, according to Jonathan's report, David receives the courtiers
who come to congratulate him on Solomon's coronation (1 Kgs 1:47-8):

> "Moreover the king's servant's came to congratulate *(brk)* our lord King David,
> saying, 'Your God make the name of Solomon more famous than yours and
> make his throne greater than yours'. And the king bowed himself upon the bed.
> And the king also said, 'Blessed be Yahweh the God of Israel, who has granted
> one of my offspring [text: Gray, 1970:64] to sit on my throne this day, my
> own eyes seeing it'".

In the simplicity of his response (no rhetorical flourish in return – just a bow which
serves both to acknowledge the visitors and to preface his brief thanksgiving) and the
ascription of all that had happened to Yahweh, there is a sense of genuineness and an
appeal such as we met, for example, in the king who fled from Jerusalem. Here is the

humility of the man who places the gift of the kingdom in Yahweh's hands. But the very next word in the narrative is *wyhrdw* ("and they trembled"):

Then they trembled and arose, did all the guests of Adonijah, and each went his own way. And Adonijah feared Solomon; and he arose and went and caught hold of the horns of the altar.

We are sharply reminded of the context of the report, and made acutely aware of a new perspective: the giving of the kingdom to Solomon is now an occasion not for blessing but for fear. And if the narrator conveyed a sense of simple spontaneity on David's part so here with a superb economy of words he creates a powerful sense of gut-reaction terror /22/. For Adonijah in particular the gift to Solomon clearly means death; and as we presently discover, his intuition proves to be correct.

This abrupt juxtaposition of blessing and terror forces us to re-think our response. Is there not something strikingly ingenuous about David? Does he not see that the occasion of blessing, the granting of the throne to this particular offspring, must also be one of mourning for the death of the elder son? What kind of divine "gift" is this that can create such a pall of fear, such a negative reaction (cf. Brueggemann, 1972b:167)?

A simple reflection makes it plain that the attitude expressed in the thanksgiving matches little the actuality. It was David and David alone who made the appointment (1:35): "for he shall be king in my stead; I have appointed him to be ruler over Israel and over Judah". Moreover, the speech of thanksgiving contains within itself a hint of the tension here between the ascription of all to Yahweh and the primary orientation of the speaker: "Blessed be Yahweh, the God of Israel, who has granted one of *my* offspring to sit on *my* throne this day, *my* own eyes seeing it". The phrase "*my* throne" (or variations thereupon; 1:13, 17, etc.) has punctuated the narrative. Any sense of the gift being Yahweh's to give has in fact been almost totally subordinated. The dominant view of the king is clear: the kingdom is *his* to give. Where, we may ask, looking back to earlier episodes, are the men of Israel now (cf. Fohrer, 1959:6; Delekat, 1967)? Even the opportunity to express an impotent disapproval is denied them.

But the ambivalence of the pivotal action is greater than this. For from yet another perspective David's *giving* of the kingdom is in fact illusory. Typically, the narrator allows this, perhaps the most important perspective of them all, to depend upon a crucial question of interpretation. "Go in at once to King David", says Nathan to Bathsheba (1:13), "and say to him, 'Did you not, my lord the king, swear to your maidservant, saying "Solomon your son shall reign after me, and he shall sit upon my throne"?'". The question is, *did* he so swear? And, as various critics have noted, there are good indications in the narrative that the claim is to be seen as fabricated for the occasion.

Certainly it is remarkable that any other reference to thus crucial promise is missing from the story. Moreover the manner of its introduction here seems calculated to raise our suspicions. Nathan's opening words to Bathsheba, obviously designed to galvanize her into taking desperate measures, are not (as far as we can judge in terms of the narrative) strictly true; despite a rather ominous (and teasing) parallel with the circumstances of Absalom's rebellion (and the murder of Amnon), Adonijah's feast at En-Rogel is not in fact a coronation feast, at least not yet /23/. Then it is noticeable that it is Nathan who puts the words of the alleged promise in Bathsheba's mouth. There is nothing about Bathsheba knowing or remembering such a promise, simply Nathan's instructions, "Go in at once to king David, and say to him . . . . " And finally the way in which he stage-manages an apparently independent confirmation appears highly contrived /24/.

The strong possibility exists, therefore, that we are witnessing an act of deliberate deception, an ingenious ploy by the Solomonic party. Where David in his senility imagines that he is bestowing the kingdom, in actuality it is being taken from him, not by violence this time (as in Absalom's case), but *taken* all the same.

So Solomon succeeds where Absalom failed. Thus ironically it is the son of Bathsheba who brings to final expression the theme of seizure established originally by David's taking of Bathsheba /25/. Moreover, David had taken Bathsheba and secured his position by effecting the murder of her husband; so now Solomon takes the kingdom and reinforces his hold on it by having the heir apparent (2:15, 22) murdered.

Any initial elements of rejoicing and blessing, whether by the people (of Jerusalem), Solomon's lieutenant, Benaiah /26/, or David himself, are appropriately undercut by the mood of fear which introduces the last movement of the story (1:49 ff.), a movement towards death (David, Adonijah, Joab, Shimei). The sudden shift of perspective from the gift as a source of blessing to the gift as a source of terror obliged us to reconsider our assessment of David's role in the matter. Similarly with Solomon, for we are now presented with Solomon as a person of speech and individual decision for the first time (1:52-3).

At one level his response to the news about Adonijah, like that of King David to the overblown rhetoric of his courtiers in the immediately preceding segment, is apparently simple and straightforward. In fact it is far from that: King Solomon responds to a straightforward question ("Let King Solomon swear to me first that he will not slay his servant with the sword") with evasion ("If . . . if . . . "). The audience may perhaps be reminded of the day of David's restoration after Absalom's rebellion: to Abishai's demand that Shimei be put to death for his opposition the king could reply (2 Sam 19:23), with a flash of that magnanimity which marked him at his best, "Shall anyone be put to death in Israel this day? For do you not know that I am this day king over Israel?" The contrast now is savage.

The reply is evasive not only because it is conditional but also because the apparent simplicity of the condition (if he prove good he shall be safe, if bad he dies) is totally deceptive. What precisely might constitute "worthiness" and "wickedness", and who is to be the arbiter? The reader has been too much made aware of the complexity of moral perspectives to be taken in by the sham simplicity of the utterance. "If wickedness is found in him", says Solomon. And any surmise that this really means "found by *me*" will presently be confirmed in the course of events.

Just as David clothed his deceitful involvement in Uriah's death with public expressions of righteous indignation at the manner of the death, so now we see his son putting a public face on the forthcoming murder, with highsounding phrases of moral rectitude. When the murder is finally engineered the motive is made crudely apparent (2:22):

> "And why do you ask Abishag the Shunammite for Adonijah? Ask for him the
> kingdom also; *for he is my elder brother, and on his side are Abiathar the priest
> and Joab the son of Zeruiah*".

Expediency is all. Here it demands that he first break his oath to Bathsheba and then
have recourse to violent means in order to provide himself with a more secure grasp
on what he considers is now his to hold. Clearly we are back also with the tone of the
dying moments of the Absalom rebellion, the attitude of David towards Sheba, of
Joab towards Amasa.

In the last analysis, then, David appears dominated by a life-style that stands
over against that which breathed life into him at earlier moments in the story: it is an
attitude which cannot risk anything, which must possess and go on possessing. Kittel
(1896:175) comments aptly that David is

> *an old man, hardly any longer capable of making up his own mind,
> quite in the hands of his court and harem – a society not over nice as to its
> aims and means.*

As though to underline this decline the narrator finally punctuates his story with
the accounts of the deaths of Joab and Shimei /27/. While it is Solomon who is the
agent of death (through Benaiah) the focus lies upon David, the instigator /28/, the
more so since the stance of David towards Joab and Shimei is now findamentally no
different from that of Solomon towards Adonijah. Solomon is little more than an
alter ego of David.

Having made, so he imagines, the gift, David now tidies it up: there is to be no
risk of bloodguilt on *his* throne (Pedersen, 1926:423-5; Montgomery and Gehman,
1951:89; Koch, 1962), nor can the Benjaminite who cursed him be allowed to remain
as a living reminder of a conflicting view of David's claim (and so Solomon's) to the
kingdom. Those former moments of graciousness and freedom, when David rebuked
Abishai for threatening Shimei's life, are now annulled. David has now adopted
Abishai's view and it is merely a question of how to find a way round his own oath
guaranteeing the man's life. The answer is a nice piece of equivocation (the effective
revocation of his promise to Shimei reminds us of Solomon's broken oath to
Bathsheba): he himself is sworn, his son is not. Solomon will find a suitable way to
achieve the desired end.

The case against Joab is similarly equivocal. Joab has murdered Abner and
Amasa, "avenging in time of peace blood which had been shed in war", and putting
"innocent blood" upon David (2:5 [Gray, 1970:98]; cf. 2:32-3 where Solomon
elaborates). Once again (compare the answer to Adonijah, 1:52) the moral categories
are simple, the case persuasive. Yet, as I have already shown earlier in the discussion,
in both instances this is merely one, convenient, perspective. From another
perspective the blood is hardly "innocent" nor the killings "without cause".

While, therefore, there is a strong element of poetic justice in the nature of
Joab's death – a fitting one for a man who epitomized the use of violent means in
the cause of political expediency and who happens now to be on the losing side, the
story as it concerns him having come full circle – we may pass no simple judgement

on him. He is no more villain than he is hero. The fraudulent blacks and whites against which he is finally pictured serve only to highlight the greyness of those who do the picturing. In reality, David, Solomon and Joab all now belong totally to the same world.

With the extinction of that crucial, radical difference that characterized, even if only momentarily and partially, the earlier David, we see in effect the extinction of the character himself. Death comes to him fittingly.

PROVIDENCE

I have offered some thematic exploration of this story of David and his kingdom in terms of the interaction of his public and private worlds and of the giving and grasping that is woven into the whole fabric of his life. No doubt there are other important dimensions yet to be explored. For the present I am content to touch briefly on one further such dimension.

Like Whybray (1968:49-50) I would doubt that the narrative was primarily composed for a specifically religious purpose. Ridout's argument (1971:220) that the "major thrust" of the narrative is theological depends heavily upon his inclusion of 2 Sam 7 within its boundaries, and as argued above (Chapter Four) this is an unlikely inclusion, except at a redactional level. On the other hand it is difficult to dispute Von Rad's insistence (1944/1966: 198-202) upon the theological significance of the three passages (2 Sam 11:27; 12:24 and 17:14) where the author draws attention to Yahweh's involvement in the whole pattern of events.

If the connection between David's adultery and the murder of Uriah, on the one hand, and the subsequent events, on the other, is seen as the working out of a kind of nemesis, it is not a nameless, impersonal nemesis but the operation of Yahweh's retribution. In 11:27 we are told that "the thing that David had done displeased the Lord". Nathan's prophecy of death and sexual outrage to come (12:9-12) then makes clear that this displeasure will have its consequences, and in retrospect the connection between subsequent events and the prophecy is plain enough. How precisely Yahweh achieves this, however, is never made clear. Is it through some hidden divine pressure on characters, or is the prophecy more a matter of Yahweh's foreknowledge – David's sons will inevitably imitate their father's actions? One senses that positive involvement on the part of Yahweh is envisaged. On the negative side (Yahweh's retribution) such involvement is given as the clear explanation of the death of the child of adultery consequent upon the prophecy of death (12:14). On the positive side (Yahweh's providential protection) we have the apparent election of Solomon – "and Yahweh loved him" (12:24) – many hazardous events away from his final enthronement. One is reminded of Jeremiah's call: "Before I formed you in the womb I knew you, and before you were born I consecrated you, I appointed you to be a prophet of the nations". At one level of reality both Solomon and Jeremiah have no choice in their destiny. Similarly Hushai arrives at the Mount of Olives, the answer to David's prayer – "O Lord, I pray you, turn the counsel of Ahithophel to foolishness". Von Rad rightly stresses the providential (i.e. not accidental) nature of this meeting, a point underlined by the fact that the prayer is

answered "at the summit, where God was worshipped". Hushai then defeats the
counsel of Ahithophel, and it is no ordinary defeat. As far as Ahithophel is concerned
it is a mortal one, which is not surprising since the author makes clear in 17:14 that
his opponent was none other than Yahweh himself: "For the Lord had ordained to
defeat the good counsel of Ahithophel, so that Yahweh might bring evil upon
Absalom". Somehow Hushai has become the instrument of Yahweh, though it is no
simple matter of divine control — after all, although Hushai had arrived at the oppor-
tune moment it was still David's instruction that had returned him to Jerusalem.
     Von Rad sums up (p. 201):

> The author depicts a succession of occurrences in which the chain of inherent
> cause and effect is firmly knit up — so firmly indeed that human eye discerns
> no point at which God could have put in his hand. Yet secretly it is he who
> has brought all to pass; all the threads are in his hands; his activity embraces
> the great political events no less than the hidden counsels of human hearts. All
> human affairs are the sphere of God's providential working.

     Perhaps a little more can be said. While I would question Brueggemann's
confident location of the narrative in a tenth-century political context, I think his
recent explorations of the theological dimensions of the story (cf. especially 1972a,
1972c, 1974) are stimulating and in essence many of his insights stand independently
of the tenth-century hypothesis. Instructive is his discussion of 2 Sam 16. He argues
that Shimei stands for a "sacral" world view "in which divine curse and intervention
to punish is an awesome threat which is taken seriously and regarded as effective.
Shimei's response is not unlike that of Nathan in 2 Sam 12:10-12. Guilt will be
punished. This is the simplest form of confidence in the efficacy of divine will and
consequently divine curse". By contrast Abishai represents a view of things "which
rejected any meaning beyond those shaped by human effort and power". David,
however, is not prepared to accept uncritically either view. On the one hand, he
cannot accept the view of Abishai that repayment and retribution is for man to take
into his own hands. On the other hand, while accepting that Yahweh does indeed
play a decisive role in the shaping of events he is not prepared to bow to a hopeless
determinism, as though once cursed he can hold out no further hope of a life beyond
that curse. Thus "he rejects Shimei's assumption that 'repayment' by Yahweh must
necessarily be judgement following guilt. Indeed the statement of Nathan in 12:14
suggests that his repayment is not consistently judgemental . . . . David dares to
affirm that Yahweh's governance of men's actions and destinies may not be in the
precise calculating scale as Shimei presumes. Thus he fully affirms Yahweh's
authority and involvement but rejects the ready assumption that we know how that
manifests itself. David's faith makes room for Yahweh's freedom". He does not
deny his own offence; rather he looks to the possibility that Yahweh in his
graciousness may choose to dispense with a rigid connection between guilt and
judgement.
     As I have made clear at an earlier stage in this book, my own interpretation of the
story owes much to Brueggemann's insight (1974) concerning the significance of "freedom". At his best David grants to others the freedom to choose. Hence in the retreat
from Jerusalem (as indirectly in the episode of the death of the child of adultery) he

affirms his belief in Yahweh's freedom to repay as he chooses. In fact, as we have seen, there would seem to be some connection between David's gift of freedom to others and Yahweh's gracious response to him, even in the context of a misfortune (the rebellion of Absalom) which can be traced, via Nathan's prophecy, to David's own prior sin (Bathsheba and Uriah). Retribution and providential care are not, for David, mutually exclusive aspects of Yahweh's dispensation. Providence is not a matter of a mechanical predestination. In a sense the view is one that we meet so often in the Old Testament, namely that blessing may come out of curse. Put another way, Yahweh is the God of the unexpected.

Yet the author's presentation of Yahweh's involvement in human affairs retains a major element of mystery. Yahweh's choices may appear arbitrary, unjustified, even immoral. Why does Yahweh love Solomon? Why should the gift of an heir be made the issue of the most compromised episode in David's life? To be sure it may be seen as something to do with David's repentance — genuine penitence is shown to be as significant as the most heinous sin. Moreover David here is the king who submits without question to the judgement of Yahweh's prophet (hence the Deuteronomistic Historian's interest in the story). Even so there remains for a more mundane morality many loose threads. As observed, the outcome of the story prompted us to ask, earlier, What reflection does Solomon's eventual enthronement have upon Uriah's dignity as a human being? Has he not become a mere pawn in a process played out by God, kings and princes? Is Yahweh himself some kind of conspirator in this story of intrigue?

Such questions are but old ones in different guise. How does one reconcile belief in a God who controls human events with a view of man who has freedom to shape his own affairs? How is God's activity related to the moral order? Is it related at all? Is God compromised by the actions of those whom he has chosen?

Obviously the story of King David offers no ready-made answers to such questions. Rather it simply affirms the presence of Yahweh and his involvement in human affairs, spells out the awesome extent of his retribution and above all points to the radical generosity with which he can break the expected order of things. In this last respect we come close to David himself. Perhaps, for our author, Yahweh is rather like David.

CONCLUSION

The story tells how David gained the throne (it was given to him), how it was taken away from him but restored, though somewhat uneasily, and how finally he himself gave it away, or alternatively, as we are invited to see it, how it is again, but now successfully, taken from him. But it is not only the story of the kingdom and David the king. It is also a story of David the man. Thus the way in which the political and personal spheres of his life were interrelated, often creating a tension through the conflict of political and personal (especially family) interests, is of central interest in the narrative. The action concerns the gaining, displacement and bequeathal of status or authority, themes which come to concrete expression in specific political or personal forms.

Such an analysis leads to the suggestion that while the rubric, "the king and the private individual", defines the subjects of thematic interest, "giving and grasping" defines their mode of treatment and, indeed, provides a key to David's fortunes. Over against the David who is content to allow the kingdom to be the gift of others (both initially and in the flight from Jerusalem) is set the David who is willing to use violence to seize the wife of Uriah. The grasping expressed in this latter pivotal episode is worked out at both political and private levels for David in the events that follow, culminating in the Solomonic succession, an affair of some ambivalence but essentially an act of seizure.

The author, through the texture of his prose, the significant juxtaposition or paralleling of events, speeches and characters, and in some cases through the presentation of crucial events on a purely inferential basis, is continually exploring the range of perspectives open to the participants in, and the interpreters of, the situations that constitute the stuff of his story. We find in the narrative no simple *Tendenz* or moralizing but rather a picture of the rich variety of life that is often comic and ironic in its contrasting perspectives and conflicting norms. Not that the author is amoral or immoral; but his judgement is tempered by his sense of the intricacy and ambivalence of the situations that confront his characters — a sense, also, that is not without significance for his treatment of Providence in the story. He has a powerful, yet sympathetic, sense of the frailty of man, and this, I believe, sums up his treatment of David, the "hero" of the story. However biting the irony of some of the earlier scenes (especially the Bathsheba episode), and however bleak the final scenes, it remains the case that David is the one truly engaging character in the story. However momentarily, he confronts us with a manner of action that breaks out of the mundane.

This is the work of no propagandist pamphleteer nor moralizing teacher: the vision is artistic, the author, above all, a fine teller of tales.

APPENDICES

NOTES

BIBLIOGRAPHY

INDEXES

Appendix A

OBSERVATIONS ON RECENT LITERARY/REDACTION–CRITICISM OF THE
NARRATIVE

The following observations relate to the discussion in Chapter Two above on
recent redactional hypotheses by Würthwein (1974), Veijola (1975) and Langlamet
(1976ab). My discussion dealt with criticisms in principle of the methods employed
by these scholars to produce their hypotheses. What follows are some particular
instances of the kind of difficulty I find in their approach.

(1) Much depends, for the discrimination of postulated redactional passages, on
pressing the logic of a given passage to the utmost. For example, Würthwein argues
(in his chapter four) that since we are told in 15:12 that Ahithophel, David's
counsellor, had joined the conspirators and is clearly a figure of importance it is
obvious that David would have learnt of his defection when the news of the rebellion
came to David in 15:13. Accordingly, so the argument runs, an inner tension in the
text is exposed when we read in vs. 31 that it was announced to David that Ahithophel
was amongst the conspirators. Against this may simply be observed (a) that the
messenger might have deliberately kept back such information, as the Cushite did on
a later occasion (2 Sam 18), or he may simply not have known anything about
Ahithophel who may initially have kept his presence on the rebel side quiet, or (b),
much more to the point, that by saving up the news of Ahithophel's defection until
the retreat the author is able to add blow upon blow to David as well as to achieve a
masterly dramatic effect by juxtaposing the arrival of this news with the utterance of
David's prayer on the Mount of Olives and the timely arrival of Hushai.
Würthwein's discussion then goes on to postulate a redactional "doublet". David,
he claims, has two reactions to this news about Ahithophel: (a) he prays that God
should "turn the counsel of Ahithophel to foolishness" (15:31), and (b) he sends
Hushai to "defeat for [him] the counsel of Ahithophel" (15:34). To the first
corresponds the counsel of 16:21-3 regarding the concubines, regarded by Würthwein
as foolish advice, since it would offend the moral susceptibilities of his supporters
and cause delay, while to the second corresponds the (wise) counsel in 17:1-4 regarding the necessity of rapid pursuit of David. This latter counsel is countered by
Hushai's argument for delay, in 17:5-14. But, Würthwein argues, there is a further
difficulty here. David forewarned of the danger that he runs, presses on to cross
the Jordan (17:17-22), whereas, since it is said in vs. 24 that Jonathan crossed the
Jordan at the same time as David arrived in Mahanaim (17:24 – $w^e d\bar{a}vid\ b\bar{a}^\circ$
$mah^a n\bar{a}y^e m\bar{a}h\ w^e ab\check{s}\bar{a}l\bar{o}m\ \bar{a}bar\ ^\circ et\text{-}hayard\bar{e}n$), it is clear that Absalom must have
pursued him without delay, in which case Hushai's advice of a general mobilization

(17:7-13) has been strangely disregarded. The "solution" is to postulate that 15:31 (David's reception of the news of Ahithophel's defection, and his prayer), 16:21-3 (Ahithophel's advice concerning the concubines), and 17:5-14, 15b, 23 (Hushai's counsel) are redactional additions to the original narrative.

The original narrative, therefore, contained no mention of David's prayer but simply recounted how he met Hushai and instructed him to return to Jerusalem in order to co-operate with the sons of Zadok as spies. Ahithophel advised Absalom to pursue David immediately, which he did, except that Hushai had sent Ahimaaz and Jonathan to forewarn him in time. Thus at a stroke the heart has been cut out of von Rad's exegesis of 15:30-7, whereby Hushai is shown by the narrator, with great finesse, to be the answer to David's prayer. With the disappearance of the prayer itself goes one of those often remarked-on moments when David's spontaneous faith is glimpsed (an excision foreshadowing the removal of most of the similar material in chapter 16). So too with the remarkable intrusion of the author in 17:14 ("For Yahweh had ordained to defeat the good counsel of Ahithophel, so that Yahweh might bring evil upon Absalom"), another lynch-pin in von Rad's exploration of the theological dimensions of the narrative.

The question remains, however, whether the evidence warrants such drastic conclusions. To my mind, far from there being any tension in the "two reactions" they wonderfully complement each other, since Hushai's arrival on the hill "where God was worshipped" is providentially connected with the prayer. It is highly debateable whether the counsel concerning the concubines was foolish (this is essential to Würthwein's case) — it may well have been envisaged as a means of gaining total commitment to Absalom's cause by making it clear that there was to be no turning back, that there would be no reconciliation between Absalom and his father. As for the matter of the delay entailed by this action there is nothing in the text to prevent us from seeing the action as a formal gesture, (and in any case how long does Würthwein imagine it might take to pitch a tent and "go in"?). However, at another level of argument, I would argue that this discussion tries to press a strict chronology out of a story where such chronological precision is irrelevant. Only if the text is treated as a kind of newsreel does it make sense to persevere with such a point.

The second argument about time, viz. that the delay proposed by Hushai seems not to have been observed (hence, it is argued, the speech by Hushai is an addition), could be said to find some further backing in the fact that when the messengers reach David they make no mention of Hushai but say "Arise and go quickly over the water; for thus and so has Ahithophel counselled against you". Again, however, I believe these arguments stretch the point unduly. I would readily agree that there is less than complete consistency in the marriage of two elements in the plot here, viz. the role of Hushai and that of Ahimaaz and Jonathan. Yet this is a minor blemish, easily comprehensible in a relatively elaborate story (and, I would add, typical of oral tradition) and does not seriously affect the flow of the story. David has planned to camp at the Jordan. Ahithophel advises immediate pursuit that night. Hushai's advice delays this pursuit sufficiently for David to be warned and for him to press on. By daybreak his last man was across and the pursuing army not yet on the scene, as it might well have been had the advice not been taken.

(2)   Veijola (1975:16; supported by Langlamet, 1976b:490-4) postulates 1 Kgs 1:46-8 as an addition to the original text. In fact the excision of this passage is the starting point of his literary criticism (cf. Langlamet, 1976b:490).

What is the evidence that vss. 46-8 are redactional? The argument is as follows. By the end of vs. 45 Joab knows the answer to his question as to the meaning of the uproar in the city (i.e. the criterion being used here is a false one, viz. that what is most economically expressed is the original). Moreover, it is claimed that vss. 46-8 exhibit the "breathless" style of an oral message (and, according to Veijola, the use of $w^e gam$ in vss. 46-7 is itself an index of addition − a judgement reversed by Langlamet), while vss. 43-5 exhibit a more "sustained" style. Furthermore, the message as a whole does not make a good parallel with the messages in 1 Sam 4:17 and 2 Sam 1:4 (but why should it?), whereas the first part of the message does. Essentially these few points constitute the whole case − a case that is a crucial one for both Veijola and Langlamet. Once vss. 46-8 are counted as redactional the way is open for an argument which proceeds by means of the correlation of vocabulary and eliminates most of the other passages employing expressions suggesting David's piety and his clear designation of Solomon as successor. But if one is not struck by the postulated differences of style in these few verses, or if one does not find any variation incompatible with the flow of the speech as a whole, the centre of the argument collapses. Quite contrary to the redactional view, I suggest in Chapter Five, above, that this speech may be seen as a carefully co-ordinated unit where vs. 46 is the pivot, with the focus on the human direction of events in vss. 43-5 deliberately counterpoised with the claim to a divine direction in vss. 47-9 in order to achieve some rich ironies.

(3)   Aesthetic considerations receive too little attention in the analysis of texts regarded as redactional. We have already seen how the aesthetic explanation, in terms of dramatic effect, for the withholding from David of the news of Ahithophel's desertion is given no place in Wurthwein's discussion of 15:31. Another example (the list could be extended) is found in Langlamet's analysis of 1 Kgs 2:13-18. Vss. 14-15 are claimed to be additions because (a) $wayy\bar{o}mer$ in vs. 13b is repeated without change of subject in 14a; (b) vs. 14 is "direct", vs. 16 (which parallels it) "vague"; (c) vss. 14-5 are claimed to be not indispensable to the narrative − vs. 16 is sufficient to lead up to the request in vs. 17;   and (d) vs. 14, the "doublet", is unnecessary and difficult to explain as the politeness of court speech. It is the last two points that really concern me here. As already observed, what is minimally required for sense is not evidence for the way a story might originally have been related. Repetition there is here, but it is very much to the point: it acts as a retarding element in the narration. What is Adonijah going to ask for? The repetition (which forms a nice *inclusio*) allows just a moment's delay longer and teases us accordingly. It also gives us just a hint of nervousness on Adonijah's part.

(4)   Recourse to vocabulary-stock is very much part of the approach particularly of Veijola and Langlamet. Mettinger (1976:22) has rightly expressed reservations about this use of vocabulary as a major criterion. I too find it difficult to accept that there is statistical significance in ratios of word-use of the order of two or three to one, out of samples of even eight or ten instances of the term being used (cf., for

example, Langlamet [1976a:120]: five occurrences of a given term in passages previously determined as "redactional" against three occurrences in "original" texts count as evidence for the redactional nature of a further passage under examination where the same term occurs).

[Since completion of the present book another paper by Langlamet has appeared in which he further develops his redactional thesis: see Langlamet, 1977.]

Appendix B

BOUNDARIES: ADDITIONAL EVIDENCE ON STYLE

The material in this appendix relates to the discussion in Chapter Two, Section D.

Inclusio and chiasmus in 2 Sam 2:8 - 5:3

(a)   2 Sam   2:19   And Asahel *pursued* (after) Abner.
                           . . . (death of Asahel: note play on *ʾḥr*).
                    24   And Joab and Asahel *pursued* (after) Abner.

(b)   2:23/4   And all who came to the place . . . *stopped*
                           (took up a stand: *ʿmd*); and Joab and
                           Asahel *pursued* Abner.
                           . . . (confrontation between Joab and Abner).
                           And all the army *stopped (ʿmd);* and they
                    28   *pursued* Israel no more, nor did they fight any more.

(c)   2:29   And *Abner and his men went (hlk)* by the
                           Arabah *all that night;* they crossed the
                           Jordan and *went (hlk) all the forenoon,*
                           and came to *Mahanaim* (i.e. destination).
                           . . . (details of aftermath of battle).
                    32   And *Joab and his men went (hlk) all night,*
                           and *daybreak* for them was at *Hebron* (destination).

(d)   2 Sam   3:8   Am I a dog's head in Judah? (i.e. oath?)
                           Today I am showing loyalty to Saul's house . . .
                           and have not given you into the hand of David;
                           yet you charge me with a fault concerning
                           a woman *today.*
                           + oath (vs. 9)   [This example noted also by König, 1900:300]

(e)   3:12   *To whom* (does) the *land* (belong)?
                           Make *your* covenent *with me (ʾty);*
                           and behold *my* hand is *with you (ʿmk),*
                           to bring over *to you* all *Israel.*

(f)   3:24-5   What have you done? *(mh ʿśyth)*
                           . . . (accusation about Abner: he came to spy and to know)

what you are doing.   *(ʾt kl ʾšr ʾth ᶜšh)*

(g)   32-4   They buried Abner at Hebron; and the king lifted up
                         his voice and wept at the grave of Abner:

    ⎛ And all the people wept;
    ⎨ ... (David's lament)
    ⎝ And all the people wept over him again.

(h) 2 Sam 4:8   Behold the head of Ishbosheth (a), son of Saul (b),
                        your (c) enemy, who sought your (c) life;
                        but Yahweh (d) has granted
                        my lord the king (c) vengeance this day
                        on Saul (b) and on his seed (a).

(i)   4:9-11   (The first and last segments pose a somewhat ironic contrast).

    As *Yahweh lives,* who has *redeemed my life*
    from every adversity,

(a)   When one told me, *"Behold Saul is dead,"*
(b)   and he was as one bringing (good?) *news
       (mśrh)* in his eyes,
(a)   I seized him and *slew* him *(hrg)* in Ziklag,
(b)   which was my reward/*news (bśrh)* for him;
(a)   How much more, when evil men have *slain
       (hrg)* a righteous man in his own house upon
       his bed.

    And now, *shall I not* seek his blood from your
    hands and *destroy you* from the earth.

Vocabulary: 2 Sam 2:8 - 5:3 and the "Succession Narrative"

    The following items from the vocabulary stock of 2 Sam 2:8 - 5:3 appear to have
a particular affinity with that of the "Succession Narrative" as it is conventionally
defined (2 Sam 9-20 + 1 Kgs 1-2).

ymyn ("right") + *śmʾl* ("left").   In Sam: 1 Sam 6:12
         (Deut. Hist.?); *2 Sam 2:19,21; 16:6.*
ʾhrwnh ("last").   In Sam. 1 Sam 29:2; *2 Sam 2:26; 19:12, 13; 23:1.*
         Not in Jud; in Kgs only 1 Kgs 17:13.
špr ("trumpet").   In Sam: 1 Sam 13:3; *2 Sam 2:28;* 6:15; *15:10;*
         18:16; 20:1, 22 (and cf. *1 Kgs 1:34, 39, 41).*
tqᶜ ("blow" e.g. a trumpet).   In Sam: 1 Sam 13:3; *2 Sam 2:28;*
         18:16; 20:1, 22 (and cf. 1 Kgs 1:34, 39).
ᶜrbwt ("steppes").   In Sam: 1 Sam 23:24; *2 Sam 2:29; 4:7; 15:28* (Q); *17:16.*

qbr ("tomb").   In Sam: *2 Sam 2:32; 3:32; 4:12; 17:23; 19:38;*
          21:14.
dl ("weak").   In prose narrative: Jud 6:15; *2 Sam 3:1; 13:4.*
          Occurs mostly in poetry (e.g. 14 times in Prov).
klb ("dog").   Used of person, in Sam: 1 Sam 24:15; *2 Sam 3:8;*
          9:8; 16:9.
ʾ*ḥz* ("grasp").   In Sam: 2 Sam 1:9; *2:21; 4:10;* 6:6; *20:9*
          (and cf. *1 Kgs 1:51*).
ḥmš ("belly"?).   In OT: *2 Sam 2:23; 3:27; 4:6; 20:10.*
nqy ("innocent").   In Sam: 1 Sam 19:5; *2 Sam 3:28; 14:9.*
nbl ("foolish").   In Sam: *2 Sam 3:33; 13:13.* Occurs mostly in
          poetry. Cf. *nblh* ("folly"); in Sam: 1 Sam 25:25;
          2 Sam 13:12.
brh ("eat").   In OT: qal: *2 Sam 12:17; 13:6, 10;* piel: Lam 4:10;
          hiph.: *2 Sam 3:35; 13:5.*
ṭᶜm (to "taste", "perceive").   In OT: 1 Sam 14:24, 29, 43, 43;
          2 Sam 3:35; 19:36; Prov 31:18; Job 12:11; 34:3; Jon 3:7.
mʾḥry kn ("afterwards"?).   In OT: *2 Sam 3:28; 15:1;*
          2 Chron 32:23.
šlm (piel: "pay, requite, reward").   In Jud-Kgs: Jud 1:7;
          1 Sam 24:20; *2 Sam 3:39; 12:6; 15:7;* 1 Kgs 9:25;
          2 Kgs 4:7; 9:26.
rph (vb. or adj.: "be weak", "weak").   In Sam: *2 Sam 4:1; 17:2.*
          Not in Jud or Kgs. Mostly in poetry.
šmwᶜh ("news").   In Sam: 1 Sam 2:24; 4:19; *2 Sam 4:4; 13:30*
          (and cf. 1 Kgs 2:28). Not in Gen-Jud. Mostly in poetry.
mškb ("bed").   In prose narrative: Exod 7:28; *2 Sam 4:5, 7, 11;*
          11:2, 13; 13:5; 17:28; 1 Kgs 1:47; 2 Kgs 6:12; 2 Chron 16:14.
ḥdr ("chamber").   In Sam: *2 Sam 4:7; 13:10, 10* (and cf. 1 Kgs 1:15)
swr rʾš ("behead").   In OT: 1 Sam 17:46; *2 Sam 4:7; 16:9.*
pdh npš ("redeem one's life").   In OT: *2 Sam 4:9; 1 Kgs 1:29;*
          Job 33:28; Pss 55:19; 71:23; 49:16; 34:23. Note the exact
          phrase in 2 Sam 4:9 and 1 Kgs 1:29 ("As Yahweh lives, who
          has redeemed my life from every adversity"), peculiar to
          these two passages.
mgyd (hiph. part. of *ngd*).   In OT: Gen 41:24; Jud 14:19; 2 Sam 1:5, 6, 13;
          4:10; 15:13; 18:11 + Est, Pss, 2 Isa, Jer, Amos, Zec.
bšr ("bear tidings").   In Sam: 1 Sam 4:17; 31:9; 2 Sam 1:20 (poem);
          4:10; 18:19,20,20,26, (and cf. 1 Kgs 1:42).
          Not in Gen-Jud, nor elsewhere in Kgs.
bšwrh ("tidings", "reward for news"?).   In OT: *2 Sam 4:10;*
          18:20,22,25,27; 2 Kgs 7:9.
ṣdyq ("righteous").   In Sam: 1 Sam 24:18; *2 Sam 4:11;* 23:3 (poem);
          (and cf. 1 Kgs 2:32). Not in Jos-Jud. Mostly in poetry.
tlh ("hang").   In Sam: *2 Sam 4:12; 18:10;* 21:22.
          Not in Jud or Kgs.

Notes to Chapter One
Introduction

/1/   Private communication. Ackroyd argues that the text of the books of Samuel show that the final redaction in the sixth century has made much deeper impact on the presentation than has often been supposed. Such impact is to be found, e.g., in the presentation of David the exiled king in the Absalom narrative, where the underlying historical tradition, now only dimly discernible in a complex wealth of separate and sometimes disparate elements (e.g. in the Ahithophel/Hushai section — here he follows Würthwein, 1974), has been developed in conjunction with the cultic motif of the humiliation and withdrawal of the true king. In this story, he argues, we find an historification of themes found, e.g., in Ps 89 which provide a basis for the interpretation of the humiliation of the exile in their use in the servant passages of 2 Isaiah. As I make clear in Chapters Two and Three, below, I am not persuaded that significant redactional activity can be isolated within this particular story of King David, but I am wholly sympathetic to the view that the story as it now exists may have developed in ways that have led to its relation to the underlying historical events being far from straightforward, as Ackroyd suggests.

Notes to Chapter Two
Genre: Prevailing Views

/1/   Cf. Petersen (1973:34-5): "The genre label is a preliminary hermeneutical tool which helps us narrow down our meaning expectations to those which might have been expressed by the author".

/2/   Cf., e.g., Miller, 1976:13 n.30; Soggin, 1976:192-3.

/3/   Rebellion by north only: Alt, 1930/1966:228-9; Soggin, 1967:75; Flanagan, 1975:108-9; cf. Mauchline, 1971:281-2. North and south: Noth, 1960:201-2; Bright, 1972:204; Weingreen, 1969:263-6; Cohen, 1971:96, 107; Bardtke, 1973:1-8; Mettinger, 1976:122-3.

/4/   In seeking textual support for this interpretation Whybray places much weight upon the remarks of Benaiah, complimentary to Solomon, in 1 Kgs 1:37 (1968:51-52; cf. Rost, 1926/1965: 234); this depends on the large assumption that Benaiah is the author's mouthpiece.

/5/   See also Schulte (1972:138-80) whose recognition of this negative perspective contributes to a depiction of the author's political stance as essentially "neutral".

/6/   E.g. Wellhausen, 1885:262; Kittel, 1896:175-6; von Rad, 1944/1966:195; Hertzberg, 1964: 341, 378; McKane, 1963:276.

/7/   Cf. e.g. the well known case of Jean Anouilh's play, *Antigone,* which first appeared in France during the German occupation (World War II) and served as a rallying point for many Frenchmen "who could see their own struggle reflected in the conflict between the uncompromising attitude of Antigone with the spirit of freedom, and Creon with the Vichy government" (Pronko, 1961:xvii); others, however, maintained that the author was on Creon's side (hence permission for the play to be produced). There remains some doubt, however, that Anouilh intended his play to have the political meaning that was found in it.

/8/   The following list gives some indication of material that may be regarded as redactional according to (a) Würthwein: 2 Sam 11:27b-12:15a; 12:24b*; 14:2-22; 15:24-6, 29, 31; 16:5-13, 21-3; 17:5-14, 15b, 23; 18:2b-4a, 10-14; 20:8-13; 1 Kgs 2:5-9, 31b-3, 44-5; (b) Veijola (on 1 Kgs 1-2): 1 Kgs 30*, 35-7, 46-8; 1 Kgs 2:1-3, 4a*, 5-12, 22b, 24, 26b-7, 28a*, 31b-3, 37b, 42a*, 44-5; (c) Langlamet: 2 Sam 15:8(?), 16b-17a, 24*, 25-6, 31, 34*, 35a*, 16:1-14, 15a, 16a, 20b*, 21-3; 17:5-14, 15b, 17, 18a*, 19-20, 21a*, 21b*(?), 23, 24b(?), 25, 27-9; 18:2b, 3, 4a, 10-14, (18); 19:14, 17-40, 41ab*, 42b*; 20:3-5, 8-13, (23-6); 1 Kgs 1:5a*b, 6ab*, 12a*b, 13a*, 17a*, 21, 29b*, 30a*b, (34*?), 35, 37, (45a*?), 46-8, 51b*, 52; 1 Kgs 2:1, 2-4, 5*, 6, 7(?), 8-9, 11, 14-15, 16a*, 22a*b, 23, 24a*, 26-7, 28a*, 31b-3, 37b, 44-5, For Langlamet the process of growth is as follows (1976b:519): (1) history of Absalom's rebellion: 2 Sam 15-20* (old material); (2) first succession history: 2 Sam 10-12*, 13-14* + 15-20* + 1 Kgs 1-2:35*; (3) Second succession history (already a history of David?): ... 2 Sam 9 + 10-20*; 1 Kgs 1-2:35* + 2:36-46* [i.e., inserted at stage (3): 2 Sam 9; 16:1-14* (old material); 19:17-41a* (old material) or 19:17-31*].

/9/   The interpreter of the story of King David might read with profit this particular essay ("The Public World: First Observations", pp. 26-44) as also Knight's essay, "Shakespeare" (1971: 30-51).

/10/   In effect I am merely employing here the same argument Whybray uses (p. 50) against the depiction of the work as a moral tract (as e.g. by M. Smith, 1951).

/11/   See e.g. Scott, 1970:34-5; Mauchline, 1971:240-1; Gray, 1970:21-2; Brueggemann, 1972a: 5-6, 1974:175; Roth, 1972:180; Vawter, 1974:480; Kaiser, 1975:156.

/12/   See e.g. McKane, 1965:23-47; Scott, 1971:13-15. The hypothesis, while attractive, is necessarily speculative. See further Whybray's study (1974) casting doubt on the use of $ḥākām$ as a designation of a professional class of royal counsellors (see pp. 31, 54) and assessing the evidence on the existence of schools in ancient Israel (pp. 32-43); also McKane's vigorous response (1975.).

/13/   See pp. 72, 95, 111. Crenshaw (1969:130-2) has commented upon some of the problems of definition raised by this and other studies of "wisdom literature", though it is not obvious that his own proffered definition — "the quest for self-understanding in terms of relationships with things, people, and the Creator" — in any way settles the matter (as observed also by Whybray 1974: 3 n.5).

/14/   See 1971:148 n. 16. Nor does Brueggemann (1972b:97 n. 16; 1974:175 n. 1) offer a substantial rebuttal. Whybray(1974:89-90) merely argues that most of the "representatives" of wisdom (i.e. those who are called "wise" — by his own argument *not* a technical term) play more important roles than Crenshaw will allow. But that they are more than the "minor" characters that Crenshaw suggests is very doubtful (contrast Jonadab or the woman of Tekoa, both called "wise", with David, Joab or Absalom). The net result of the accompanying word study for the "Succession Narrative" is that apart from the occurrence of $ḥkm$ (8 times), taken to be a charcteristic term of the "intellectual tradition" (but by no means exclusive to the so-called "wisdom" literature, and, as Whybray owns [p. 5], "no infallible guide" to the designation of such literature), the only other relevant terms are from his category 2, especially $bîn$ and $ʿēṣā$; but words in this category are of little value for the purpose in hand "in view of their wide dissemination in various traditions of the Old Testament" (so Whybray, p. 50). I can see here no significant support for the thesis of the earlier book.

/15/   Furthermore the subsuming of "evidence" under certain key criteria lacks control. We are told (Whybray, p. 58) that "Every incident [in the narrative] illustrates either the application of wisdom and/or counsel to a particular situation, or the consequences of not applying it ...''; but examples are then given of acting without wisdom (e.g. David's adultery) which makes it clear that *any* action a reader judges to have been not wise may come under this head since the element of actually *taking counsel* is optional. A similar observation can be made concerning the ensuing claim that "in almost every other incident in the book the characters act only after they have calculated their chances of success and the probable consequences" (e.g. David's killing of Uriah; or his sending back to Jerusalem Hushai and the priests): for an action to qualify it is not necessary for the calculation of the chances of success (etc.) to be actually expressed in the text; moreover the consequences may fall within the range success to failure. Hence almost any action taken by a character in any situation could qualify for inclusion under this criterion.

/16/   Crenshaw (1969:139 n. 41) notes that Nathan's oracle is "one great exception to Whybray's thesis about special revelation, as he himself admits (p. 69)''.

/17/   Lefebvre (1949:VII) terms the story *histoire romancée* or *roman;* Harris (1971:232) describes it as a "novel" and lists "adventure, psychology and sentiment" as its most characteristic ingredients.

/18/   This line of argument arising from Posener's study of the work's (claimed) political and social background is briefly restated by Aldred (1961:112-20), who takes the argument a step further than Posener though without adducing any further evidence.

/19/   See e.g. Whybray, 1968:11; Mettinger, 1976:24, 31. Eissfeldt (1965:140-1) is a notable exception — he suggests, tentatively, a ninth century date (cf. McKane, 1963:19-21). Note also the caution expressed by Wagner, 1972:136. Hölscher's ninth century date (1952:77-80, 98) is dependent on his analysis of the material as part of a "J" source, concluding with 1 Kgs 12. Similarly Carlson's late dating (1964) is bound up with his thesis of an exile "D-work" of which the narrative is a unified part, having passed through an earlier oral pre-Deuteronomic stage. I follow neither thesis. Flanagan's argument (1975:112-13), that the 2 Samuel part of the story was written by Davidic scribes, depends on his separation of the "Solomonic" sections (2 Sam 10-12 and 1 Kgs 1-2) from the rest of the narrative; see my criticisms below, Chapter Four, n. 19. Apart from the matter of this dependence, I remain unconvinced that the usage of the phrase *kol yiśrā'ēl* gives any indication of date, for a number of reasons, including (a) the difficulty, recognized by Flanagan (p. 108), in determining whether the term is used for Israel and Judah together or for the northern kingdom alone, and (b) the further difficulty in determining at any given point whether the phrase is being used as a technical term for the name of a kingdom or being used to mean something like "many Israelites" (whether from the North or from North and South).

/20/   In a similar vein is von Rad's argument (1944/1966:195): "[The author] must have been one who had an intimate knowledge of what went on at court. His portrayal of personalities and events breathes an atmosphere which must silence any doubts as to the reliability of his account". Cf. e.g. Driver, 1913a:183; Pfeiffer, 1952:356-7; Weiser 1961:165; Bright, 1972:179.

/21/   See also Eissfeldt (1965:140-1), though he is more reserved in his criticism: "This argument must be limited to the point that an eye-witness account underlies it". Cf. Whybray, 1968:12, 15-6; Würthwein, 1974:54-5.

/22/   See e.g. Wolff (1966:133-4) and the critique by Wagner (1972:120-1); cf. also Winnett (1965: 3-5). The study by Schulte (1972), following Hölscher (1952) but with important differences, re-opens the question in a radical way, as does the recent work of Rendtorff (1975, 1977) and Schmid (1976) – see the discussion in *JSOT* 3 (1977).

/23/   I note with interest that J. L. Crenshaw has also cast doubt on the existence of this "Enlightenment" in a paper ("The Solomonic Enlightenment – or the Emperor's New Clothes") presented to the Southern meeting of the S.B.L. in March, 1975 (reported in *Religious Studies Review* 2 no. 2 [1976]9).

/24/   See further the criticisms of Carlson (1964:136-9); but his own attempt to identify the "ideological tendency" of the material with that of the Deuteronomic school is somewhat forced.

/25/   So e.g. AV and the English version of the Jewish Publication Society of America (Philadelphia, 1955), both following MT.

/26/   The excision of 14:25-7 is not as straightforward as sometimes supposed. As is noted by Budde (1902:268), vs. 28 recapitulates vs. 24; such ring composition *(Wiederholung)* presupposes the existence of vss. 25-7. In fact vss. 24-8 as a whole has a chiastic structure. The preferable alternative, if Hertzberg's argument be not accepted, is to treat 18:18 as a secondary, aetiological, insertion (following Carlson, 1964:187).

/27/   See note 3 above; and cf. Flanagan (1975:108-9) on the difficulty of determining the meaning of "all Israel" (see also note 19 above).

/28/   Cf. especially 2 Sam 15:1-13; 17:1-15; 18:6-7, 16-17; 19:8-14, 22, 40-3; 20:1-2, 14; also 1 Kgs 1:3, 20, 28-35.

Notes to Chapter Three
Genre: An Alternative View

/1/   But I differ on the details: see below, Chapter Five. The extent of the structural unity in the narrative has been challenged by Flanagan (1972), though in my view he fails to account convincingly for the material in 1 Kgs 1-2 which forms a direct link with the subject matter, characters and style of 2 Sam 13-20. Note also the earlier treatment of this material as compounded of several self-contained narratives (especially Gressmann, 1910:164, 167, 178-85; Caspari, 1909:317-25, 332-33).

/2/   Notice the hint of formulaic language here: "Now, then, let me pin him to the ground with one stroke of the spear and I shall not strike him twice" (26:8). Cf. Joab's killing of Abner in 2 Sam 20:10.

/3/   So McKane, 1963:256: "the saying is directed against Joab as well as Abishai".

/4/   Napier (1955:143-4) describes it as "an antithetical relationship" and "a relationship involving tension". Schulte (1972:150-4; followed by Würthwein, 1974:43-4) characterizes these passages (16:10, 19:23 and also 3:29) as later redactional insertions designed to vindicate David over against the sons of Zeruiah, particularly Joab (the original hero of the story); but she is hard pressed to find warrant for the excision in the texts themselves – her strongest point is the repetitious nature of 2 Sam 3:28-39. For analyses showing how 16:10 is an integral part of the larger context see Ridout, 1971:56-70, and Bruggemann, 1974:177-81.

/5/   There are textual problems in this passage, especially at the end of vs. 15 and beginning of vs. 16. See Driver, 1913b:353; H. Smith, 1899:377-8; Mauchline, 1971:304. With most commentators (against Driver) I accept the end of vs. 15 as it stands in MT *(wyᶜp dwd)*, and see it as providing the particular motivation for the attempt to kill David (so also e.g. Hertzberg, 1964:386).

/6/   Cf. in 1 Sam 24, the "variant" of 1 Sam 26, where again it is the "men" who are in tension with David.

/7/   Note that the motif of David and Joab at cross-purposes is characteristic of many of the stories of Joab: in addition to those already mentioned are (a) the end of the story of the Ammonite war (cf. esp. 12:26), (b) the story in 2 Sam 14 of Joab's ploy to bring Absalom back from exile, (c) the story in 2 Sam 24 (cf. esp. vss. 3-4) of the census, and above all, (d) the death of Joab (1 Kgs 2) as a legacy of David.

/8/   On the use of personal names to literary effect see Clines, 1972. It is a curious fact that the "sons of Zeruiah" are never known by a patronymic; such exclusive use of a matronymic is rare in the OT (cf. the effective use of "Adonijah, son of Haggith" in 1 Kgs 1). Whatever the reason for this it is clear that the usage suits the narrative tradition perfectly. Possibly the usage arose originally in a "narrative" context for these literary reasons. Van Seters (1976b:25) speculates, against both Samuel and Chronicles, that "sons of Zeruiah" was originally a patronymic.

/9/   However, like Hoftijzer (1970:420 n. 3), I do not find these other parallels altogether clear and convincing, certainly not in the case of the Jeremiah passage which lacks entirely any aspect of "disguise" in the presentation of the parable.

/10/   Cf. p. 221: "The legal issue . . . is the hallmark of this literary *genre*"; and p. 226: "Nathan's story should be examined for traces of a real legal problem justifying its being brought by a third party (the prophet) to the notice of the king".

/11/   It is a similar focus that leads Hoftijzer to argue (1970:421 and cf. pp. 421-3, esp. 423 n. 1), against Simon as it happens, that "this procedure only makes sense, if one presupposes that the decision of the king in a special juridical case was also binding for parallel cases. This means that in fact the king himself was bound by such a precedent". This seems to me to be a quite unnecessary inference, especially once one has put the legal aspect in its proper perspective (see further below).

/12/   Hoftijzer (1970:442-4) rightly notes the "vulnerable position" of the woman and the difference between her situation and that of the prophets.

/13/   Simon, 1967:221: it is "a disguised parable designed to overcome man's own closeness to himself, enabling him to judge himself by the same yardstick that he applies to others".

/14/   It must be close to the "real" situation yet not so close as to be obvious to the person to whom it applies. See also Simon, 1967:221.

/15/   They do not in themselves serve primarily to teach some general doctrine or belief. Cf. Rofé, 1974:154: ". . . in the specific case of prophetical parables . . . the ideas represented are doctrines or beliefs relevant to the prophetic activity".

/16/   Cf. Budde, 1902:265 (quoting Nöldeke — but from which work is not clear) for a similar story from an Arab source. Gunkel (1921:132-3) recognized the folktale *(Märchen)* character of the motif and suggested in addition (pp. 35-6) that the story of the poor man's ewe was itself a folktale, on the grounds that it has a certain poetic quality and that it is not entirely apt in its present context.

/17/   Most of his discussion, however, is concerned specifically with the wiles (not all of which lead to death, according to his examples) of the *foreign* woman. He also draws attention to the theme in Proverbs 1-9 of the "foreign/strange woman" whose way leads to death. See also McKane, 1970:334-41, 360-9.

/18/   Abishag also presides over David's death. Blenkinsopp does not include the Rizpah incident (he is looking only at 2 Sam 9ff.), but cites Absalom's rebellion and occupation of his father's harem as an instance of the "pattern"; this, however, seems to me to lack the catalyst quality of the other incidents. Moreover, I cannot accept that Blenkinsopp's definition of the pattern (in terms of "sin externalized in a sexual form which leads to death"; death in each case is "punishment") adequately corresponds to the presentation of the material in the narrative as it stands; particularly in Adonijah's case there is no suggestion in the text of sexual *sin,* and it is a moot point (and indeed, as I have suggested earlier, deliberately so presented) whether we should infer rebellious intentions in him (Blenkinsopp, 1966:48). There are similar difficulties with Leach's interesting analysis of the story (1969:74-9) in terms of these "sexual incidents" (he traces themes of sex relations and political relations developing in parallel).

/19/   Van Seters (1976b:27) objects that this pattern of deaths "certainly does not apply to Gen 34 where all the males of the city were killed". For one who so liberally applies Olrik's so-called "laws" of oral composition (Van Seters, 1975:Part II; cf. Gunn, 1976b:159; Culley, 1976a:28-30) this is a remarkable quibble. It remains the case that, apart from Dinah, Hamor and Shechem are the only two named, active role-playing, characters from the city.

/20/   The main similarities are noted briefly by Klaehn (1914:39) who is interested, however, in a literary connection (the "Yahwist") between the two blocks of material. Auzou (1968:392 n. 37) observes that the one story recalls the other. On the Rahab story in oral tradition see Tucker, 1972: 83-6.

/21/   For the two motifs see Thompson, 1955-8: K649 and K646, respectively; cf. also K515 (and 516-39) and K640-9. The two motifs are not in fact incompatible — the searchers could have asked the whereabouts of the spies, been told that they had gone, doubted this and searched the house, and, having found nothing, taken the false directions as the truth.

/22/   Van Seters insists (1976b:28) that this kind of plot inconsistency (he calls it a "blind motive"

— cf. Van Seters, 1975:163) is a criterion for direct literary dependence. That it is in fact highly characteristic of oral-traditional composition, probably through the special reliance on standard patterns or motifs as building blocks for the narrative (see e.g. Lord, 1938:439-45; Lang, 1969; Gunn, 1970; Hansen, 1972), appears to be unknown to Van Seters. I hope to deal more fully elsewhere with this feature and other "criteria" for oral composition and literary dependence as utilized by Van Seters in Part II of his recent book (1975).

/23/   See also Ridout, 1971:97: "This remarkable elaboration of what could have been told quite briefly serves the purpose of creating suspense for the listener and gives him ample time to ponder how David is likely to receive the report of the momentous events of that day". Cf. p. 102: "We see that the entire episode is built on the ironic contrast of good tidings over against bad tidings. The [bśwrh] [the key word, bśr, appears 9 times] has been good news for David's forces, for they have been victorious in battle. But for David the [bśwrh] was bad, for his son died".

/24/   Though their situations are not directly comparable in that these men claim to be more than just messengers.

/25/   Note also Parry and Lord, 1953-4:I 419-20 ([7] and [16]), p. 325 (note the parallel in the news being distorted so as to gain a reward) and p. 209.

/26/   Auzou (1968:393) describes Ahimaaz here as "extremely sensitive and knowing how to have regard for a father's feeling [coeur]". Klopfenstein (1964:330, 345) claims that this evasion is motivated by consideration for the king rather than by fear of being struck down, but he offers no special justification for his opinion.

/27/   Others concern his application of Olrik's so-called "epic laws" as criteria for determining oral composition and thus a system of priority in the new scheme of literary dependence which Van Seters postulates for constituent segments of Genesis (cf. Gunn, 1976b:159; Culley, 1976a:28-30); also his use of the "blind motive" as a criterion. See also above, n. 22.

/28/   Cf. Shorter Oxford English Dictionary: "tell: relate in spoken or written words, as tell me a tale, a story". Similarly the word "literature" is regularly used without prejudice to the question of its oral or written provenance. The problem is that the language does not provide us with clearly differentiated equivalents: "story-writing" or "story-composition" (neutral) are scholarly manufactures.

/29/   See e.g. Parry and Lord, 1953-4:I Notes, passim (cf. Thompson, 1974:187-9); de Vries, 1963:22-3, 194-209; Culley, 1972.

/30/   For some methodological implications, see further Gunn, 1976b:157-8. Culley (1976a:65) is quite right to emphasize this blend of stability and flexibility as characteristic of this kind of oral composition. He is mistaken, I believe, when he adds that "There is here, perhaps, the danger of turning difficulties into virtues by explaining differences as well as similarities as evidence of oral transmission". On the contrary, it is precisely the differences in the context of similarity that constitutes the blend of stability and flexibility which is the hallmark of this type of composition (or transmission) and which is often very difficult to explain on grounds of direct literary dependence (as I try to show in this chapter).

/31/   In poetry: cf. Parry, 1936; Lord, 1951, 1960; Gunn, 1971. In prose: Sokolov, 1966:405, 407-8, 432 (and cf. 305); Dégh, 1965:xxxii; Radlov, 1866-1904:V xvi ff. (cf. Chadwick, 1932-40: III 181-3); Delargy, 1945:208-9; Bruford, 1969:182-209. See further Lord, 1974; Culley, 1976a: 1-25. While studies, over the last decade, in oral African literature are clearly of interest for a general theory of oral literature (if such be possible), it has to be said that generically speaking little that has been published bears much resemblance to the type of prose story we are concerned with in the books of Samuel (or elsewhere in the OT, for that matter) see also Culley, 1976a:17-19.

/32/   See Kennedy, 1903:1571-2; also Budde, 1902:275; H. Smith, 1899:347; Driver, 1913b:318. LXX has phoinikes, "dates", for qayiş in 2 Sam 16:1 but not elsewhere.

/33/   Methodologically, there is nothing improper in setting to one side the two non-equivalent items in order to emphasize the correspondence between the other four items, though if the ratio of non-equivalent to equivalent were the other way round one would have reason to suspect the procedure. See also above, n. 30.

/34/   This is a difficult question which need not be settled here. Apart from bread and wine the items in question occur in the OT as follows: *smqym* − 1 Sam 30:12;1 Chron 12:41; *qyṣ/dbḷh* − Amos 8:1-2; Jer 40:10, 12; 48:32; Mic 7:1; Isa 16:9; and 1 Sam 30:12; 1 Chron 12:41, respectively. The term used to describe the quantity of wine, *nbl-yyn*, occurs in only three other contexts − 1 Sam 1:24; 10:3; Jer 13:12.

/35/   Thus when we turn to a comparable list of food, 1 Chron 12:41 − comparable in terms of general context and content (the bringing of provisions, which are listed, for the maintenance of some soldiers in connection with David) − we find that though we again come across the *ṣmqvm* and *dblym* there are no quantities given, let alone similar ones. Nor is there any correspondence with the order of the items in 1 Sam 25 and 2 Sam 16 (cf. also Gen 43:11; 32:13-15 or the presents in Gen 45:21-23, 2 Kgs 8:9).

/36/   Van Seters (1976a:152) calls for an explanation for the "remarkable inconsistency" between my 1974a paper, where I followed the conventional analysis of 2 Samuel in ascribing chapters 2-4 to an author other than that of the "Succession Narrative", and a later essay (1975), where I indicated that I believed these chapters to be integral to the latter narrative. The explanation is simple: between writing one paper and the other (the 1974a paper was two years "in press") I made a study of the boundaries of the narrative which led to a not especially remarkable change of view.

/37/   For the relation of this analysis to the discussion of the so-called "battle report" by Richter (1966a:262-6), Plöger (1967:16-9), and Van Seters (1972: 188), see further Gunn, 1974a:286-8; Van Seters, 1976a; Gunn, 1976b.

/38/   In the analysis of this and other patterns I have found it convenient to use the terms "element" "structure" and "language". The elements are the narrative or descriptive segments which together constitute the pattern (as itemized, e.g., in the passages at present under discussion). The structure is the particular arrangement or order of the elements, and more especially the most important of these. The language is the actual verbal expression, the wording, of the elements.

/39/   It is possible, though this cannot be demonstrated here, that it may be redactional, deriving from the transformation of a story about the death of Eli and his sons into one primarily concerned with the capture of the ark, the object being to build a bridge between the material of chapters 1-3 and that of 5ff. Most commentators see the process as rather the reverse, but see now Davies, 1977: 10-14.

/40/   Perhaps, following Richter (1966a:262-6), this element of initial movement should be included as standard.

/41/   For element 1, see the analysis of 1 Sam 4:10; 2 Sam 2:17 and 2 Sam 18:6 above. In the case of 2 Sam 18:6, I count *wyṣ' . . . lqr't* as much a part of element 1 as *wthv hmlḥmh*. 1 Sam 31 has *wplštym nlḥmym byśr'l*; cf. 1 Sam 4:10: *wylḥmw plštym*. The note about the ark is omitted from 1 Sam 4:10.

/42/   The variation here (cf. 1 Sam 4:17; 31:1; 2 Sam 2:17; 18:7) may be governed by a desire to avoid the rather crude repetition of "Philistines" that we find, e.g., in 1 Sam 31:1-2.

/43/   Both 2 Sam 2 and 18 lack an equivalent summary statement of element 2(c). The latter proceeds directly to its elaborated account of Absalom's death. The language of the former momentarily raises the possibility that the three sons of Zeruiah are going to be thus singled out ("and there were there the three sons of Zeruiah . . . "), and although this turns out to be, in fact, the introduction to a scene of pursuit, in the end the death does occur, and indeed it is Asahel, one of the three sons, who dies. Note that he is on the *winning* side, unlike the others whose deaths are related in these passages, though whether it is to be his or the defeated Abner's death that is recounted hangs for a time in the balance. There may be a deliberate artistic counterpointing here.

/44/   Similarities between these two passages are noted in passing by Klostermann, 1887:129; Nowack, 1902:35, 36 and 194; Schulz, 1923:30-1; Caspari, 1926:394. A little fuller are the observations of Löhr, 1898:121: he notes not only the description of the messenger but also the question, and, to a limited extent, the form of the message *(ns... wgm... wgm)*. So also Kennedy, 1904:192.

/45/   The expression "earth on the head" occurs again only in 2 Sam 15:32 (the "Succession Narrative") and in Neh 9:1 (where it is associated with fasting and sackcloth and thus more a sign of contrition). Elsewhere it is ashes (see however Jastrow, 1900) or dust that is put or thrown upon the head to signify humiliation, contrition or mourning. Cf. the recent discussion by de Ward, 1972: esp. 6-8. On the tearing of clothes, see *ibid.*, 8-10; note again the connection with 2 Sam 15:32, both the phrase as a whole and the use of *qrᶜ* in the Qal part. pass.:

  1 Sam 4:12   *wmdyw qrᶜym*
  2 Sam 1:2   *wbgdyw qrᶜym*   *wᵓdmh ᶜl rᵓšw*
  2 Sam 15:32   *qrwᶜ ktntw*
  Cf. *qrᶜy bgdym* in 2 Kgs 18:37//Isa 36:22, and Jer 41:5.

/46/   Reading *mhnh* with LXX; MT has *mᶜrkh*, perhaps a dittography from the next clause. Cf. Driver, 1913b:48. This also noticeably improves the balance of the prose.

/47/   E.g., the drawing up of the opposing ranks, details of weapons, of who attacked first, or how long before one side fled. Hence also Van Seters' point (1972:188) about the lack of any "contest" in OT battle reports, in contrast with what he calls "heroic" style; on the other hand we do find quite elaborate accounts of the *aftermath* of the battle, as in 2 Sam 2 and 18.

/48/   1 Sam 31 plunges straight into the account of the battle, while 1 Sam 4 has a preliminary skirmish and a scene in the Philistine camp, and 2 Sam 18 the episode concerning who is to lead the army in the field together with a description of the army marching out under review. 2 Sam 18 and 1 Sam 31 elaborate the aftermath of the scene of the battle, particularly in connection with the death of the leading character concerned (the former in considerable detail); but no details are given of the deaths of Hophni and Phineas.

/49/   A kind of "dischronologization" *(Nachholung)* results. Though this is by no means without precedent in OT narrative (cf. e.g. Schulz, 1923:10-1; Baumgartner, 1923:150-5, 157; Martin, 1969) it is rarely successful just because chronological sequence is far and away the normal mode of narration and one which, therefore, the reader or listener comes to expect. 2 Sam 18 avoids the clumsiness by proceeding directly with the *detailed* account of the death. Clearly the structure in its most basic form, i.e. with a summary account of element 2(c), is most suitable in a passage such as 1 Sam 4:10 where there is no further elaboration.

/50/   It is interesting to note that the use of standard patterns in oral-traditional composition can lead to similar, and sometimes grosser, infelicities: see also above, note 22.

/51/   I take 1 Sam 31 and 2 Sam 1 to be most probably from different sources. A recent discussion (with bibliography) is that of Grønbaek (1971:216-21), who takes a different view. The problem lies in the conflicting accounts of Saul's death. A clear presentation of the case against the harmonizing solution, whereby the Amalekite's story is taken as a falsehood, is that by Kennedy (1904:191-2; and cf. H. P. Smith, 1899:254-5). Other, more atomistic, analyses have been made (cf. Cook, 1899-1900:146-7; Budde, 1902:193-5; Van Seters, 1976a:146), but in my view these carry little conviction because they are essentially arbitrary; there is no compelling evidence of composite authorship *within* 2 Sam 1 itself.

/52/   An interesting example of this kind of argument is van den Born's examination (1954:209-14) of Jud 19: he argues in view of the many similarities between this story and the Sodom story in Gen 19 that it is a "pastiche" of Gen 19. (Similarly Jud 20 is "an artificial creation" based on Jos 7-8). Van Seters has taken up this approach extensively in his recent book on the Abraham stories in Genesis, though in my view (as already indicated above) his attempt fails because of inadequate premises. See further the recent review of this type of explanation by Culley, 1976a:Part II.

/53/   2(a) — *wyngp(w)... lpny ᶜbdy dwd*: where the close parallel lies in the construction and language of the element as well as in the distinctive subject matter, viz. "the servants of David".

2(b) – *bywm hhw³*

/54/   Against Van Seters, Porter's discussion (1968:20) is pertinent; see especially n. 16, where he comments regarding those Hittite royal inscriptions which have been regarded as most resembling Hebrew "historical composition": "their narrative-form and style . . . are quite different from the vivid use of dialogue and the dramatic scene construction, which mark the Hebrew prose stories" (cf. also Schulte, 1972:6). Van Seters (1976a:148) responds to my stress on the "story" form of the OT material: "I frankly find it much easier to see how a scribal convention which was in common use for constructing annals and chronicles could be adapted to a literary use in composing a story about warfare than for an oral story-teller's device to be taken over for the completely non-narrative function of composing chronicles". I do not accept that Van Seters has demonstrated any clear link between the Assyrian or Babylonian "battle reports" and the battle scenes we are concerned with in the OT. More important, his point only has cogency if the OT texts in which we find these scenes are assumed to be, in fact, *chronicles,* which is precisely what I have been at pains to deny.

/55/   See e.g. Allen (1971) and especially the admirably balanced analysis of saga literature by Lönnroth (1976). For a Turkish case of a "written" narrative genre emerging from an oral-traditional one see Eberhard, 1955:3, 58; cf. Harvey (1974) on the Spanish novel of chivalry.

/56/   On writing and literacy see the evidence set out with clarity by Millard, 1972; in my view, however, the weight of this evidence is against both widespread literacy in Israel and any widespread use of writing for "formal literature", at least prior to about the eighth century.

/57/   Jackson (1965:184) also is not happy with a sharp distinction between the "Succession Narrative" and stories "just the other side of the 'borderline' between legend and history"; he refers to Jud 3-4 and cites the important study by Alonso Schökel (1961). Whybray (1968:115) affirms that "the Succession Narrative stands firmly in the line of development of the Israelite narrative tradition". One of Schulte's aims (1972) is to show that "the seed bed of Israelite history writing [*Geschichtsschreibung* – the "Succession Narrative" is included in a loose definition of this term; cf. e.g. p. 219] is not the court chronicle *(Hofchronik)* but the popular tale *(volkstumliche Erzählung)*". See also Bentzen, 1952:I 243-51; Gray, 1970:17-8, 86; Schulz, 1923. Perhaps a major distinction between my own view and those of these critics is that I do not believe it is possible for us, given our relative ignorance of Israelite history (because of dating problems), to know where in this "line of development of the Israelite narrative tradition" the "Succession Narrative" stands.

/58/   See authors cited in n. 31, above. On individual variation in a given tradition, see e.g. Campbell, 1890:I 1; Lord, 1960; Dégh, 1965:xxxii (and cf. Culley, 1976a:10-3); Gunn, 1971:1-14.

/59/   See also the interesting discussion of "traditional" literature by Scholes and Kellogg, 1966: 50ff.

/60/   Cf. the review of evidence concerning this official's functions by Mettinger (1971:52-62). Such a combination of bureaucratic and artistic functions as I am suggesting is not difficult to parallel: for an ancient Irish example, see Murphy, 1966:102-3; cf. Gunn, 1974b:515.

/61/   Cf. Schofield, 1950:28-9. E. F. Campbell (1975:22-3) explores the possibility that such stories as this were narrated by women, especially the "wise women".

Notes to Chapter Four
The Boundaries of the Story

/1/   See further Rost, 1926/1965:184-9 and 193-200; Carlson, 1964:144-62; Noth, 1968:8-13; Gray, 1970:15-16.

/2/   Against this view: Hölscher, 1952:288 (he adds 1 Kgs 3:4a, 16-8 + 12:1, 3b-14, 18-9); and Mowinckel, 1963:11-4 (he takes 1 Kgs 1-2 as the beginning of a Solomon saga).

/3/   See also Hempel, 1964:30; Hertzberg, 1964:297, 299, 376; Rendtorff, 1971:429, 432, 437-9; Richter, 1966a:264. Cf. earlier, H. Smith, xxvi and 267-8; Budde, 1902:xvi; Nowack, 1902:xvii-xxiii; Pfeiffer, 1952:342-59; Caird, 1953:859-60.

/4/   It is almost universally excluded, even by Vriezen (1948:170, 187) who includes almost everything else from 1 Sam 16:14 to 2 Sam 21:15.

/5/   The link with 2 Sam 6 was earlier suggested, tentatively, by Wellhausen, 1878:222; and cf. Kittel, 1896:46.

/6/   As Mowinckel (1963:10) is not slow to observe. See the recent criticisms by Schulte (1972: 138-9) and on chapter 6, Carlson (1964:92-6) with further literature cited there. For acceptance of Rost's suggestion see e.g. von Rad, 1944/1966:176-7; Noth, 1957:62; Weiser, 1961:164; Hertzberg, 1964:376; (?) Auzou, 1968:364; (?) Delekat, 1967:26. Jackson (1965:183, 186) gives qualified support to the chapter 6 connection but finds little warrant for linking chapter 7. Ridout (1971: see esp. 171-6) ignores chapter 6 but includes the whole of chapter 7. Most recently, Mettinger (1976:60, 62) has suggested that vss. 1-7 may have formed the opening of the "Succession Narrative".

/7/   For criticism of his analysis of chapter 7, see Noth, 1955. My own view is close to that of Mowinckel (1963:10-1; so also Bentzen, 1952:II 94), without necessarily endorsing the details of his "cultic" argument that the chapter is "an aetiological legend, a typical, theological, learned one"; it is, moreover, largely a literary unit and source analyses such as Rost's lack convincing support in the text.

/8/   Caird (1955:856) contrasts the "turgid verbosity" of 2 Sam 7 with "the superb narrative prose" of 2 Sam 9-20; similarly Pfeiffer, 1952:341; 1937:308; cf. Bentzen, 1952:II 94. In my view, Ridout's undoubted literary tact deserts him at this point in his thesis: his perspective here is primarily theological or ideological.

/9/   Indeed the inclusion of material through the same thematic process need not stop with chapters 6 and 7: Eybers argues (1971:28-30) that "Unity [of most of 1 and 2 Samuel + 1 Kgs 1-2] may also be found in the purpose, if this was to indicate that Solomon was the legitimate king of all Israel, for this does not depend on II Sam 7 only, but also on the very origin of the monarchy, which was instituted by Samuel. Therefore the relevant history starts with Samuel and reaches a climax near the middle of the book (II Sam 7), followed by a detailed description of how God's promise to David was fulfilled".

/10/   Ward (1967), discussing chapters 2-4 as part of a proposed source narrating the story of David's rise (in both 1 and 2 Samuel), observes (p. 140) that it is the finest piece of writing in the whole composition. It is worth noting also that Luther (1906:194-9) puts this material (2:8-3:1,

6-39 + 4:1-12) in the same class of narrative as 2 Sam 13-19 (i.e. *novellistische Geschichtsschreibung*).
/11/ Note the caution shown by Kennedy, 1904:234; Eissfeldt, 1965:277-8; Mauchline, 1971:241-2. Against: Segal, 1918-9:54-5; Hertzberg, 1964:381.
/12/ Cf. however Carlson (1964:198-203), though it is not altogether clear whether this is precisely what he is claiming; also Schulte, 1972:139, 166-9; Pfeiffer, 1952:353; Caird, 1955:859; (?) Auzou, 364; Soggin, 1976:192.
/13/ It appears to me that Carlson's criticisms (1964:199-200) of Segal (1918-9:54-5) merely highlight the literary discontinuity of the two stories (21:1-14 and Chapter 9); in which case questions of "priority" become simple historical ones, irrelevant for our enquiry.
/14/ No other son of Saul is mentioned, not even when Abner is quarrelling with Ishbosheth; the murder of Ishbosheth in 4:4 implies that, as far as the story is concerned, Mephibosheth is now the last possible contender for the throne (and cf. 2 Sam 16:3 where the same assumption underlies the narrative), and it makes clear that he has been taken into hiding and out of the public (and David's) eye.
/15/ This is also discussed by Segal (1964-5:323 n. 5). In my view the author has seen the opportunity to include this piece of (foreshadowing) information following his momentary pause to add the gloss (of his own making) about Beeroth; the transition to Mephibosheth comes through the note of *fleeing*. Then when he picks up the narrative proper he reintroduces his characters by giving them their *full* names (vs. 5a, and cf. the end of vs. 2; virtually ring-composition). This passage is generally taken as a gloss or transposition from chapter 9: see e.g. Wellhausen, 1878:222; H. Smith, 1899:283-5; Budde, 1902:216; Hertzberg, 1964:264.
/16/ Notice too that the incident mentioned in connection with Abiathar's punishment (1 Kgs 2:26) is also one that is narrated in the larger narrative (reading *ʾrn*, "ark", with MT and not *ʾpd*, "ephod" as suggested by Gray, 1970:108-9). I find quite unconvincing Noth's rather extravagant analysis (1968:8-13); followed by Gray, 1970:16; cf. e.g. Würthwein, 1974:12-17; Mettinger, 1976:28) which takes vss. 26-35, together with 13-25 and 36-46a, as secondary, and vss. 5-9 as tertiary, elaborations of the story. Ridout's excision (1971:76-7) of vss. 26-7 on structural grounds has more to commend it.
/17/ Note that the pattern observed in the "Succession History" by Blenkinsopp (1966:48-9) whereby each major episode contains an important incident involving a woman and an ensuing death (he expresses it in terms of "sin externalized in a sexual form which leads to death") may be observed here also — the quarrel over the former king's concubine, Rizpah, leads eventually to Ishbosheth's death. We are reminded of the *final* episode (Solomon's coup) where Abishag, formerly David's concubine, is the catalyst in Adonijah's death.
/18/ Schulte (1972:166) recognizes the difficulty and suggest that either 2 Sam 5:6-9 belongs to the story (but she rightly doubts this) or one or more episodes are missing from the extant compilation.
/19/ This "break" provides a starting point for Flanagan's argument (1972) that 1 Kgs 1-2 was originally separate from 2 Sam 9-20, which itself contains an originally distinct unit, 2 Sam 11-12. While I accept that Flanagan is right to emphasize once more (so earlier, Luther, Gressmann, Caspari; and cf. Eissfeldt, 1965:139, 270) the loosely structured, episodic nature of the narrative, and to stress the fragility of the "succession" theme in 2 Sam 13-20 (so also Blenkinsopp, 1966:47), I do not find his main thesis of a major redaction convincing. My major criticisms is that he fails to account for the material in 1 Kgs 2 which forms a direct link with the subject matter and characters of 2 Sam 13-20 (and 2-4, as I argue in this present chapter) and, with the exception of a few verses (esp. vss. 2-4, 10-11, 27) is extremely difficult to distinguish in terms of outlook and style from the rest of the "Succession Narrative" (Whybray, 1968:8-9; against Noth, 1968:8-11).
/20/ Cf. Flanagan, 1971:50. He links 10:1-5 with 11:1 but still sees this as part of a basic account of the war concluded in 12:26-31 and separate from the Bathsheba story.
/21/ According to Schulte, the "David-Saul-story" is found in 1 Sam 16-20, 21-3, 27, 29-30, 2

Sam 1-2:8, and 2 Sam 5 (these references are approximate only), though this has undergone a certain development and two stages *(Teile)* may be distinguished, particularly in chapters 16-20. 2 Sam 2:10a, 11; 3:1(?), 2-5, 10, 30; 4:2b, 4 are considered not original to the major narrative of chapters 2-4 (i.e. from 2:12, the beginning of the "David-Story"); cf. pp. 165-6.

/22/   Indeed the whole episode comes as something of a surprise after 1 Sam 31 where the implication is that the house of Saul has come to an end (cf. 31:2, 6-7).

/23/   Most of them belong to larger hypotheses concerning the composition of the narratives in both 1 and 2 Samuel relating to the so-called "story of David's rise" *(Geschichte vom Aufstieg Davids)*, seen variously as running from 1 Sam 15 or 16 to 2 Sam 5, 7, 8, or even 9. Cf. recently Nübel, 1959; Weiser, 1966; Ward, 1967; Grønbaek, 1971; and see further the literature cited and the summary of hypotheses in Schicklberger, 1974:255-8.

/24/   Otherwise in the OT: Gen 29:14; Jud 9:2; cf. Gen 2:23; Job 2:5.

/25/   As e.g. Schulte's "David-Saul-Story".

/26/   The note about the ᵓpwd bd (vs. 14b), whatever this object was, probably belongs originally to the ark story.

/27/   1 Chron 15:29 reads wyhy instead of the curious whyh at the beginning of the verse; see Titkin, 1922:47.

/28/   Notice the use of the term "city of David": it occurs in Samuel only here and in 2 Sam 5:7, 9.

/29/   Cf. also 1 Kgs 1:40 (Solomon): "And all the people went up after him, playing on pipes [cf. 2 Sam 6:5] and rejoicing with great joy"; also 2 Kgs 11:14 (Joash): "and when she looked, there was the king standing beside the pillar . . . and all the people of the land rejoicing and blowing trumpets".

/30/   Another possibility is to separate 3:12-16 from its present context, as Flanagan suggests (1971: 46), and link it with 3:17-19 and 5:1-3. But the "covenant" motif in vss. 12-13 seems to belong naturally to vs. 21 and, more important, the key word šlḥ links it with the whole of vss. 20ff.

/31/   Cf. the lists of word usage in Schulte, 1972:90-4; see also e.g. Budde, 1902:XVI; Segal, 1964-5:324-32.

/32/   Notice too the quite different role of David in this warfare: his absence from the military activity of chapter 2 conforms better to the pattern of chapters 11, 15 and 18.

/33/   I use the term "style" with some hesitation as it is clear that a definition of style and the nature and value of stylistic analysis of literature are matters of some considerable debate. See e.g. Spencer, 1964; Babb, 1972; Chatman, 1971. In what follows I am mainly interested (as is Rost) in what might be termed "rhetorical devices" (but also in lexical stock and irony); see further Muilenburg, 1953; Alonso Schökel, 1961:143-7; Blenkinsopp, 1966:48-9; Ridout, 1971:Chapter 1.

/34/   See Driver, 1913b:242. If yhdw is indeed "hardly possible" after wypgšwm it is simpler to read wayyipᵉgᵉšû than to delete yhdw.

/35/   yhdw is no insignificant word — it encapsulates the peculiarity of the anecdote. Notice also the way in which the narrator uses simple repetitions to convey the "double" nature of the action: wyṣᵓ, yṣᵓw; ᵓlh ᶜl hbrkh mzh, wᵓlh ᶜl hbrkh mzh; wyᵓmr ᵓbnr ᵓl ywᵓb yqwmw, wyᵓmr ywᵓb yqmw.

/36/   The examples set out in Appendix B, below, may be compared with those presented by Ridout, 1971:36-47. He discusses 2 Sam 14:25-7; 20:1-22; 20:16-20; 12:13b-14; 1 Kgs 2:26; 2 Sam 16:7b-8; 19:12-3; 1 Kgs 1:24-7; 2 Sam 13:32-3; 1 Kgs 2:42-3; 2 Sam 17:8-10; in that order. Rost merely lists his examples (p. 221): 2 Sam 11:20-1; 11:25b; 13:32-3; 15:19-20; 16:7-8, 10-11; 18:19-31; 19:12-13; 1 Kgs 1:24-7; 2:42-3.

/37/   I am not arguing here that these techniques which have been singled out by others as characteristic of the "Succession Narrative" are necessarily the exclusive preserve of this narrative but simply that chapters 2-4 share these characteristics and cannot on that account be distinguished from chapters 9-20 + 1 Kgs 1-2, as Rost's analysis implies.

/38/   See Ridout (1971:24-5) where he summarizes: "In the case of phrases and longer units, repetition is normally varied in successive occurrences through the use of synonyms, omissions, additions, or alterations of word order. The great variety which is introduced into repeated phrases, sentences and paragraphs is so pervasive as to force us to conclude that our author has consciously attempted to modify these iterations".

/39/ Cf. a similar structure in 2 Sam 18:20-23 (Ridout, 1971:99). Notice also that it is after the third statement about Asahel not turning aside that the killing is recounted – cf. Ridout, p. 120: "There is considerable evidence that the third repetition of a series was a favoured climactic point for our author".

/40/ On the text of this example see Driver, 1913b:248. I follow LXX in omitting *lpny* after *ky ʾm.*

/41/ Note that the chiasmus has a single element at the centre and that this is the focal point of the speech. Cf. Ridout, 1971:48-9: "In practically all the examples of chiasm which we have identified in the Succession Narrative, the structure has a single element in the centre which is not paired with another element . . . . Furthermore, it can be said that the centre of the chiasm is normally the most important part of the structure . . . ."

/42/ He discusses 1 Kgs 2:12-46 (25, 34, 36); 2 Sam 14:13-20 (17b, 20b); 20:4-13 (7, 10b, 13b); 18:17; 19:9 and 15:13-16:14 (complex and discussed in some detail).

/43/ The text of 4:6 is difficult. For various attempts to resolve the problems (none wholly convincing) see Driver, 1913b:255; Hertzberg, 1964:264-5; Mauchline, 1971:213. Adoption of LXX (so e.g. Driver [1913b], RSV) would mean the elimination of our particular phrase.

/44/ On distinctive authorship in a narrative tradition that employs stock patterning such as this, see above, Chapter Three.

/45/ Flanagan (1971), who follows some of the earlier "literary" critics in assuming a two source theory in 2:12-32, remarks (45-6) that "the episode described in vv. 17-23 is not mentioned when Joab and Abner meet in vv. 24-28, as would be expected if it were from the same tradition". But it is precisely because the author does not develop the vengeance theme at this point that he is allowed the subtle luxury of foreshadowing the death of Abner (in 2:22) while yet managing to retain in the account of his death an element of shock. Moreover the failure to mention the Asahel scene in 2:24-8 is entirely in keeping with Joab's character as presented in the "Succession Narrative" – above all he is a man of deeds not words (the significant exception is in 2 Sam 19:1-9), and it is clear in 2:24-8 that he realizes that Abner is safely out of his reach, short of a desperate battle.

/46/ Acceptance of the "succession" nature of the narrative, particularly as it has been formulated by Rost (by no means the first to trace such a theme: cf. e.g. Wellhausen, 1878:224-5; Driver, 1913a: 182-3) is almost a matter of course amongst commentators: see, recently, Fohrer, 1970:222; Gray, 1970:15; Mauchline, 1971:240; Ridout, 1971:212-3. Cf. also Flanagan, 1971:97-8 and 1972:172-3: he however sees this theme as superimposed by redaction (the addition of Solomonic sections), upon an earlier literary unit, "a Court History, that was intended to show how David maintained legitimate control over the kingdoms of Judah and Israel" (see above, n. 19). Blenkinsopp, (1966: 47) also has suggested a separation of "legitimation" and "succession" themes. M. Smith (1951) describes the work as "a moral tract", a "story of crime and punishment": the plot stems from David's sin in the Bathsheba episode, and "succession" is a major element only in the final episode (Solomon established on the throne) where it is subsumed under the theme of reward and punishment. Carlson's criticism of Rost (he does not accept the existence of "a special *Thronfolgegeschichte* in 2 Sam") is somewhat diffuse but the importance of the "succession" theme does not appear to come under particular attack (cf. esp. pp. 131-9, and 167). Jackson is strongly critical of Rost's account of the purpose of the story (i.e. it is written to the greater glory of Solomon) and argues that though the narrative does indeed provide an answer to the question how it came about that Solomon gained the throne, this is of only peripheral interest – the story is much more concerned with the delineation of character and themes such as "life and death, love and hatred, honour and dishonour" (1965:194-5; cf. 185-6). The most recent criticism of Rost's definition of the narrative as a "succession" story is that of Schulte (1971:see esp. 138). Würthwein (1974) and Langlamet

(1976b) while attacking Rost's pro-Solomonic interpretation of the narrative, do not appear to doubt that it is a "succession" story.

/47/ Moreover when Whybray (1968:21) writes of this episode (Sheba) as reminding us "of the latent possibility . . . that David would not have *any* successor to sit on his throne" it seems to me that he could not claim to be isolating the primary focus of the material. Where Sheba poses a threat it is clearly to David's grip on his kingdom: "Now Sheba . . . will do us more harm than Absalom; . . . pursue him, lest he get himself fortified cities, and cause us trouble" (2 Sam 20:6). See further above, p. 90.

/48/ Cf. Blenkinsopp, 1966:47-8; also Carlson's exposition of 2 Sam 10-20 (24) in terms of the theme of "David under the Curse" (1964:140ff.). Note also von Rad's comment (1944/1966:196 n. 40) minimizing the importance of source problems in this section of chapter 12; with this I concur.

/49/ Jackson, 1965:185 n. 15: "It can hardly be regarded as laudatory to proclaim publicly the circumstances surrounding Solomon's birth". The point is emphasized by Delekat (1967), Würthwein (1974:49) and Langlamet (1976b:525-6).

/50/ Cf. Whybray (1968:27) on the Absalom episode: "Ostensibly the central character in these chapters is Absalom; yet in a deeper sense the reader is made to feel that it is David whom the author seeks to portray . . . ." So too Brueggemann (1974:176) on 2 Sam 15-19.

/51/ Hence of course the claims that the story is written *in majorem gloriam Salomonis* (Rost, 1926/1965:234; so Whybray, 1968:53; Fohrer, 1970:222; and many others).

/52/ He attempts to overcome this difficulty by appeal to (hypothetical) circumstances of composition. Rost fails to see the problem.

/53/ Cf. Whybray, 1968:22: "Bathsheba and her son retire into the background" — which might well be termed an understatement.

/54/ If we are to go by the lists of 2 Sam 3:2-5 and 5:13-6 he was at best ninth or tenth in line of succession. See also Jackson, 1965:185.

/55/ In the present discussion I trust that I have not used the term "theme" in a way that differs significantly from Rost's use of the term *Thema*. "Theme" answers the question, What is the work *about?* But it is not simply a classification of subject-matter or a synopsis of plot — rather it encapsulates something of the significance or implication of the subject-matter and plot; it is more like "plot with the emphasis on meaning" (Clines, 1976a:485). Clearly discussion in this area of literary interpretation has to contend with terminological difficulties; in Chapter Five, e.g., I have sometimes used "theme" (or "sub-theme") where others might have preferred "motif". I doubt, however, that such difficulties in fact bar access to the interpretation itself. For a most useful discussion of "theme" see Clines, 1976a:483-7; amongst the questions he raises, one which remains for me is the extent to which all statements of theme in a literary work must be capable of integration into a single statement.

Notes to Chapter Five
An Interpretation of the Story

/1/   For this chapter I have revised and built upon my 1975 essay, especially by attempting further to explore and clarify the following topics raised there: (a) the "kingdom" theme (accession, rebellion and succession); (b) the correlation and interaction between the public (political) and private spheres of David's life; and (c) the ways in which these and other thematic aspects of the story exposed in the essay (e.g. the "giving and grasping" theme) are integrated.

As the reader will recognize, much of this chapter depends in one way or another on the insights and stimulation of other critics, so much so that I have felt it difficult to know where acknowledgement of indebtedness or simple agreement might reasonably stop. In the event, and in the interests of "readability", I have severely curtailed such reference (which may still be found, for part of the essay at least, in the original 1976 version) but wish to acknowledge here particular indebtedness to the following writers: Kittel (1896); Luther (1906); Rost (1926/1965); von Rad (1944/1966); Napier (1955); Jackson (1965); Delekat (1967); Whybray (1968); Auzou (1968); Ridout (1971); and finally Brueggemann (especially 1972abc, 1974), who, perhaps more than any other, offers an insight into the essential David.

Since this chapter was drafted two further papers of interest have come to hand, those of Roth (1977) and Gros Louis (1977). I have not been able to take these into account here, but it is gratifying to see that Gros Louis' paper also develops the "public and private" theme along lines most congenial to my own view (though his starting point, the final form of the text from 1 Sam 16 to 1 Kgs 2, is rather different). Roth's structuralist account of 2 Sam 10-12 provides a valuable analysis of what I would call the "ambivalence" of David.

/2/   The scene also takes us back to the beginning of the story, the quarrel over Rizpah (2 Sam 3); see chapter 4 n. 17 above.

/3/   David's request for Michal appears to provide the excuse for Abner's visit. That it was a specially significant move in establishing a claim to the throne, as seen by many commentators (e.g. Carlson, 1964:51; Hertzberg, 1964:259; Mauchline, 210; cf. the caution of McKane, 1963:195), is not evident in the story as it stands.

/4/   It is often asserted that Abner's dealings with Rizpah in some way constituted a legal claim to the throne (or could be so construed); see e.g. H. Smith, 1899:275; Hertzberg, 1964:257; Fohrer, 1959:5; Note however the caution expressed by Tsevat, 1958:241; McKane, 1963:190; Mauchline, 1971:208-9. In support of the claim reference is usually made to 2 Sam 16:21-2 (Absalom and David's concubines) and 1 Kgs 2:13-25 (Adonijah's fatal request for Abishag). But why should Abner go through such a rigmarole when he was already a close relative and power was his to seize at will? Any why is there absolutely no hint of such an understanding in Ishbosheth's rebuke? Similarly such interpretation requires the implication that both Adonijah and Bathsheba (in 1 Kgs 2) are to be viewed as imbeciles. In the latter case Solomon's reply to Bathsheba may be quite simply understood in terms of "ask an inch, take a mile": any request for anything would have served to trigger Solomon's paranoia. 2 Sam 16:21-2 pictures a quite different situation:

Absalom has *already* rebelled and claimed the throne; the public possession of the harem is, as the text explains, a propaganda exercise designed to show that his rebellion was past the point of no return; he behaves now as though he were indeed the king.

/5/   Cf. H. Smith's observations (1899:311) about the numbers of sons and servants and the implied extent of the estate, and McKane's query (1963:224) about the state of the text ("The difficulty is that, if Mephibosheth is to enjoy David's hospitality, he does not appear to stand in need of the produce of his estate in the way presupposed by the preceding half of the verse [i.e. vs. 10]"). The text needs no emendation.

/6/   Certainly the clues are laid in such a way as to suggest that it is Ziba who is lying (Hertzberg, 1964:345; Klopfenstein, 1964:327-8; Ridout, 1971:161-7). In my judgement the primary clues are (a) the insistence on Mephibosheth's lameness (9:3, 13; 19:27) in which respect he was at the mercy of Ziba; and (b) the otherwise gratuitous note about his apparent state of mourning (19: 24). Gressmann (1910:180, 183), however, sees it the other way round; and McKane (1963:273) comments that "there is no means of ascertaining whether the truth was with Ziba or Mephibosheth".

/7/   Deception and clandestine activity (and the related theme of conspiracy), i.e. the attempt to prevent someone from confronting the true state of affairs, play an important role in the narrative as a whole. Death by deception is the lot of Asahel, Abner and Amasa. The deaths of Abner and Amasa, moreover, as well as that of Ishbosheth, are covert affairs, at least (the story stresses) in relation to the key figure, David. Indeed, in the case of Abner and Ishbosheth, the fact that the deed was, from David's point of view, covert, and that it was seen publicly to be so, is equally as important in its consequences as the deed itself. Deceit marks both of David's attempts to pass on to Uriah the paternity of the illegitimate child and the manner of Uriah's death (also a clandestine act), no less than the manner of David's reaction to this news. The Ammonites are sure that David's embassy is an act of deception just as Joab apparently cannot believe that Abner could have come to David's camp with anything but ulterior motives. By deception and clandestine dealing Amnon creates the opportunity to rape Tamar, Absalom the opportunity to murder Amnon, and Joab the opportunity to secure Absalom's return to court. The woman of Tekoa deceives the king, just as Nathan had done in an earlier scene, while a little later Hushai makes possible the return of David by an elaborate deception. Nor is the account of the death of Absalom free from this persistent motif: the altercation between Joab and the man who brought him the news of Absalom's plight in the tree involves the question of whether or not the king can be deceived, while Ahimaaz, bringing the news to David, does in fact attempt just this (18:29, cf. vs. 20). Deception is the mainspring of the Mephibosheth and Ziba story as we have just noted. And, of course, the last main conspiracy of the story (1 Kgs 1) moves from the covert meeting of Nathan and Bathsheba to what seems to be one of the boldest acts of deception of them all (see further, below). What we are witnessing in all this material is a concentration of interest on the way men's lives and responsibilities are bound up in a world where what "seems to be" competes often on equal terms with "what is". A basic datum dogs the observer (and evaluator) of this world and its inhabitants: man has a remarkable capacity for distorting or curtailing the perspectives of others.

/8/   There is a problem about the originality of this passage: see e.g. Carlson (1964:157-9; cf. Budde, 1902:254-5) who takes 12:7b-12 as a Deuteronomic addition. He observes (p. 190), however, that even without these verses it is possible to interpret the misfortunes which come upon David in 2 Sam 13-1 Kgs 2 as "retribution 'in full measure' for David's crime in 2 Sam 11f.". So also von Rad (1966:196 n. 40: "the editorial addition would be wholly in keeping with the spirit of the original") and Whybray (1968:23-4).

/9/   This perspective is explored by Delekat, 1967:33-6. It should not be merely assumed, as by von Rad (1944/1966:198-203; widely followed), that the few expressions of Yahweh's attitude (displeasure, love, etc.) are to be identified with the author's own view. Moreover it is easy to exaggerate the significance of the few passages where the narrator speaks of Yahweh's action or attitude (von Rad singles out 2 Sam 11:27; 12:24; 17:14; cf. Schulz, 1923:196-7): to say that

Solomon was beloved by Yahweh, or that Yahweh ordained that the counsel of Ahithophel be defeated does certainly add a providential dimension; it hardly warrants the claim that Yahweh is the primary focus of interest (cf. von Rad, 1966:202-3).

/10/ See further Schulz, 1920:113; Ridout, 1971:153, 157. Indeed the ironic contrast with the faithful Joab and David's servants goes further (11:2): "it happened late one afternoon, *when David arose from his couch . . . .*"

/11/ Segal (1964-5:331) rightly notes the parallel between the last clause and 1 Sam 20:8b. There are other parallels in the same segment: father-son confrontation, threat to the throne, absence at a sacrifice used as an excuse.

/12/ I disagree with Whybray (1968:28) who takes the brevity in the narrative here to indicate how cold and formal the reception was.

/13/ The phrase encapsulates the problem of Absalom's conspiracy against Amnon. That the author is interested in the *variety* of ways of viewing this action is most obviously demonstrated within the narrative by the arguments of the woman of Tekoa and the action of Joab. Commentators are apt to make rather facile judgements about David's failure here (cf. e.g. Hertzberg, 1964:335; von Rad, 1944/1966:182; Ridout 1971:148). For a somewhat melodramatic account of Absalom here as a kind of "type" of the evil "seducer" *(Verführer)* in the Bible (linked with the Satan of the Gospels) see Voeltzel, 1961:33-4.

/14/ See especially Napier, 1955:139-40; Hertzberg, 1964:378; McKane, 1963:253-4, 257-8; Brueggemann, 1972ac, 1974 (so e.g.: "It is a mature faith which lets him function without needing to function where he cannot. Great freedom and responsibility are combined with an ability to leave other matters completely in the hands of Yahweh" – 1972c:41-2).

/15/ The following two passages (15:24-9; 16:5-13) are often cited in illustration of a "positive" side of David: cf. Napier, 1955:139-40; McKane, 1963:253-4, 257-8; Auzou, 1968:389; Brueggemann, 1969:495; 1972a:14-17; 1972c:41-2; 1974:175-92, esp. 177-81.

/16/ Bewer (1962:29) calls him a "child of luck". Whybray (1968:37) asks, Was it "real greatness, or was it luck . . . which preserved David's kingdom?". Cf. Pedersen's analysis (1926:188-90) of David's character in terms of his "blessing".

/17/ This is a point against those who see David in this episode as shrewdly calculating, an initiator and strategist: see McKane (1963:253-4); cf. Mauchline (1971:277) and Napier (1955:140: "he is still able to exercise the astute powers of strategy always characteristic of him").

/18/ Contrast, e.g., the scene of lament over Abner's death (3:31-9). Two other occasions where inner emotion is revealed directly are 13:37, 39 and 1 Kgs 1:50. Schulz (1923), who discusses this feature of narrative style in Samuel as a whole, cites (p. 199) 19:1 as a normal case of grief indicated by externals, presumably taking *wayyir^{e}gaz* in a purely literal sense (to quiver, shake). The metaphorical meaning is well attested (*BDB*, 919; Driver, 1913b:333) and in my view better fits the context here.

/19/ Von Rad misses entirely this deteriorating movement and observes romantically (1944/1966: 187) that "the noble behaviour of the king, purified as he is by suffering, shines like a brilliant light on all around him". Similarly deficient is Brueggemann's attempt (1971:328-31) to analyse the restoration of David in terms of a symbolic restoration of *šālôm* (order and stability) – "The king is the source of health, order and life for the community" – though it is possible that such a mythic pattern *underlies* our present story.

Note also a function both here and earlier of the Mephibosheth sub-plot. David's gain of the throne of Israel brings in its wake the gift of Saul's land to Mephibosheth. On the journey from Jerusalem David makes a simple judgement against the Saulide. By it (a gift in fact to Ziba) David's loss of his kingdom finds its parallel in Mephibosheth's deprivation: "The king said to Ziba, 'Behold, all that belonged to Mephibosheth is now yours'". On the return journey the corresponding judgement is now characteristically a compromise. And its terms ominously foreshadow what is soon to threaten David's fortune: "And the king said to Mephibosheth ' . . . I have decided: you and Ziba shall divide the land'''.

/20/   I take "man of Belial" in 20:1 to mean a "reckless" person, one who disregards the proprieties or disturbs the *status quo* (cf. Hannah, 1 Sam 1:16; Nabal, 1 Sam 25:17). Notice that nowhere is it said that Sheba actually engaged in an armed rebellion, merely that he called for the men of Israel to disband and go home, though of course the implication is secession. Caird (1955:1151) rightly notes that when we next see Sheba he is accompanied only by his own clan. For a negative view of David in this episode see also Schulte 1972:179.

/21/   Cf. Hertzberg, 1964:372; Napier, 1955:143; Jackson, 1965:180; Auzou, 1968:396. It is surprising how little is said of Amasa. In fact, we are merely told of his parentage (he was closely related to both Joab and David) and of his appointment, first over Absalom's army, and second over David's; then (nothing about his role in the disastrous battle in the forest of Ephraim) of his commission to muster the men of Judah (presumably for the pursuit of Sheba). It is not until this point in the narrative that we are expressly told of any action actually taken by Amasa (previously he is simply the object of someone else's action or address). The story-teller wastes no words: "So Amasa went to summon Judah; but he delayed beyond the set time which had been appointed him" (20:5). He next appears at Gibeon. Again we see him, fleetingly, in action: "And Amasa came to meet him . . . And Amasa did not observe the sword which was in Joab's hand . . . and he died" (20:8-10). There is something almost cruelly comic about the portrait; Amasa was the man whose loss of a battle gained him a command, who failed to keep an appointment, and who could not spot the sword in his rival's hand.

/22/   Notice the balance between vss. 49 and 50 with the verbs of "rising" and "going" being repeated but the key element of "fearing" varied *(ḥrd, yrʾ)*. The focus of the narrative moves significantly from the more general (the guests of Adonijah trembled and went their way) to the particular (Adonijah feared Solomon and went to the altar).

/23/   The parallel with Absalom in vss. 5 and 6 is broadened (after mention of the existence of political factions) to include not only his action at the time of his rebellion but also of his conspiracy against Amnon: he holds a feast (sacrifice) to which "all his brothers, the king's sons" *except* " Solomon, his brother" are invited (1:9-10; cf. 2 Sam 15:7-12 and 13:23-7). Just as Amnon in 13: 23-7 is singled out for special mention, so now Solomon in 1 Kgs 1:9-10. While, therefore, nothing explicit gives us grounds for seeing the feast in terms of conspiracy, by the end of the passage this possibility dominates our perspective. It is thus only too easy for us to accept Nathan's version of the event, as do Bathsheba and David in the narrative itself (so also many commentators when judging Adonijah's intentions: cf. e.g. Rost, 1926/1965:195-7; Whybray, 1968:23, 52; Montgomery and Gehman, 1951:70, 73; Ridout, 1971:151-2); only with our growing suspicion about Nathan's own actions is there an incentive to look again with other eyes at what has been recounted.

This carefully constructed parallel between the two sons and its subtle dramatic contribution is a strong argument against Flanagan's dissociation of 1 Kgs 1-2 from 2 Sam 13-20. His attempt (1972:174-5) to play down the extent of the parallel by claiming that any comparison must be between Absalom and Sheba, not Absalom and Adonijah, depends upon an historical, not a literary, analysis.

/24/   Cf. e.g., Kittel, 1896:179-82; Ehrlich, 1914:213-5; Gray, 1970:88; Langlamet, 1976b:330-7. Two other points: (1) Adonijah later says to Bathsheba, and is not contradicted (indeed Bathsheba's willingness to act for him suggests perhaps a certain attitude of remorse):"You know that the kingdom was mine, and that all Israel fully expected me to reign" (2:15); (2) Šanda (cited by Montgomery and Gehman, 1951:75) may well be right in suggesting that Solomon's reluctance to allow Adonijah the gift of Abishag may be connected, in part at least, with the fact that Abishag is the only witness to the conspiracy. Why else is Abishag mentioned in this crucial scene (1:15)? Montgomery and Gehman offer the unlikely suggestion that the mention is designed to reinforce the point that Abishag was not a proper concubine (i.e. the king had not had sexual intercourse with her) since if she had this status, they claim, no visitors would have been allowed in the chamber.

/25/ The parallel with Absalom is also drawn at the personal as well as the political level. Just as Absalom killed his brother Amnon, so Solomon has Adonijah murdered. In terms of the theme of giving and grasping there is a further touch of irony in the fact that the occasion (pretext) for the murder is a *gift* – the gift of Abishag.

/26/ Whybray (1968:50-2) depends heavily upon the identification (unjustified, as I try to show) of Benaiah's expressed viewpoint (1:36, 47) with that of the author, in order to show that the narrative was written in support of Solomon's accession.

/27/ The accounts of the fates of Adonijah, Abiathar, Joab and Shimei are much more than mere "appendices" allowing the "pulling together of all the strings" (Whybray, 1968:39) following the conclusion of the real ("succession") theme: on my interpretation they play a key role in portraying the kind of ethos that finally prevails over David. Similarly Mettinger's "beautifully rounded off work" (1 Kgs 1-2 divested of all reference to its victims) is not one for which I have much enthusiasm – quite apart from the fact that I fail to see the "inconsistencies" in the text which justify the excisions (see Mettinger, 1976:28).

/28/ Solomon's speech concerning Joab (2:31-3) constantly reminds us of David: cf. "my father's house", "without the knowledge of my father David", "to David and to *his* descendents and to *his* house and to *his* throne".

Bibliography

Aldred, C.
1961   *The Egyptians,* Ancient Peoples and Places 18; London: Thames &
               Hudson.
Allen, R. F.
1971   *Fire and Iron. Critical Approaches to* Njáls saga; Pittsburgh: University
               of Pittsburgh Press.
Alonso Schökel, L.
1961   "Erzählkunst im Buche der Richter", *Bib* 42:143-72.
Alt, A.
1930/1966   "The Formation of the Israelite State in Palestine", *Essays on Old
               Testament History and Religion,* trans. R. A. Wilson (this essay first
               appeared in German in 1930); Oxford: Blackwell. 171-237.
1951   "Die Weisheit Salomos", *TLZ* 76: cols. 139-44.
Arnold, M.
1895   "The Study of Poetry", *Essays in Criticism. Second Series,* London.
Auzou, G.
1968   *La danse devant l'arche. Étude du livre de Samuel,* Connaissance de la
               Bible; Paris: Editions de l'Orante.
Babb, H. S. (ed.)
1972   *Essays in Stylistic Analysis,* New York: Jovanovich.
Bardtke, H.
1973   "Erwägungen zur Rolle Judas im Aufstand des Absalom", *Wort und
               Geschichte,* AOAT 18; ed. H. Gese, H. P. Rüger; Kevalaer.
Baumgartner, W.
1923   "Ein Kapitel vom hebraischen Erzählungstil", *Eucharisterion, Studien
               zur Religion und Literatur des Alten und Neuen Testaments, Hermann
               Gunkel... dargebracht* I, FRLANT XIX/1; Gottingen.
Bentzen, A.
1952   *Introduction to the Old Testament,* 2nd edn.; Copenhagen: Gad.
Bewer, J. A.
1962   *The Literature of the Old Testament,* 3rd edn. rev. E. G. Kraeling;
               New York & London: Columbia University Press.
Blenkinsopp, J.
1964   "Jonathan's Sacrilege. 1 SM 14, 1-46: A Study in Literary History".
               CBQ 26: 423-49.
1966   "Theme and Motif in the Succession History (2 Sam. XI 2ff.) and the
               Yahwist Corpus", *VTS* 15: 44-57.
Born, A. van den
1954   "Études sur quelques toponymes bibliques", *OTS* 10: 197-214.
Brayley, I. F. M.
1976   Review of Veijola, 1975, in *JTS* N.S. 27: 427-8.

Bright, J.
1951   "I and II Samuel", (= "Studia Biblica XVI"), *Interp* 5: 450-61.
1972   *A History of Israel*, 2nd edn.; OTL; London: SCM.
Brueggemann, W.
1968   "David and his Theologian", *CBQ* 30: 156-81.
1969   "The Trusted Creature", *CBQ* 31: 484-98.
1970   "The Triumphalist Tendency in Exegetical History", *JAAR* 38: 367-80.
1971   "Kingship and Chaos (A Study in Tenth Century Theology)", *CBQ* 33: 317-32.
1972a   "On Trust and Freedom. A Study of Faith in the Succession Narrative", *Interp* 26: 3-19.
1972b   "Life and Death in Tenth Century Israel", *JAAR* 40: 96-109.
1972c   *In Man We Trust*, Richmond, Virginia: John Knox.
1974   "On Coping With Curse: A Study of 2 Sam 16:5-14", *CBQ* 36: 175-92.
Bruford, A.
1969   *Gaelic Folktales and Mediaeval Romances*, = *Bealoideas* 34 (1966-9); Dublin.
Bruno, A.
1935   *Das Hebräische Epos. Eine Rhythmische und Textkritische Untersuchung der Bücher Samuelis und Könige;* Uppsala.
Budde, K.
1897   *Richter*, KHC; Freiburg.
1902   *Die Bücher Samuel*, KHC; Tübingen & Leipzig.
Caird, G. B.
1953   "The First and Second Books of Samuel", *The Interpreter's Bible* II; New York: Abingdon. 853-1176.
Campbell, A. F.
1975   *The Ark Narrative (1 Sam 4-6; 2 Sam 6). A Form-Critical and Traditio-Historical Study*, SBL Dissertation Series 16; Missoula, Montana: Scholars Press.
Campbell, E. F.
1974   "The Hebrew Short Story: A Study of Ruth", *A Light Unto My Path. Old Testament Studies in Honor of Jacob M. Myers*, ed. H. N. Bream, R. D. Heim, C. A. Moore; Philadelphia: Temple University Press. 83-101.
1975   *Ruth*, AB; Garden City, N.Y.: Doubleday & Co.
Campbell, J. F.
1890   *Popular Tales of the West Highlands*, 4 vols.; London.
Caspari, W.
1909   "Literarische Art und historischer Wert von 2 Sam. 15-20", *Theologische Studien und Kritiken* 82: 317-48.
1926   *Die Samuelbücher*, KAT; Leipzig.
Carlson, R. A.
1964   *David, the chosen King. A Traditio-Historical Approach to the Second Book of Samuel*, Stockholm: Almqvist & Wiksell.
Chadwick, H. M. and N. K.
1932-40   *The Growth of Literature*, 3 vols.; Cambridge.
Chatman, S. (ed.)
1971   *Literary Style: A Symposium*, London: Oxford University Press.
Clines, D. J. A.
1972   "X, X ben Y, ben Y: Personal Names in Hebrew Narrative Style", *VT* 22: 266-87.

1976a	"Theme in Genesis 1-11", *CBQ* 38: 483-507.
1976b	*I, He, We, and They: A Literary Approach to Isaiah 53,* JSOT Supplement Series 1; Sheffield: JSOT.

Cohen, M. A.
1971   "The Rebellions During the Reign of David. An Inquiry Into Social Dynamics in Ancient Israel", *Studies in Jewish Bibliography, History, and Literature, in Honor of I. Edward Kiev,* ed. C. Berlin; New York: Ktav. 91-112.

Cook, S. A.
1899-1900   "Notes on the Composition of 2 Samuel", *AJSL* 16:145-77.

Crenshaw, J. L.
1969   "Method in Determining Wisdom Influence Upon 'Historical' Literature", *JBL* 88: 129-42.

Culley, R. C.
1963   "An Approach to the Problem of Oral Tradition", *VT* 13: 114-25.
1967   *Oral Formulaic Language in the Biblical Psalms,* Near and Middle East Series 4; Toronto: University of Toronto Press.
1972   "Oral Tradition and Historicity", *Studies on the Ancient Palestinian World,* Toronto Semitic Texts and Studies 2; ed. J. W. Wevers, D. B. Redford; Toronto: University of Toronto Press. 102-16.
1976a   *Studies in the Structure of Hebrew Narrative,* Semeia Supplements 3; Missoula, Montana: Scholars Press.
1976b   "Oral Tradition and the OT: Some Recent Discussion", *Semeia* 5: 1-33.

Davies, P. R.
1977   "The History of the Ark in the Books of Samuel", *Journal of Northwest Semitic Languages* 5: 9-18.

Dégh, L.
1965   *Folktales of Hungary,* Folktales of the World; Chicago: University of Chicago Press.

Delargy, J. H.
1945   "The Gaelic Story-Teller", *Proceedings of the British Academy* 31: 177-221.

Delekat, L.
1967   "Tendenz und Theologie der David-Salomo-Erzählung", *Das ferne und nahe Wort,* ed. F. Maas; BZAW 105; Berlin: Töpelmann.

Dietrich, W.
1972   *Prophetie und Geschichte. Eine redaktionsgeschichtliche Untersuchung zum deuteronomistischen Geschichtswerk,* FRLANT 108; Göttingen: Vandenhoek & Ruprecht.

Driver, S. R.
1913a   *An Introduction to the Literature of the Old Testament,* 9th edn.; Edinburgh.
1913b   *Notes on the Hebrew Text and the Topography of the Books of Samuel,* 2nd edn.; Oxford.

Eberhard, W.
1955   *Minstrel Tales from Southeastern Turkey,* Folklore Studies 5; Berkeley and Los Angeles: University of California Press.

Ehrlich, A. B.
1914   *Randglossen zur hebräischen Bibel* 7; Leipzig.

Eissfeldt, O.
    1931   *Die Komposition der Samuelisbücher,* Leipzig.
    1948   *Geschichtsschreibung im Alten Testament,* Berlin.
    1965   *The Old Testament, An Introduction,* trans. P. R. Ackroyd (from 3rd German edn. 1964); Oxford: Blackwell.

Eybers, I. H.
    1971   "Some Remarks Concerning the Composition of the Historical Books of the Old Testament", *De Fructu Oris sui: essays . . . van Selms,* Pretoria Oriental Series 9; Leiden. 26-45.

Flanagan, J. W.
    1971   *A Study of the Biblical Traditions Pertaining to the Foundation of the Monarchy in Israel,* Diss. University of Notre Dame, Indiana; Ann Arbor: University Microfilms.
    1972   "Court History or Succession Document? A Study of 2 Samuel 9-20 and 1 Kings 1-2", *JBL* 91: 172-81.
    1975   "Judah in All Israel", *No Famine in the Land. Studies in Honor of John L. McKenzie,* ed. J. W. Flanagan, A. W. Robinson; Missoula, Montana: Scholars Press. 101-16.

Fohrer, G.
    1959   "Der Vertrag zwischen König und Volk in Israel", *ZAW* 71: 1-22.
    1970   *Introduction to the Old Testament,* trans. D. Green (from Sellin's *Einleitung,* 10th rev. edn. 1965); London: S.P.C.K.

Gray, J.
    1967   *Joshua, Judges and Ruth,* New Cent. B; London: Oliphants.
    1970   *I & II Kings,* 2nd edn.; OTL; London: SCM.

Gibert, P.
    1974   "Légende ou Saga?", *VT* 24: 411-20.

Gressmann, H.
    1910   *Die älteste Geschichtsschreibung und Prophetie Israels,* SAT II/1; Göttingen.

Grønbaek, J. H.
    1971   *Die Geschichte vom Aufstieg Davids (1. SAM. 15 - 2. SAM.5). Tradition und Komposition,* Acta Theologica Danica X; Copenhagen: Munksgaard.

Gros Louis, K. R. R.
    1977   "The Difficulty of Ruling Well: King David of Israel", *Semeia* 8: 15-33.

Gunkel, H.
    1921   *Das Märchen im Alten Testament.* Tübingen.
    1931   "Sagen und Legenden' II. In Israel", *Die Religion in Geschichte und Gegenwart V,* 2nd edn., ed. H. Gunkel, L. Zscharnack; Tübingen. Col. 49-60.

Gunn, D. M.
    1970   "Narrative Inconsistency and the Oral Dictated Text in the Homeric Epic", *American Journal of Philology* 91: 192-203.
    1971   "Thematic Composition and Homeric Authorship", *Harvard Studies in Classical Philology* 75: 1-31.
    1974a   "Narrative Patterns and Oral Tradition in Judges and Samuel", *VT* 24: 286-317.
    1974b   "The 'Battle Report': Oral or Scribal Convention?", *JBL* 93: 513-8.
    1975   "David and the Gift of the Kingdom", *Semeia* 3: 14-45.
    1976a   "Traditional Composition in the 'Succession Narrative'", *VT* 26: 214-29.

1976b "On Oral Tradition: A Response to John Van Seters", *Semeia* 5: 155-61.
Hansen, W. F.
1972 *The Conference Sequence. Patterned Narration and Narrative Inconsistency in the Odyssey,* Berkeley & Los Angeles: University of California Press.
Harris, J. R. (ed.)
1971 *The Legacy of Egypt,* 2nd edn.; Oxford: Clarendon.
Harvey, L. P.
1974 "Oral Composition and the Performance of Novels of Chivalry in Spain", *Forum for Modern Language Studies* 10: 270-86.
Hempel, J.
1964 *Geschichten und Geschichte im Alten Testament bis zur persischen Zeit,* Gütersloh: Gütersloher Verlagshaus.
Hermisson, H.-J.
1971 "Weisheit und Geschichte", *Probleme biblische Theologie,* ed. H. W. Wolff; München: Kaiser. 136-54.
Herrmann, S.
1953-4 "Die Königsnovelle in Ägypten und in Israel. Ein Beitrag zur Gattungsgeschichte in den Geschichtsbüchern des Alten Testaments", *Wissenschaftliche Zeitschrift Universitäts Leipzig* 3, Gesellschafts- und Sprach- wissenschaftliche Reihe, Heft 1: 51-62.
Hertzberg, H. W.
1964 *I & II Samuel,* trans. J. S. Bowden (= ATD 10, 2nd edn. 1960); OTL; London: SCM.
Hoftijzer, J.
1970 "David and the Tekoite Woman", *VT* 20: 419-44.
Holoka, J. P.
1973 "Homeric Originality: A Survey", *Classical World* 66: 257-93.
Hölscher, G.
1952 *Geschichtsschreibung in Israel. Untersuchungen zum Yahwisten und Elohisten,* Lund: Gleerup.
Jackson, J. J.
1965 "David's Throne: Patterns in the Succession Story", *Canadian Journal of Theology* 11: 183-95.
Jacob, E.
1955 "Histoire et Historiens dans l'Ancien Testament", *RHPR* 35: 26-34.
Jastrow, M., Jr.
1900 "Dust, Earth and Ashes as Symbols of Mourning among the Hebrews", *JAOS* 20: 136-41.
Kaiser, O.
1975 *Introduction to the Old Testament,* trans. J. Sturdy (from 2nd German edn. 1970 with further revisions 1973); Oxford: Blackwell.
Kennedy, A. R. S.
1903 "Fruit", *Encyclopaedia Biblica,* ed. T. K. Cheyne, J. Sutherland Black; London. 1567-75.
1904 *Samuel,* Cent. B; Edinburgh.
Kittel, R.
1896 *A History of the Hebrews* II, trans. H. W. Hogg, E. B. Speirs (from German edn. 1892); Theological Translation Library VI; London.
Klaehn, T.
1914 *Die sprachliche Verwandtschaft der Quelle K der Samuelis- bücher mit der*

Quelle J des Heptateuch. Ein Beitrag zur Lösung der Frage nach der Identität beider Quellen, Borne-Leipzig.

Klopfenstein, M. A.
1964   *Die Lüge nach dem Alten Testament. Ihr Begriff, ihr Bedeutung und ihre Beurteilung,* Zürich & Frankfort a.M.: Gotthelf-Verlag.

Klostermann, A.
1887   *Die Bücher Samuelis und der Könige,* SZ; Nördlingen.

Knights, L. C.
1959   *Some Shakespearean Themes,* London: Chatto and Windus.
1971   *Public Voices,* London: Chatto and Windus.

Koch, K.
1962   "Der Spruch 'Sein Blut bleibe auf seinem Haupt' und die israelitische Auffassung vom vergossenen Blut", *VT* 12: 396-416.
1969   *The Growth of the Biblical Tradition. The Form-Critical Method,* trans. S. M. Cupitt (from 2nd German edn. 1967); London: A. & C. Black.

König, E.
1900   *Stilistik, Rhetorik, Poetik in Bezug auf die Biblische Litteratur,* Leipzig.

Lang, M. L.
1969   "Homer and Oral Techniques", *Hesperia* 38: 159-68.

Langlamet, F.
1976a   Review of Würthwein, 1974, and Veijola, 1975, in *RB* 83: 114-137.
1976b   "Pour ou Contre Salomon? La Rédaction Prosalomonienne de I Rois, I-II", *RB* 83: 321-79, 481-528.
1977   "Absalom et les Concubines de son Pere. Recherches sur II Sam., XVI, 21-22", *RB* 84: 161-209.

Leach, E.
1969   "The Legitimacy of Solomon", *Genesis as Myth and Other Essays,* London: Jonathan Cape. 25-83.

Lefebvre, G.
1949   *Romans et contes égyptiens de l'epoque pharaonique,* Paris.

Leimbach, K. A.
1936   *Die Bucher Samuel,* HS III/1; Bonn.

Löhr, M. (ed.)
1898   *Die Bücher Samuels* (O. Thenius, 3rd rev. edn.); KeH; Leipzig.

Lönnroth, L.
1976   *Njáls Saga. A Critical Introduction,* Berkeley & Los Angeles: University of California Press.

Lord, A. B.
1938   "Homer and Huso II: Narrative Inconsistencies in Homer and Oral Poetry", *Transactions of the American Philological Association* 69: 439-45.
1951   "Composition by Theme in Homer and Southslavic Epos", *Transactions of the American Philological Association* 82: 71-80.
1953   "Homer's Originality: Oral Dictated Texts", *Transactions of the American Philological Association* 84: 124-34.
1960   *The Singer of Tales,* Cambridge, Mass.: Harvard University Press.
1974   "Perspectives on Recent Work on Oral Literature", *Forum for Modern Language Studies* 10: 187-210.

Luther, B.
1906   "Die Novelle von Juda und Tamar und andere israelitische Novellen",

Macdonald, D. B.   *Die Israeliten und ihre Nachbarstämme*, ed. E. Meyer; Halle. 177-206.

1933   *The Hebrew Literary Genius. An Interpretation*, Princeton.

Maier, J.
1965   *Das altisraelitische Ladeheiligtum*, BZAW 93; Berlin: Töpelmann.

Martin, W. J.
1969   "Dischronologized narrative in the Old Testament", *VTS* 19: 179-86.

Mauchline, J.
1971   *1 and 2 Samuel*, New Cent. B; London: Oliphants.

McCarthy, D. J.
1965   "II Samuel 7 and the Structure of the Deuteronomic History", *JBL* 84: 131-8.

McKane, W.
1963   *I & II Samuel*, Torch B; London: SCM.
1965   *Prophets and Wise Men*, SBT 44; London: SCM.
1970   *Proverbs. A New Approach*, OTL; London: SCM.
1975   Review of Whybray, 1974, in *JSS* 20: 243-8.

Mettinger, T. N. D.
1971   *Solomonic State Officials. A Study of the Civil Government Officials of the Israelite Monarchy*, Coniectanea Biblica: OT Series 5; Lund: Gleerup.

1976   *King and Messiah. The Civil and Sacral Legitimation of the Israelite Kings*, Lund: Gleerup.

Millard, A. R.
1972   "The Practice of Writing in Ancient Israel", *BA* 35: 98-111.

Miller, J. M.
1974   "Saul's Rise to Power: Some Observations Concerning 1 Sam 9:1 - 10:16; 10:26 - 11:15 and 13:2 - 14:46", *CBQ* 36: 157-74.

1976   *The Old Testament and the Historian*, Philadelphia: Fortress.

Montgomery, J. A. and Gehman, H. S. (ed.)
1951   *A Critical and Exegetical Commentary on the Books of Kings*, ICC; Edinburgh: T. & T. Clark.

Mowinckel, S.
1963   "Israelite Historiography", *ASTI* 2: 4-26.

Muilenburg, J.
1953   "A Study in Hebrew Rhetoric: Repetition and Style", *VTS* 1: 97-111.

Murphy, G.
1953   *Duannaire Finn* III, Irish Texts Soc. 43; Dublin: Educational Co. of Ireland.

1966   "Saga and Myth in Ancient Ireland", *Early Irish Literature*, ed. E. Knott, G. Murphy; London: Routledge & Kegan Paul. 97-142.

Napier, B. D.
1955   *From Faith to Faith. Essays on Old Testament Literature*, New York: Harper & Bros.

Noth, M.
1955   "David und Israel in II Samuel, 7", *Mélanges Bibliques . . . André Robert*, Travaux de l'Institut Catholique de Paris 4; Paris: Bloud & Gay. 122-30.

1957   *Überlieferungsgeschichtliche Studien*, 2nd edn.; Tübingen: Max Niemeyer.
1968   *Könige*, BKAT IX/1; Neukirchen-Vluyn: Neukirchener Verlag.

Nowack, W.
1902   *Die Bücher Samuelis,* HK I/4; Göttingen.
Nübel, H. -U.
1959   *Davids Aufsteig in der frühe israelitischer Geschichtsschreibung,* Diss.
                       Bonn.
Olrik, A.
1909   "Epische Gesetze der Volksdichtung", *Zeitschrift fur deutsches Altertum
                       und deutsche Litteratur* N.F. 51: 1-12 (English trans. in *The Study of
                       Folklore,* ed. A. Dundes; Englewood Cliffs: Prentice-Hall; 1965; 129-41).
Parry, A.
1971   Introduction to *The Making of Homeric Verse. The Collected Papers of
                       Milman Parry,* ed. A. Parry; Oxford: Clarendon. ix-lxii.
Parry, M.
1930   "Studies in the Epic Technique of Oral Verse-Making: I. Homer and the
                       Homeric Style", *Harvard Studies in Classical Philology* 41: 73-147.
1932   "Studies in the Epic Technique of Oral Verse-Making II. Homeric
                       Language as the Language of an Oral Poetry", *Harvard Studies in
                       Classical Philology* 43: 1-50.
1936   Review of W. Arend, *Die Typischen Scenen bei Homer* (1933), in
                       Classical Philology 31: 357-60.
Parry, M. and Lord, A. B.
1953-4   *Serbocroatian Heroic Songs* I and II, Belgrade and Cambridge, Mass.:
                       Harvard University Press and the Serbian Academy of Sciences.
Pedersen, J.
1926   *Israel. Its Life and Culture* I-II, London and Copenhagen: Oxford
                       University Press and Branner.
Peet, T. E.
1929   *A Comparative Study of the Literature of Egypt, Palestine and
                       Mesopotamia,* Schweich Lectures 1929; London.
Petersen, D. L.
1973   "A Thrice-Told Tale: Genre, Theme and Motif", *Biblical Research* 18:
                       30-43.
Petrie, W. M. F.
1895   *Egyptian Tales Translated from the Papyri,* First and Second Series;
                       London: Methuen.
Pfeiffer, R. H.
1937   "Midrash in the Books of Samuel", *Quantulacumque. Studies presented
                       to Kirsopp Lake,* ed. R. P. Casey, S. Lake, A. K. Lake; London.
1951   "Facts and Faith in Biblical History", *JBL* 70: 1-14.
1952   *Introduction to the Old Testament,* 2nd edn.; London: A. & C. Black.
Plöger, J. G.
1967   *Literarkritische, formgeschichtliche und stilkritische Untersuchungen
                       zum Deuteronomium,* BBB 26; Bonn: Peter Hanstein.
Porter, J. R.
1968   "Pre-Islamic Arabic Historical Traditions and the Early Historical
                       Narratives of the Old Testament", *JBL* 87: 17-26.
Posener, G
1956   *Littérature et Politique dans l'Égypte de la XIIe Dynastie,* Paris:
                       Librairie ancienne Honoré Champion.

Pritchard, J. B.
    1956   *Ancient Near Eastern Texts relating to the Old Testament,* 2nd edn.;
                                 Princeton, N. J.: Princeton University Press.
Pronko, L. C.
    1961   *The World of Jean Anouilh,* Prespectives in Criticism 7; Berkeley and
                                 Los Angeles: University of California Press.
Rad, G. von
    1953   "Josephsgeschichte und altere Chokma", *VTS* 1: 120-7.
    1962   *Old Testament Theology,* trans. D. M. G. Stalker (from 1st German edn.
                                 1957, incl. revisions for 2nd edn.); Edinburgh: Oliver & Boyd.
    1944/1966   "The Beginnings of Historical Writing in Ancient Israel", *The Problem of
                                 the Hexateuch and other essays,* trans. E. W. Trueman Dicken (from 1st
                                 German edn. 1958; this essay first pub. in *Archiv für Kulturgeschichte*
                                 32 (Weimar 1944) 1-42); Edinburgh: Oliver & Boyd. 166-204.
    1972   *Genesis,* trans. J. H. Marks (= ATD 2-4, 9th edn. 1972); 3rd edn.; OTL;
                                 London: SCM.
Radlov, V. V.
    1866-1904   *Proben der Volkslitteratur der türkischen Stämme und der dsungarischen
                                 Steppe,* 10 vols., St. Petersburg.
Raglan, Lord
    1936   *The Hero. A Study in Tradition, Myth and Drama,* London.
Rendtorff, R.
    1971   "Beobachtungen zur altisraelitischen Geschichtsschreibung anhand der
                                 Geschichte vom Aufstieg Davids", *Probleme biblischer Theologie,* ed.
                                 H. W. Wolff; Munchen: Kaiser. 136-54.
    1975   "Der 'Jahwist" als Theologe? Zum Dilemma der Pentateuchkritik", *SVT*
                                 28: 158-66.
    1977   *Das überlieferungsgeschichtliche Problem des Pentateuch,* BZAW 147;
                                 Berlin: de Gruyter.
Richter, W.
    1966a   *Traditionsgeschichtliche Untersuchungen zum Richterbuch,* BBB 18;
                                 2nd edn.; Bonn: Peter Hanstein.
    1966b   "Urgeschichte und Hoftheologie", *BZ* N.F. 10: 96-105.
Ridout, G. P.
    1971   *Prose Compositional Techniques in the Succession Narrative (2 Sam. 7,
                                 9-10; 1 Kings 1-2),* Diss. Graduate Theological Union; Ann Arbor:
                                 University Microfilms.
Robbins, R. H. (ed.)
    1960   *The Hundred Tales. Les Cent Nouvelles Nouvelles,* New York: Crown
                                 Publishers.
Rofé, A.
    1970   "The Classification of the Prophetical Stories", *JBL* 89: 427-40.
    1974   "Classes in the Prophetical Stories: Didactic Legenda and Parable",
                                 SVT 26: 143-64.
Rost, L.
    1926/1965   "Die Überlieferung von der Thronnachfolge Davids", *Das Kleine Credo
                                 und andere Studien zum Alten Testament,* Heidelberg: Quelle & Meyer.
                                 119-253. (This essay orig. pub. as BWANT III/6, 1926).
Roth, W. M. W.
    1972   "The Wooing of Rebekah", *CBQ* 34: 177-87.

1977   "You are the Man! Structural Interaction in 2 Samuel 10-12", *Semeia* 8: 1-13.

Schicklberger, F.
1974   "Die Davididen und das Nordreich. Beobachtungen zur sog. Geschichte vom Aufstieg Davids", *BZ* N.F. 18: 255-63.

Schmid, H. H.
1976   *Der sogennante Jahwist*, Zürich: Theologischer Verlag.

Schmidt, L.
1970   *Menschlicher Erfolg und Jahwes Initiative: Studien zu Tradition, Interpretation und Historie in Überlieferungen von Gideon, Saul und David*, WMANT 38; Neukirchen-Vluyn: Neukirchener Verlag.

Schofield, J. N.
1950   "'All Israel' in the Deuteronomic Writers", *Essays and Studies Presented to Stanley Arthur Cook*. ed. D. W. Thomas; London: Taylor's Foreign Press. 25-34.

Scholes, R. and Kellogg, R.
1966   *The Nature of Narrative*, New York: Oxford University Press.

Schulte, H.
1972   *Die Entstehung der Geschichtsschreibung im alten Israel*, BZAW 128; Berlin: de Gruyter.

Schulz, A.
1920   *Die Bücher Samuel*, EH; Münster in Westf.: Aschendorff.
1923   "Erzählungskunst in den Samuel-Büchern", *Biblische Zeitfragen* 11 (heft 6/7): 161-208.

Scott, R. B. Y.
1970   "The Study of the Wisdom Literature", *Interp* 24: 20-45.
1971   *The Way of Wisdom in the Old Testament*, New York: Macmillan.

Seebass, H.
1974   "Nathan und David in II Sam 12", *ZAW* 86: 203-11.

Segal, M. H.
1918-9   "Studies in the Books of Samuel. II. The Composition of the Book" *JQR* 9: 43-70.
1964-5   "The Composition of the Books of Samuel", *JQR* 55: 318-39.

Simon, U.
1967   "The Poor Man's Ewe-Lamb. An Example of a Juridical Parable", *Bib* 48: 207-42.

Smith, H. P.
1899   *A Critical and Exegetical Commentary on the Books of Samuel*, ICC; Edinburgh.

Smith, M.
1951   "The So-Called 'Biography of David' in the Books of Samuel and Kings", *HTR* 44: 167-9.

Soggin, J. A.
1967   *Das Königtum in Israel. Ursprünge, Spannungen, Entwicklung*, BZAW 104; Berlin: de Gruyter.
1976   *Introduction to the Old Testament*, trans. J. Bowden (from 2nd Italian edn. 1974); OTL; London: SCM.

Sokolov, Y. M.
1966   *Russian Folklore*, trans. C. R. Smith (from 2nd Russian edn. 1941); Hatboro, Pennsylvania: Folklore Associates.

Spencer, J. (ed.)
    1964   *Linguistics and Style,* London: Oxford University Press.
Steblin-Kamensky, M. I.
    1967   "On the Nature of Fiction in the Sagas of Icelanders", *Scandinavica* 6: 77-84.
    1973   *The Saga Mind,* trans. K. H. Ober; Odense: Odense University Press.
Taylor, A.
    1964   "The Biographical Pattern in Traditional Narrative", *Journal of the Folklore Institute* 1: 114-29.
Thompson, S.
    1955-8   *Motif-Index of Folk Literature,* 6 vols., Copenhagen: Rosenkilde and Bagger.
Thornton, T. C. G.
    1968   "Solomonic apologetic in Samuel and Kings", *ChQR* 169: 159-66.
Thompson, T. L.
    1974   *The Historicity of the Patriarchal Narratives,* BZAW 133; Berlin: de Gruyter.
Titkin, H.
    1922   *Kritische Untersuchungen zu den Büchern Samuelis,* FRLANT N.F. 16: Göttingen.
Tsevat, M.
    1958   "Marriage and Monarchical Legitimacy in Ugarit and Israel", *JSS* 3: 237-43.
Tucker, G. M.
    1971   *Form Criticism of the Old Testament,* Philadelphia: Fortress.
    1972   "The Rahab Saga (Joshua 2): Some Form-Critical and Traditio-Historical Observations", *The Use of the Old Testament in the New and Other Essays,* ed. J. E. Efird; Durham, N.C.: Duke University Press. 66-86.
Van Seters, J.
    1972   "The Conquest of Sihon's Kingdom: A Literary Examination", *JBL* 91: 182-97.
    1975   *Abraham in History and Tradition,* New Haven: Yale University Press.
    1976a   "Oral Patterns or Literary Conventions in Biblical Narrative", *Semeia* 5: 139-54.
    1976b   "Problems in the Literary Analysis of the Court History of David", *JSOT* 1: 22-9.
Vaux, R. de
    1961   *Les Livres de Samuel,* La Sainte Bible; 2nd edn.; Paris: Les Éditions du Cerf.
Vawter, B.
    1974   "History and Kerygma in the Old Testament", *A Light Unto My Path. Old Testament Studies in Honor of Jacob M. Myers,* ed. H. M. Bream, R. D. Heim, C.A. Moore; Philadelphia: Temple University Press. 475-91.
Veijola, T.
    1975   *Die ewige Dynastie. David und die Entstehung seiner Dynastie nach der deuteronomistischen Darstellung,* Helsinki: Suomalainen Tiedeakatemia.
Voeltzel, R.
    1961   *Das Lachen des Herrn. Über die Ironie in der Bibel,* Hamburg-Bergstedt: Herbert Reich Evangelischer Verlag.

Vries, J. de
    1963   Heroic Song and Heroic Legend, trans. B. J. Timmer (from the Dutch
                        edn. 1959); London: Oxford University Press.
Vriezen, T. C.
    1948   "De Compositie van de Samuël-Boeken", Orientalia Neerlandica. A
                        Volume of Oriental Studies, ed. (?) Netherlands' Oriental Society;
                        Leiden: A. W. Sijthoff. 167-89.
Wagner, N. E.
    1972   "Abraham and David?", Studies on the Ancient Palestinian World,
                        Toronto Semitic Texts and Studies 2; ed. J. W. Wevers, D. B. Redford;
                        Toronto: University of Toronto Press. 117-40.
Ward, E. F. de
    1972   "Mourning Customs in 1, 2 Samuel", JJSt 23: 1-27.
Ward R. L.
    1967   The Story of David's Rise: A Traditio-Historical Study of I Samuel xvi
                        14 - II Samuel v, Diss. Vanderbilt University; Ann Arbor: University
                        Microfilms.
Weingreen, J.
    1969   "The Rebellion of Absalom", VT 19: 263-6.
Weiser, A.
    1961   Introduction to the Old Testament, trans. D. M. Barton (from 4th German
                        edn. 1957); London: Darton, Longman & Todd.
    1966   "Die Legitimation des Königs David", VT 16: 325-54.
Wellhausen, J.
    1878   Einleitung in das Alte Testament (F. Bleek, 4th rev. edn.); Berlin. (The
                        section on Judges-Kings is repr. in Die Composition des Hexateuchs und
                        der historischen Bücher des Alten Testaments, 3rd edn. 1899).
    1885   Prolegomena to the History of Ancient Israel, trans. J. S. Black, A.
                        Menzies (from 2nd German edn. 1883); Edinburgh.
Wenham G. J.
    1972   "B^e tûlāh 'a girl of marriageable age'", VT 22: 326-48.
Whybray, R. N.
    1968   The Succession Narrative, SBT 2nd Series 9; London: SCM.
    1974   The Intellectual Tradition in the Old Testament, BZAW 135; Berlin: de
                        Gruyter.
Wilcoxen, J. A.
    1974   "Narrative", Old Testament Form Criticism, ed. J. H. Hayes; San Antonio:
                        Trinity University Press. 57-98.
Winnett, F. V.
    1965   "Re-examining the Foundations", JBL 84: 1-19.
Wolff, H. W.
    1966   "The Kerygma of the Yahwist", Interp 20: 131-58. (Orig. in German in
                        Evangelische Theologie 24: 73-97).
Würthwein, E.
    1974   Die Erzählung von der Thronfolge Davids--thologische oder politische
                        Geschichtsschreibung?, Theologische Studien 115; Zürich: Theologischer
                        Verlag.

Index of Modern Authors

Index of Biblical Passages

Index of Biblical Names

Index of Subjects